D1617277

The Postwar Japanese Economy

The Postwar Japanese Economy

Its Development and Structure, 1937–1994

Second Edition

Takafusa Nakamura

UNIVERSITY OF TOKYO PRESS

This book was originally published in Japanese by the University of Tokyo Press under the title *Nihon Keizai: Sono Seicho to Kozo* (1980, 1993).

English translation © by UNIVERSITY OF TOKYO PRESS, 1995
First edition published 1981; second edition, 1995

ISBN 4-13-047063-9
ISBN 0-86008-514-7

Printed in Japan

99 98 97 96 95   6 5 4 3 2 1

Contents

List of Tables

List of Figures

Preface

The purpose of this book is to concisely summarize the course of the Japanese economy and its inner workings from the Second World War to the present day. Fifty years have passed since the conclusion of World War II. If one reckons the time from the day Japan plunged into war with China, then nearly sixty years have elapsed. During that time, Japan, which was absolutely devastated at the time of its military defeat, rose again, achieved a high rate of growth and the world's second largest GNP, and survived two oil price crises and a dramatic appreciation in the value of its currency to emerge in the 1990s with a strong and stable economy.

Part I of this book presents a historical account of the Japanese economy during the wartime, postwar, and rapid growth periods. A chapter on the war years has been included in order to give the reader an idea of how much the postwar economy inherited from conditions prevailing prior to and during the war, as well as an appreciation of how ruinous was the wartime destruction. Of unquestionably great significance, the reforms implemented following the war may without exaggeration be termed revolutionary. With new reforms carried out atop a foundation of institutions and technology handed down from prewar days, and in an environment conducive to world-wide economic growth and technological progress, the postwar Japanese economy was able to pursue its course of rapid growth in long, swift strides. This has been so much the case that Americans and Europeans seem to have fallen prone to thinking that Japan, Incorporated, holds the patent on rapid economic growth. It is a fact that government policies, government and private sector cooperation, good labor-management relations, and so on were instrumental in the achievement of rapid growth. However, I believe that the prewar and wartime legacy, the favorable international environment, and the efforts of the Japanese people also served extremely well in this process, and I have attempted to explain the reasons for this as persuasively as possible.

Taking a structural view of the subject, Part II divides the problems which arose during the course of growth into one chapter on fiscal and monetary topics and another concerning labor, agriculture, and small business. Rapid economic growth produced swift changes in Japan's economy and society. These chapters attempt to examine from several perspectives what happened in the midst of those changes. An aim of this section is to give some general consideration to issues frequently taken up overseas, such as the "dual structure."

Part III takes up Japan since the 1970s. The conditions conducive to rapid growth collapsed at the beginning of this period. Due to worldwide inflation, the abandonment of the 360-yen-to-the-dollar exchange rate which had been maintained since 1949, and resource limitations as symbolized by the oil crisis of 1973, Japan departed from the path of rapid growth and began to follow a course of so-called "stable" growth. However, the conditions for rapid growth, which had been so propitious earlier, now added to Japan's difficulties when the growth rate began to decline. Chapter Six analyzes the course of events in the 1970s leading up to Japan's encounter with the oil crisis. Taking up the changes and he trial-and-error policy-making process in the wake of the oil crisis, Chapter Seven describes the lengthy adjustment process whereby the new economic superpower, initially at a loss amid mounting international friction, worked out a set of policies to respond to its drastically altered situation. Chapter Eight brings the story up to the 1990s and the collapse of the inflated economic boom of the 1980s.

If the primarily overseas readers of this book are able to gain a general understanding of the Japanese economy via its pages, nothing could give me greater pleasure.

My sincere appreciation for their efforts in the preparation of this book is due first to the translator of the first edition, Jacqueline Kaminski, and to Professor Kozo Yamamura of the University of Washington, who took on the task of editorially supervising the English version. I am also grateful to numerous economists in Japan who have reviewed the Japanese edition of this book and have made helpful corrections, and to Roger Northridge, who translated numerous new passages for the updated second edition. I would also like to thank Ishii Kazuo and Susan Schmidt of the University of Tokyo Press, who undertook the work of editing and compiling the English edition.

Part I

Rising from the Ashes

1

Preparation through Destruction: The Wartime Economy

1. The Origins of Direct Wartime Controls

From the outbreak of the war with China in July of 1937 until the defeat in August 1945, Japan poured all its strength into the war and, in so doing, was destroyed. As stringent direct economic controls were imposed with the beginning of the war in China, the nation's economic power was mobilized for the prosecution of the war. To that end, the industrial structure was distorted into a swollen military production sector and a subsistence commodities sector squeezed to the utmost. The best labor power was conscripted into military service only to become cannon fodder on the front lines, while the citizenry at home barely survived at the most minimal level only to face the need to escape from air raids. Even now a revulsion against recalling those days persists. Combined with the limited availability of source materials, this feeling has often resulted in the omission of the war years from treatments of the Japanese economy, which are divided into the two simple periods "prewar" and "postwar." Japanese economic development has even been discussed in terms of one long wave which links the years 1935–36 with 1952–53.[1]

If only because the economy of the 1930s concealed in embryo a variety of elements that tie into the postwar economy, the war years cannot be ignored in a consideration of the postwar period. To a great extent, the system created during the war was inherited as the postwar economic system. The industries developed during the war became the major postwar industries; wartime technology was reborn in the postwar export industries; and the postwar national lifestyle, too, originated in changes that began during the period of conflict.

Let us begin with a simple overview of the wartime economy. After six years of military conspiracies in Manchuria and Shanghai and the *coup d'état* of February 26, 1936,[2] no political power in the government was strong enough to question or oppose the Army, which moved

3

to gain implementation of its Five-year Plan for Key Industries, giving priority to basic industries such as steel, coal, and synthetic petroleum (see Table 1.1). The Plan was based on the ideas of Ishiwara Kanji, Chief of Operations at the Army General Staff Office and one of the leaders in the 1931 Manchurian Incident, and was intended as preparation for expected war with the Soviet Union. Ishiwara showed drafts of this plan to such important political leaders as future wartime Prime Minister Konoe Fumimaro and financial figures like Ikeda Shigeaki of the Mitsui zaibatsu and Yūki Toyotarō of the Yasuda zaibatsu, building up a consensus on its general outlines. When the Hirota Cabinet, itself noted for its ties with the Army, fell in January 1937, the puppet cabinet of General Hayashi Senjūrō installed Yasuda's Yūki as Finance Minister and Mitsui's Ikeda as Governor of the Bank of Japan, with the intention of thereby bringing about implementation of the Army's Five-year Plan. This is the situation to which Yūki was referring when he remarked around that time that the military and financial worlds had to "throw themselves into each other's arms." When Konoe Fumimaro formed his cabinet in July 1937, it also had to take as one of its appointed tasks the fulfillment of the Army's Production Capacity Expansion Plan.

Japan was at this time already on the verge of bankruptcy in its international payments. The situation is clear from the data in Table 1.2. During the first half of the decade there had been some deficits, but they were generally covered by surpluses in the non-trade accounts. However, between 1936 and 1937 the trade deficit expanded drastically, and the balance of payments equilibrium was completely destroyed. The Japanese yen was the dominant currency within the yen bloc, and the exchange rate was fixed at parity between the yen and the yuan used in Manchuria and North China. Hence Japan received nothing but yen from its yen-bloc trading partners where its trade accounts were in the black, while it had to make payments in foreign currency or in gold to third-country nations with which it was running a trade deficit. So the actual balance-of-payments situation was even worse than the total trade balances indicate. The government increased the power of its foreign exchange administration, but as the deficits continued unabated, it was reduced to shipping gold payments abroad after March of 1937.

The increased imports which were producing these deficits were stimulated by the large-scale military expansion budget drawn up by Finance Minister Baba Eiichi of the Hirota Cabinet. Baba drafted the budget with the ideas of the military in mind, and it called for expenditures of ¥3.04 billion, compared with ¥2.20 billion for the

Table 1.1. Industrial Capacity Expansion Targets in the 1937 Five-year Plan for Key Industries

	Production target			Present capacity			Rate of expansion		
	Total	Japan	Manchuria	Total	Japan	Manchuria	Total	Japan	Manchuria
Automobiles (1000s)	100	90	10	37	37	—	2.7	2.4	—
Machine tools (1000s)	50	45	5	13	13	—	3.8	3.5	—
Steel products (1,000 tons)	1,300	900	400	485	440	45	2.7	2.0	8.9
Oil (10,000 kilolitres)	565	325	240	36.4	21	15.4	15.6	15.5	15.6
Coal (10,000 tons)	11,000	7,200	3,800	5,556	4,200	1,356	2.0	1.7	2.8
Aluminum (1000 tons)	100	70	30	21	21	—	4.8	3.3	—
Magnesium (1000 tons)	9	6	3	0.5	0.5	—	18.0	12.0	—
Electric power (10,000 kilowatts)	1,257	1,117	140	721	675	46	1.7	1.7	3.0
Shipbuilding (10,000 tons)	93	86	7	50	50	—	1.9	1.7	—

1) The expansion rate for general machinery was about 1.8.
2) The expansion rate for oil is based on domestically produced raw materials for gasoline. A rate of expansion calculated on the basis of production capacity from imported oil (1936) would be somewhat less than 10.
3) Although not shown here, target expansion rates were 2.1 for weapons and 10 for both aircraft and military vehicles. Production targets for the latter were 10,000 aircraft and 100,000 vehicles.

Source: Nakamura Takafusa, Nihon no Keizai Tōsei [Japan's Economic Controls] (Nikkei Shinsho, 1975).

Table 1.2. Japan's Trade Balance (1930s)

(¥1,000,000s)

	Total			China trade (including Manchuria and Kwantung) (Paid in yen)			Third-country trade (Non-yen bloc; paid in gold/FX)		
	Exports	Imports	Net	Exports	Imports	Net	Exports	Imports	Net
1931	1,147	1,235	−89	221	236	−15	926	1,000	−74
32	1,410	1,431	−21	276	206	70	1,134	1,226	−92
33	1,861	1,917	−56	411	281	130	1,450	1,636	−186
34	2,172	2,283	−111	520	311	209	1,652	1,972	−320
35	2,499	2,472	27	575	350	225	1,924	2,122	−198
36	2,693	2,764	−71	658	394	264	2,035	2,370	−335
37	3,175	3,783	−608	791	437	354	2,384	3,346	−962
38	2,690	2,663	27	1,166	564	602	1,524	2,099	−575
39	3,576	2,918	658	1,747	683	1,064	1,829	2,235	−406
40	3,656	3,453	203	1,867	756	1,111	1,789	2,697	−908
41	2,651	2,899	−248	1,659	855	804	992	2,044	−1,052

Source: Ministry of Finance Customs Statistics.

previous fiscal year. Neither the Hirota Cabinet nor the succeeding Hayashi Cabinet was in a position to adopt orthodox policies that would hold down deficits through fiscal and monetary restraint because their primary mission was to expedite plant and equipment investment in "key" industries, in line with industrial capacity expansion policies. Direct government controls were the only remaining means of curbing imports. The worsening of the grave balance-of-payments situation with the advent of Baba's fiscal policies was the decisive turning point that ushered in direct and powerful government control over the economy under the Konoe Fumimaro administration.

The Kaya-Yoshino Three Principles, bearing the names of Finance Minister Kaya Okinori and Commerce and Industry Minister Yoshino Shinji in the first Konoe Cabinet (1937–39), were "balance of payments equilibrium, expansion of productive capacity, and regulation of the supply of and demand for materials." The Three Principles meant that, exceeding the powers normally available to governments under a capitalist economic system such as control of interest rates and fiscal measures, the government would directly control materials and funds, damping down production and imports of consumer goods while increasing production and imports of goods for the military, in order to channel goods and money on a priority basis into the key sectors—the "production capacity expansion" industries, paramount of which were those producing for the military.

War between Japan and China broke out near Beijing in July 1937. Seeing this as a good opportunity to realize the ambition it had harbored since the Manchurian Incident to advance into North China, the Army took a hard-line stand in favor of expanding the conflict. The Konoe Cabinet toed the Army line, and the war widened. This cabinet had to draw up a provisional military appropriation of ¥500 million immediately (in July) and ¥2 billion more in September—an amount practically equivalent to the whole 1937 revised national budget of ¥2.8 billion. As direct economic controls became unavoidable, the Temporary Capital Adjustment Act and Temporary Export and Import Commodities Measures were approved at the same time. The former law imposed controls on the establishment of companies, capital increases, payments, bond flotations, and the borrowing of long-term funds in an effort to channel long-term funds on a priority basis into the military industries. The latter gave the government the authority to control the production, processing, trading, holding, and consumption of commodities and raw materials related to imports and exports. In the spring of the following year, 1938, the National

General Mobilization Law was passed, ordering the conscription of labor power, determining wages and other working conditions, and giving directives on the production and distribution of goods. With this law, broad controls in such areas as the behavior of firms, their disposal of profits, and financial institutions' uses of funds became possible. The practical application of these laws was in most cases left to imperial or ministerial ordinances; as a result, virtually all authority over economic controls was delegated to the government bureaucracy.

The newly established Planning Agency began working on a Materials Mobilization Plan in October 1937. The plan allocated foreign exchange to a targeted value of imports, which was estimated as the balance after deducting consumption of domestic production and inventories from total demand. The latter was obtained by determining the shares of key materials—primarily those major goods dependent on imports of steel, oil, copper, aluminum, cotton, rubber, etc.—to be allocated to the Army and Navy and to private demand. The scale of imports was chiefly determined by foreign exchange income from exports, but in addition, foreign exchange on hand and gold shipments abroad were also taken into consideration. Thus, the question of how much foreign exchange could be secured in order to finance the necessary imports became the key that determined the scale of production.

Table 1.3 shows the plan for imports. The 1938 plan at first anticipated that imports of about ¥3 billion would be possible; since imports had been ¥3.7 billion in 1937, this was already a drop of about 20 percent. However, this amount had to be cut to ¥2.5 billion in June of the same year because of poor economic conditions in America, resulting in an export slump. Subsequently, Japan's ability to import fell even further. Since the Army and Navy received priority in obtaining scarce materials in spite of the shrinking total value of imports, private demand was gradually suppressed. When war began in Europe in 1939, the fear also arose that it would become impossible to procure key materials, so on-hand foreign currency was mobilized to buy up stocks of strategic goods such as gasoline, iron, nickel, and cobalt. The Bank of Japan's gold reserves hit bottom, so it then bought up privately-owned gold from the citizenry and also called in foreign stocks and bonds, allocating everything to the fund for imports.

As materials shortages grew increasingly severe, the strengthening of controls was unavoidable. They had already been strengthened once, along with cutbacks in the imports plan, when the Materials

Table 1.3. Summary of Materials Mobilization Plan

(A) Import Capacities for Key Items

(¥1,000,000s)

	1938	1938 revised	Jan.–Mar. 1938	FY 1939	FY 1940	FY 1940 3rd Qtr.	FY 1940 4th Qtr.	FY 1941 1st Qtr.	FY 1941
Steel	557.1	442.3	390.4	497.2	469.1	259.6	270.4	133.2	54.2
Non-ferrous metals	293.9	300.4	351.6	247.9	284.4	187.2	256.4	203.6	98.9
Textiles & paper	853.9	586.7	563.6	497.5	770.1	422.8	432.8	427.2	345.9*
Fuel	524.8	417.0	312.0	282.5	229.2	204.0	351.2	301.6	112.3
Food	43.9	34.3	22.3	23.9	142.4	46.0	8.0	55.6	33.3
Total**	3,056.9	2,554.3	2,230.3	2,395.0	2,629.0	1,614.0	1,846.4	1,600.0	787.6

(B) Rate of Change from Previous Period (%)

	1938	1938 revised	Jan.–Mar. 1938	FY 1939	FY 1940	FY 1940 3rd Qtr.	FY 1940 4th Qtr.	FY 1941 1st Qtr.	FY 1941
Steel	—	-20.7	-11.7	27.4	-5.7	-44.6	4.0	-50.7	-59.3
Non-ferrous metals	—	2.2	17.1	-1.1	-18.2	-34.1	36.8	-20.6	-51.4
Textiles & paper	—	-31.3	-3.9	-11.7	54.8	-45.1	1.1	-1.3	-19.0*
Fuel	—	-20.5	-25.2	-9.4	-18.8	-10.9	72.0	-14.2	-62.8
Food	—	-21.8	-34.6	4.7	496.0	-67.5	-82.7	596.9	-20.1
Total**	—	-16.4	-12.6	7.4	9.4	-38.6	14.4	-13.3	-50.8

1) Figures for three-month periods are multiplied by 4 and given as annual rates. All values are calculated from raw data and rounded. The Japanese fiscal year begins on April 1 and ends on March 31. Thus 1st-quarter data are for April–June, 2nd-quarter data are for July–September, and so on.

2) * indicates that rubber, leather, and lumber are included. **Totals include chemicals, fertilizer, machinery, and other materials in addition to the items shown in the table.

Source: Nakamura Takafusa and Hara Akira, Gendaishi Shiryō—Kokka Sōdōin (1) Keizai [Source Materials on Modern History—The National General Mobilization: (1) Economy] (Misuzu Shobō, 1969), commentary on p. 67.

Mobilization Plan was revised in June 1938. During 1939, full-scale controls were extended over the entire economy. For example, the use of cotton goods to fill private demand was as a rule prohibited, and a ration coupon system for steel and other metals was adopted. Of course these controls were accompanied by soaring market prices, which an official price system was set up to curb. But since official prices tended to be fixed at levels below the supply and demand equilibrium level, hoarding became rampant, and commodities for which prices had been fixed disappeared from the market, leaving nothing to circulate but goods outside the official price system. The authorities had no choice but to gradually extend the list of officially priced goods, and this led to an increase in black market operations. To counter the black market, an economic police force was created. In this way, once direct controls were imposed, the successive expansion of both the number of items affected and the system of control knew no bounds. In order to enforce price controls, costs had to be held down, and in order to do that, wage controls were necessary. In 1939 the "September 18 Stop Order" placed a ceiling on all prices and wages, thereby bringing them under government control.

As a result of the continued drought throughout western Japan and Korea in 1939, a crisis arose over the rice crop and hydroelectric power. A food administration system was inaugurated, rice rationing went into effect, and afterwards the ration coupon system was extended into almost all aspects of national life. Corporate profits and firms' uses of funds also became the objects of government control in 1939; people were conscripted for military production, and junior high school students were put to work in factories. Thus, the Japanese economy by about 1940 was in effect a centrally planned command economy much like that of the former Soviet Union. In the fall of that year a debate developed over the "New Economic Order" called for by Konoe Fumimaro and his followers. The plan called for separating the owners of capital from those responsible for management in order to convert businesses from private profit-seeking undertakings into "public" enterprises where production would be paramount. The idea was vehemently opposed in financial circles.

2. The Pacific War

With no imminent prospect of an end to the war with China in sight even by 1940, the second Konoe Cabinet, under the leadership of Foreign Minister Matsuoka Yōsuke, concluded the Tripartite Alliance with Germany and Italy in the belief that Germany would be victorious in Europe and would come to Tokyo's aid to negotiate a solution to the Sino–Japanese War. This effort to bring about peace on Japanese terms was countered when the Americans imposed an embargo on scrap iron and machine tool exports. Relations between Japan and the United States became very strained, and negotiations were opened in April 1941. The negotiations, however, did not progress. When the Germans attacked the Soviet Union in June of that year, the view that Japan should also go to war against Russia gained strength; but this fervor for war shifted toward Southeast Asia. In July Japanese forces entered southern French Indochina (present-day South Vietnam). The United States responded by playing its last and strongest trump cards—a complete export embargo on aircraft fuel and other petroleum products, and a freeze on Japanese assets in America.

Japan's oil reserves at the time were about 8.4 million kilolitres (approximately two weeks' supply at present-day consumption rates), only enough for the combined fleet to conduct operations for two years. The Army and Navy concluded that if matters were allowed to proceed under the oil embargo, the scanty oil stocks would decline even further; if the nation failed to go to war in the Pacific, it would lose the ability to fight. Hence, the Army felt compelled to choose between widening the war and submitting, and chose to take the plunge into war.

The basic plan when Japan embarked upon war in the Pacific was to set up an "invincible" system by advancing into Southeast Asia, occupying the Philippines and Singapore, and gaining control of the resources of the Dutch East Indies (Indonesia). The biggest question was whether or not Japan would be able to ship the raw materials obtained there back to the home islands and convert them into fighting power. The bottleneck until then had been the shortage of foreign exchange for imports, but it was replaced by the problem of shipping capacity. In 1941 Japan possessed about 6.5 million tons of ship tonnage and an annual shipbuilding capacity of 600,000 tons. It was estimated that, allowing for Army and Navy requisitions of about 3 million tons of available vessels for military operations, if the remaining 3 million tons could be secured to handle shipping from Southeast Asia, there was no obstacle to the prosecution of the war. On the other hand, annual shipping losses were estimated at 600,000 to 800,000 tons, and the decision to go to war was based on the judgment that the fleet could maintain staying power by compensating for this level of losses with new ship construction. Needless to say, this was an optimistic forecast, made for the sake of rationalizing the entry into war.

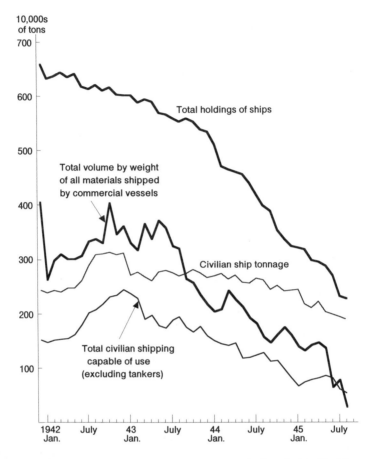

Figure 1.1. Ship tonnage and materials transport during the Pacific War
Source: Calculated from appended tables in Ōi Atsushi, *Kaijō Goei Sen* [The Convoy War at Sea] (Nihon Shuppan Kyōdō, 1953).

For half a year after the opening of hostilities Japan occupied the resource-rich areas of Southeast Asia, but how did the economy fare thereafter during the course of the Pacific War? Figure 1.1 shows wartime tonnage and volume of goods shipped, probably the best barometers of national strength. The shipping capacity which had somehow held out until the first half of 1943 fell off sharply after that, due to air and submarine attacks on supply ships. As a result, the nation's strength declined markedly, so much so that the Southeast

Table 1.4. Fluctuations in Military Production

Year	1941	1942	1943	1944	1945
Aircraft fuselages	6,174	10,185	20,028	26,507	5,823
Engines	13,022	18,498	35,368	40,274	6,509
Naval vessels (no. of ships)	48	59	77	248	101
(tonnage)	200,860	230,724	145,760	408,118	98,240
Small arms (1,000s)	729	440	630	827	209
Gunpowder & ammunition (tons)	52,342	67,461	71,574	81,324	21,279
Total (Index of real value, 1937 = 100)	474	659	923	1,406	447

Source: Kokumin Keizai Kenkyū Kyōkai (Okazaki Ayatoshi, editor), *Kihon Kokuryoku Dōtai Sōran* [Conspectus of Trends in Basic National Strength] (1953).

Asian shipping lanes were blocked in the fall of 1944. Japan was already defeated at this time. The Japanese economy "was twice destroyed—first by the blockading of imports, and second by the air raids."[3]

Beginning in 1943 Japan made a national effort, albeit belatedly, to meet a nominal production goal of 50,000 airplanes, but this effort could be sustained only for a short time (Table 1.4). Trends in the military industries and in agriculture, mining, and manufacturing are shown in Table 1.5. Steel production peaked in 1943 and then began

Table 1.5. Movements in Production Indexes (1937 = 100)

Item	1941	1942	1943	1944	1945
Agriculture & forestry	95.1	99.8	96.3	76.2	59.3
Rice	83.0	100.6	94.8	88.2	59.0
Mining & manufacturing	123.0	119.4	121.0	123.0	53.1
Mining	120.2	117.4	118.5	107.8	56.9
Manufacturing	123.1	119.6	121.0	124.2	52.7
Steel	132.0	139.5	156.1	145.8	51.8
Non-ferrous metals	114.4	126.1	153.2	170.2	63.2
Machinery	188.2	195.4	214.3	252.3	107.2
Chemicals	120.3	100.3	87.1	80.0	33.2
Paper and pulp	106.3	83.6	71.5	41.4	19.5
Textiles	60.4	47.7	31.3	16.6	6.4
Food products	78.1	69.4	57.5	47.4	31.6
Other	60.8	59.2	52.1	31.3	11.3

Sources: Official indexes of the Ministry of International Trade and Industry and Ministry of Agriculture and Forestry. Bank of Japan, *Meiji ikō Honpō Juyō Keizai Tōkei* [Hundred-year Statistics of the Japanese Economy].

to decline. Production of consumption goods such as textiles, food products, and paper (including pulp) had already fallen to 60 percent of its prewar level by the time Japan entered the Pacific War, and the subsequent decline is striking. Even agricultural production broke down in 1944. The war was begun and prosecuted at the expense of the people, and it finally ended by destroying them.

Let us now look at the control of industry. The upshot of the "New Economic Order" controversy was the formation of "Control Associations" (Tōsei Kai) in key industries beginning in 1941. Although the ordinance establishing a controlling cartel in each major industry theoretically conferred great powers on association members and called for autonomous regulation in the hands of private individuals, in actuality the government took on broad supervisory powers and made the associations function as lower-echelon mechanisms of government control. However, their effectiveness was limited, and in 1943 the Munitions Companies Act was passed in an effort to set up a system for increased aircraft production. The law designated key firms as "munitions companies" and set up a system conferring the status of public officials on company representatives, who were to increase production in conformity with national—i.e., Cabinet— directives. Compensation for losses was also provided for. Such was the final form taken by wartime controls, but the shortage of raw materials still obstructed increases in production. Furthermore, in order to increase munitions production, policies were adopted for retooling consumption goods producers, particularly the textile industry. Their factories were converted to military production, their machines scrapped, and their workers conscripted. Mobilized troop strength was 2.41 million men in 1941, 3.81 million in 1943, and 7.19 million by the time the war ended. To make up for the lost labor power, the government went as far as mobilizing all students at the junior high school level and above in 1944. Estimates of Japan's population structure by industry are given in Table 1.6. The striking decrease in the employed population in May of 1945 is impressive.

In 1945 the major cities of Japan, particularly Tokyo and Osaka, were reduced to rubble by air raids. Large numbers of people were on the verge of starvation, and securing the most minimal food supply for the population had already become a more urgent issue than military production. The remaining ships had been mobilized for the transport of food from China and Korea. While calling for "top priority dispatching of ships" to obtain grain from Manchuria and salt from mainland China, the Summary Materials Mobilization Plan for the first half of fiscal 1945 stated that, in order to prepare for "enemy

Table 1.6. Distribution of Wartime Employed Population
            (1,000 persons; figures in parentheses are percentages)

	Oct. 1940	Feb. 1944	Nov. 1944	May 1945	Dec. 1945	Oct. 1947
All industries	32,483	31,695	29,721	27,641	30,069	33,329
	(100.0)	(100.0)	(100.0)	(100.0)	(100.0)	(100.0)
Agriculture &	13,850	13,571	13,685	13,633	17,520	17,102
forestry	(42.6)	(42.8)	(46.0)	(49.3)	(58.3)	(51.3)
Fisheries	543	457	370	359	533	710
	(1.7)	(1.4)	(1.2)	(1.3)	(1.8)	(2.1)
Mining, manufacturing,						
transportation &	9,985	11,717	10,011	8,510	7,183	9,381
communications	(30.7)	(37.0)	(33.7)	(30.8)	(23.9)	(28.1)
Commerce	4,991	2,510	2,035	1.588	2,016	3,004
	(15.4)	(7.9)	(6.8)	(5.7)	(6.7)	(9.0)
Civil service & self-	2,187	2,831	2,905	2,942	2,339	2,588
employed	(6.7)	(8.9)	(9.8)	(10.6)	(7.8)	(7.8)
Domestic work	709	468	299	224	238	101
	(2.2)	(1.5)	(1.0)	(0.8)	(0.8)	(0.3)
Other	218	141	417	384	237	444
	(0.7)	(0.4)	(1.4)	(1.4)	(0.8)	(1.3)

Source: Nakamura Takafusa and Arai Kurotake, "Taiheiyō Sensōki ni Okeru Yūgyō Jinkō no Suikei: 1940–1947" [Estimates of Employed Population during the Pacific War: 1940–1947] (Tōkyō Daigaku Kyōyō Gakubu, Shakaigaku Kiyō, No. 27).

landing in the home islands" and to provide for "minimum military preparedness," "a portion of military production [would] continue" and key industries would "operate at 50 percent of the previous period's level." Japan's power to resist had already collapsed well before the dropping of the atomic bombs and the Soviets' entrance into the war.

3. The Legacy of War
The state of the Japanese economy at the time of defeat in August 1945 may be summarized as follows. First, the population. Those who died in battle or from diseases contracted at the front are estimated at 1.65 million for the Army, including 27,000 civilians in military service, and 470,000 for the Navy. Air raid casualties were 300,000 dead, and 90,000 civilians died in the battle for Okinawa, bringing the total to more than 2.5 million including the wounded and missing. If we include Japanese casualties overseas—among the internees in Siberia and colonists in Manchuria—the total approaches 3 million.

Table 1.7. Damage to the National Wealth

(¥100 millions)

	Total damages	Estimated total value in the absence of damages	Remaining national wealth at end of war	Proportion damaged (%)	National wealth in 1935 converted into current values at end of war
Total national wealth					
assets	643	2,531	1,889	25	1,867
Structures	222	904	682	25	763
Industrial machinery					
tools	80	233	154	34	85
Ships	74	91	18	82	31
Electricity & gas supplying					
facilities	16	149	133	11	90
Furniture & household					
effects	96	464	369	21	393
Products	79	330	251	24	235

Source: Economic Stabilization Board, *Taiheiyō Sensō ni yoru Waga Kuni no Higai Sōgō Hōkōkusho* [Comprehensive Report on Damage to Japan from the Pacific War], 1949.

Material losses in terms of national wealth are shown in Table 1.7. The total value of losses incurred was ¥64.3 billion. These losses amounted to a quarter of the remaining national wealth of ¥188.9 billion, an amount which was approximately equal to the total value of national wealth in 1935. Thus, the accumulation of the ten years from 1935 to 1945 was wiped out at a stroke.

Table 1.8 presents data on production capacity, comparing plant and equipment capacity in 1937 with capacities at their wartime peak and at the time of defeat. The chemical and heavy industries had far more equipment and plant capacity during the war than prior to it. The conspicuous reductions in light-industry capacity, particularly textiles, were due more to wartime conversion to military production and scrapping of equipment than to war damage. These two shifts formed the basis for the heavy and chemical industrialization following the war.

The training of engineers and workers who acquired a mastery of

Table 1.8. Production Plant Capacity for Key Materials

Production plants	Units	FY 1937 production plant capacity	Maximum wartime production capacity		Production plant capacity at end of war	Remarks
			Fiscal year	Production plant capacity		
Pig iron	100s of tons	3,000	1944	6,600	5,600	
Rolled steel	"	6,500	1944	8,700	7,700	
Copper	Tons	120,000	1943	144,000	105,000	
Aluminum	"	17,000	1944	127,000	129,000	
Oil refining	100s of kilolitres	2,320	1942	*4,157	2,130	*Crude oil refining plant capacity
Machine tools	Units	22,000	1940	*60,134	54,000	*Actual production
Bearings	Millions of yen	36	1944	320	245	
Caustic soda	"	380	1941	723	661	473
Soda ash	"	600	1941	889	835	504 Actual
Ammonium sulphate	"	1,460	1941	1,979	1,243	689 production
Super phosphate of lime	"	2,980	1941	2,846	1,721	1,141 capacity
Cement	"	12,894	1941	9,621	6,109	3,520
Cotton yarn	100s of spindles	12,165	1941	13,796	2,367	
Rayon	100s of pounds	570,000	1937	570,000	88,600	
Staple fibers	"	451,000	1941	813,000	184,000	
Cotton looms	Units	362,604	1941	393,291	113,752	
Woolen looms	"	29,185	1941	31,815	9,802	
Rayon looms	"	356,119	1942	343,845	135,582	
Rayon pulp	1000s of English tons		1940	404	201	
Paper pulp	"		1940	1,329	705	
Western-style paper	1000s of pounds	2,617,643	1940	2,617,643	1,183,000	

their technologies in these factories also directly prepared the country for postwar development. Factories that made machine guns turned to making sewing machines; optical weapons factories began turning out cameras and binoculars. In this way the facilities, technology, and skills acquired during the war exerted a tremendous influence on the subsequent direction of the economy.

The emergence of the subcontracting system, which spread so widely in the postwar era, was also a wartime phenomenon. Large firms in the military industries had at first made it a rule to produce everything in-house, including parts. But they developed a system of subcontracting parts and other work out to small and medium-sized firms as an emergency measure to facilitate production increases. This practice honed the small firms' technical skills and was an opportunity to raise production standards. It also occasioned the formation of crucial links between small and large firms. This was of decisive significance for small firms in the heavy and chemical industries, which were thus able to secure a steady stream of orders and grow accordingly. Here lie the origins of the long-term postwar relationships between small enterprises and their patron or "parent" companies.

In the spring of 1944 the "System of Financial Institutions Authorized to Finance Munitions Companies" was established. The munitions companies, which produced according to government orders, were the most powerful firms supplying military demand. The government, in turn, designated "authorized financial institutions" for the munitions companies and arranged for these institutions to provide an unimpeded supply of needed funds to the companies. The arrangement was so contrived that other financial institutions, as well as the Bank of Japan and the government, were to back the authorized institutions so they would not run short of funds. In the postwar reconstruction these relationships were to reappear and become entrenched in the form of the powerful financial groupings known as *keiretsu*. The *keiretsu* of not only the industrial combines (*zaibatsu*) like Mitsui and Mitsubishi but also of major banks like the Industrial Bank of Japan, Fuji, Sanwa, and Dai-ichi Kangyō, were all formed around this time.

The strong administrative leadership which the Ministry of International Trade and Industry (MITI) and the Ministry of Transport have come to exercise over industry can also be traced to the wartime Commerce and Industry Ministry's and Munitions Ministry's experience with controls which was passed on into the postwar period. Additional financial controls were implemented by the Nationwide Financial Control Association established in 1942. The real heart of the organization was the Bank of Japan. The Bank's experience with controls set the stage for such direct controls as Bank of Japan window guidance (discussed in greater detail in Chapter 4) in the postwar economy. It is often said that the authority and leadership of the Japanese government bureaucracy have been stronger than in other countries since before the war, but this was not necessarily the case in the prewar period. Such industries as spinning, for example, once prided themselves on their independence from the government. It was during the course of wartime controls that the "guidance" relationship was established between firms and the bureaucracy, and between private banks and the Bank of Japan.

The origins of postwar labor-management relations can also be found in the wartime era. During the war the labor unions were broken up, and in each firm Patriotic Industrial Associations (Sangyō Hōkoku Kai) were organized with the participation of both labor and management. The Associations were responsible for an industrial safety program, guidance for living, the rationing of materials, and so on. The rapidity with which it was possible to form a large number of unions when the Occupation Army ordered their establishment is attributable to the fact that these organizations already existed. Japan's labor unions were formed and have continued up to the present as company, rather than trade, unions largely because wartime associations like the Patriotic Industrial Associations simply shed their old skins but continued to exist after the war ended.

The seniority wage system and the lifetime employment system first took shape during the depression following World War I, primarily in the chemical and heavy industries, but their expansion into a nationwide system was due to the implementation of wage controls in 1940–41. A wage and price freeze was proclaimed on September 18, 1939, and thereafter, on the basis of a survey of actual conditions, everything from starting salaries of new graduates to the amounts of annual wage increases was determined by the government. By this means the system of seniority wages and promotion based on length of employment spread throughout the country.

There are other examples of "progressive" policies which had previously been impossible but were implemented because the country was at war, and which were then handed down into the postwar period. The Health Insurance Law affecting firms with 300 or more regular employees was passed in 1922, but its scope was broadened during the war years. The National Health Insurance Law was passed in April 1938 at the beginning of the war with China, and was followed by the enactment of the Personnel Health Insurance Law and the Seamen's Insurance Law in 1939. These provided Japan with an almost complete health insurance system. In 1941 the Workmen's Annuity and Insurance Law was passed, for the first time legally requiring the payment of annuities in case of old age, disability, or death. Its scope was broadened in 1944 to include staff personnel and women. The systemization during wartime of a social insurance program which, politically, could not have been achieved in peacetime was aimed at providing a minimum guaranteed living for the large labor force that had been mobilized for the war, and at giving the people "reassurance and hope" (according to Welfare Minister Kanemitsu's explanation to the Diet in 1941). This system, however, acted as a springboard for the development of the postwar social security system.

With the establishment of the Food Administration System in 1941, protective policies for farmers, particularly tenant farmers, began to be implemented in the form of rice price controls. Because of the importance of wartime food production, the government held its general rice buying price to ¥44 per *koku* (= 180.4 kilolitres); at the same time it gave ¥5 production increase subsidies to producers when it purchased rice directly from them, but gave no such subsidies when buying from landlords. Thus, the government was actually treating the producers' rice price and the landlords' rice price as two separate things and, in so doing, raised the producers' net income and sought to effect a real reduction in farm rents. The general buying price for rice remained fixed at ¥55 per *koku* until 1945, but the production increase subsidies which had started out at five yen per *koku* had reached ¥245 for producers' rice by 1945, giving producers earnings of ¥300 per *koku*. Even before the postwar land reform, the tenant farmer system had already been reduced to a mere shell, and the status of landlords had declined. This was half the reason that land reform was able to progress as smoothly as it did after the war.

Every aspect of the people's way of life changed during the war. What had once been the agricultural and traditional-industry workforce became concentrated in the cities and took up hammers or turned lathes in the heavy and chemical industries. They put on industrial overalls and learned the life of bondage to the factory whistle. Women who had been accustomed to wearing kimono also donned work pants and no longer objected to wearing Western-style clothing. As such items as rice, sake, sugar, and tobacco were rationed, consumption also became standardized. Households that had mainly lived on cereals and sweet potatoes during the war took to eating rice afterwards as a reaction against the wartime dearth of rice.

Such changes as these also prepared the way for the far-reaching penetration of urban production methods and lifestyles after the war.

From the examples given above it can be seen that, to a surprisingly large extent, the postwar social and economic system, technologies, lifestyles, customs, and so on took shape during, and were passed on from, the war years. Even if these institutions were not established with a view to the longer term in mind, they cast the die for the postwar period.

Notes

1. See, for example, Kazushi Ohkawa and Henry Rosovsky, *Japanese Economic Growth: Trend Acceleration in the Twentieth Century* (Stanford University Press, 1973).

2. On February 26, 1936, 1400 soldiers led by officers in the Army's Imperial Way faction (Kōdōha) took over the center of Tokyo, including the War Ministry and the Diet building. Two former Prime Ministers—Takahashi Korekiyo and Saitō Makoto—as well as the Inspector General of Military Education were assassinated. Prime Minister Okada Keisuke was attacked, and Grand Chamberlain Suzuki Kantarō was seriously wounded. Although the rebellion was eventually suppressed, the date of its outbreak has come to represent the incontrovertible ascendency of the military.

3. Jerome B. Cohen, *Japan's Economy in War and Reconstruction* (Greenwood Press, 1973: reprint of 1949 edition).

2

Reform and Reconstruction

1. Defeat and Devastation: Autumn 1945

With the defeat the Japanese economy faced staggering problems. The number one issue was unemployment. When the military forces were demobilized, there were over 7 million troops; the cessation of military production threw 4 million people out of work (of whom 750,000 were women); and an estimated 1.5 million were repatriated from abroad. This brought the jobless total to about 13.1 million. Even after making allowances for those who were able to return to their former jobs, particularly in agriculture, how was employment to be created for the approximately 10 million people with no jobs to return to?

It was generally expected at the time that a dramatic jump in the number of unemployed would be unavoidable. However, large-scale unemployment never actually materialized. To state the matter differently, the conditions under which people lived left no leeway for such a thing as being unemployed. Unless they had sufficient savings to live on, the demobilized troops and those thrown out of work had to find some means or other of making a living. Even if they did this by setting up open-air stalls or by becoming petty black marketeers or black market brokers, they were not "unemployed." In 1947 rural communities also absorbed a labor force of 18 million, about 4 million more than before the war. Thus, massive unemployment did not develop, but, as will be related below, the problem of the low-income "underemployed" persisted long afterwards in the form of a "dual structure" within the economy.

The next concerns were the grave shortages of energy and food. Indigenous energy sources at the time were limited to coal and hydroelectric power. Demand had fallen off with the suspension of military production, but coal output had dropped even more precipitously, from a monthly volume of about 3 to 4 million tons until the

23

defeat to barely a million tons in the autumn of 1945. The biggest
reason was that, with Japan's defeat, the Koreans and Chinese who
had been forced to work in the coal mines refused to continue, and
coal mining was virtually paralyzed. Starved for fuel, even railway
transport faced a crisis. Added to this, the 1945 rice crop was a dis-
astrously low two-thirds of average annual output; the outlook for the
nation's food supply was bleak, and it was feared that people would
starve to death. For these reasons, coal production increases and food
deliveries to the government were encouraged, and entreaties were
made to the Occupation Army for imports of food, but not much
progress was made on any of these fronts. It was only in 1947 that any
prospects for the resolution of these problems began to come into
view.

Inflation was a third major problem during this period, for several
reasons. First of all, income received during the war (including war
insurance) had been accumulated in the form of savings, public
bonds, and so on. Although it had been possible for these funds to
enter the market as effective demand during the war, they did not
actually surface due to the policy of compulsory saving. However,
after the air raids intensified in the autumn of 1944, the government
and the Bank of Japan, fearing public unrest, had no choice but to
allow the release of these funds onto the market. In addition, directly
after the defeat a large volume of funds for provisional military
expenses flowed into circulation from the salaries of demobilized
troops, payments for completed orders of military goods, advance
payments, compensation for losses, and so on. As a result of all this, a
rapid inflation developed. As rumors flew of property tax levies, a
paper currency conversion, and a freeze on bank deposits, people
began hoarding commodities, and the total value of bank deposits
went into a decline beginning in December of 1945.

To cope with the situation, the Emergency Financial Measures
Order was invoked in February 1946. It attempted to check inflation
by calling for the deposit of all cash in financial institutions, ordering
the issue of new currency, implementing a "new yen" conversion
which authorized each household to draw up to ¥500 per month in
living expenses, and levying a property tax (¥100 billion according to
the first draft, but finally amounting to about ¥30 billion). But these
measures alone could not curb the inflation, and the problem had to
await implementation of the Dodge Plan in 1949 for solution.

2. Economic Democratization

After its defeat, Japan was occupied by the Allied Powers—in reality,
the American forces. The existence of the Japanese government was

recognized, and the Occupation took the form of indirect rule, but the basic reform policies had already been drawn up in Washington. On September 6, Supreme Commander for the Allied Powers (SCAP) General Douglas MacArthur received the United States Initial Post-Surrender Policy for Japan from Washington, and on September 10 he publicly announced the policies for the administration of Japan. They consisted of a series of reforms aimed at "democratization." The following is a summary of Part Four of the Post-Surrender Policy, entitled "Economy."

First, in the interest of "economic demilitarization," the suspension and prohibition in future of military production, a ban on fleet and aircraft facilities, restrictions on the nature and scale of heavy industries, and restrictions on the possession of merchant vessels were set forth. Second, in the interest of the "promotion of democratic forces" provision was made for the promotion of labor unions and agricultural associations and for the emergence into the open of the activities of labor unions and other organizations which had until then been illegal. The next step was the "elimination of concentration" in production and in property rights in the broad sense. In addition, the policy of purging business leaders and breaking up the zaibatsu was clearly put on record. Under the third heading, "Resumption of Peaceful Economic Activity," it was first noted that Japan itself bore the responsibility for its economic plight, and that it would likewise bear the responsibility for reconstruction. Japan would furthermore be obligated to provide goods and services for the Occupation Army, to ration goods fairly, to pay reparations, and so on. The tone of the reforms was on the whole extremely severe, and the Occupation authorities lost no time in beginning to implement them.

The three major reforms, the breakup of the zaibatsu, land reform, and labor democratization, and their effects may be summarized as follows.

(1) The Breakup of the Zaibatsu
"The purpose of zaibatsu dissolution ... is to destroy Japan's military power both psychologically and institutionally." Japan's industries had been "under the control of a few great combines ... enjoying preferential treatment from the Japanese government." Moreover, the concentration of industrial control "promoted the continuation of a semi-feudal relationship between labor and management, held down wages, blocked the development of labor unions ... obstructed the creation of firms by independent entrepreneurs, and hindered the rise of a middle class in Japan." "The low wages and concentrated profits ... produced by such a structure have been inconsistent with

the development of a domestic market ..., and in consequence, Japanese business felt the need to expand its exports. This drive for exports ... has been an outstanding motive of Japanese imperialism ... and aggression." Corwin Edwards, Chief of the Zaibatsu Mission that came to Japan in January 1946, made these comments in *Report of the Mission on Japanese Combines*.

Any fair assessment must acknowledge that not all the actions taken by the zaibatsu prior to the war were harmful. For example, the zaibatsu introduced a number of new industries into Japan in rapid succession, and possessed the strength to put them on a firm footing in their new environment. It is difficult to believe that "low wages" and "restricted domestic markets" were the result of the "semi-feudal" control of the zaibatsu, and difficult to demonstrate that they "hindered the rise of a middle class." Whether or not the zaibatsu can be said to have been the advance guard of imperialism is also problematic. The principal source of the great wealth of Mitsui and Mitsubishi was trade. They were affiliated with overseas firms and hoped for cooperation with England and America. However, it is also a fact that the zaibatsu exercised privileged powers of control over the Japanese economy. Thus it is not surprising that American economists, whose watchwords in the 1930s had been the New Deal and antitrust, saw the zaibatsu as the source of all evil.

The first step in the dissolution of the zaibatsu was to break up the holding companies, which were the core of zaibatsu control, and to sell their stock to the public. The holding companies at the time (1946) possessed 167 million shares of stock, having a value of ¥8.1 billion. Since the total number of shares in all companies in the country was 443 million, this meant that the holding companies owned nearly 40 percent of the total. As a result of a series of dissolution measures, 165 million shares, valued at ¥7.57 billion, had been disposed of by 1951. The zaibatsu leaders, including members of the founding families, were purged and were prohibited from further activity in the financial world. The unrelenting nature of the zaibatsu dissolution, even to the extent of taking measures against founding family members, was contrary to the general principles of a modern democratic society.

A succession of democratization policies concerning the industrial associations was adopted. The first was the Anti-Monopoly Law of April 1947. After two revisions, in 1949 and 1953, the law was greatly relaxed, and it was 1977 before further amendments put teeth back into it. This law became a basic principle of the postwar Japanese economy. In December of 1947 the Elimination of Excessive Concentration of Economic Power Law was passed. It stipulated that if, after a review, it was determined that any of the designated companies had market control, such firms were to be reduced in size. On the basis of this legislation, 325 companies were designated for partitioning into smaller units in February 1948, but because the reconstruction of the Japanese economy became urgent as the Cold War progressed, the application of the deconcentration law was relaxed by the Occupation authorities. Only eighteen companies were ever actually split up. Among the largest of these were Nippon Steel, which was broken up into Yawata Steel and Fuji Steel, and Mitsui Mining, which was separated into Mitsui Coal Mining and Mitsui Metal Mining. The others included Mitsubishi Mining, Seika (Sumitomo) Mining, Toshiba, Hitachi Ltd., Mitsubishi Heavy Industries, Oji Paper, and Dainippon Beer.

In fact, however, even though this legislation was in practice very leniently applied, Table 2.1 shows that, with the exception of such firms as those in textiles, where there were many consolidations during the war, and the highly oligopolistic aluminum and beer industries, the concentration ratios for the top three and the top ten producers in most industries were lower after the war than they had been prior to it—particularly those for the top three producers. Once again the stock held by large corporations in affiliated companies was sold to the public and controlling relations were severed. These measures set the stage for the fierce competition which was characteristic of postwar industry in Japan. As we will see, the plant and equipment expansions and technological advances made under the pressure of competition produced economic growth.

The above-described policies exerted great influence over the entire postwar economy. It was an economy characterized by intense competition in all industries. There were some industries, such as steel and automobiles, in which the nature of the industry led to competition among a handful of oligopolistic firms, and others, like textiles, in which a large number of firms competed, but the basic trend after the war was toward a dead heat in a field of little guys, with no Gullivers in the race. This produced good market mechanisms and was a powerful factor in economic growth. Therein lay the effectiveness of this series of Occupation policies, from the zaibatsu dissolution to the deconcentration law—good examples of the kind of economic policies whose results were startling to those who drafted them.

(2) Land Reform

The large-scale decrease in tenant farm rents that was effected by the wartime food administration system has already been described. Right after the defeat, the Ministry of Agriculture and Forestry sub-

Table 2.1. Concentration Ratios for Leading Producers

(%)

	1937		1950		1962	
	Top 3 firms	Top 10 firms	Top 3 firms	Top 10 firms	Top 3 firms	Top 10 firms
Pig iron	97.8		88.7	93.0	27.7	38.4
Ferro-alloys	51.2	60.0	48.8	81.2	34.6	69.3
Hot rolled steel	56.2	81.3	49.6	77.1	49.8	78.9
Galvanized iron sheet	19.9	85.5	32.8	70.3	37.6	73.6
Electric-furnace steel	74.9	100.0	73.4	100.0	65.3	100.0
Aluminum	91.8	100.0	100.0	—	100.0	—
Bearings	100.0	—	76.3	95.4	68.7	92.6
Steel ships	67.5	96.7	39.1	94.1	37.7	75.5
Ammonium sulphate	60.6	93.5	41.2	87.3	32.7	78.2
Super phosphate of lime	46.6	80.6	47.3	89.7	32.0	72.5
Caustic soda	55.1	86.5	33.8	71.1	23.5	59.8
Synthetic dyes	56.3	70.1	75.2	92.7	64.8	88.8
Sheet celluloid	77.7	91.2	69.2	89.2	80.6	95.0
Rayon filament	36.5	76.1	70.8	100.0	60.5	100.0
Cotton yarn	33.9	59.1	35.1	88.1	16.6	48.2
Cotton textiles	16.5	30.6	18.6	44.2	6.6	17.2
Pulp	65.2	85.3	39.5	73.0	30.5	60.6
Paper	83.1	99.3	57.0	80.3	39.9	65.9
Soy sauce	20.1	28.2	16.7	23.7	25.3	30.3
Cement	40.1	78.5	55.9	91.3	47.1	82.0
Coal	35.4	60.6	35.9	59.6	31.0	55.8
Foreign trade*	35.1	51.7	13.0	30.5	24.8	50.5
Banking	25.8	61.1	21.8	59.6	19.9	54.5
Marine transport	29.8	46.8	18.1	33.1	22.8	56.6
Life insurance	41.4	81.6	47.2	83.7	43.5	85.1
Warehousing	37.8	61.4	25.2	37.4	20.6	31.2

* Prewar figures for foreign trade are averages for the years 1937–43, while postwar figures shown are for 1951 and 1957 instead of for 1950 and 1962.
Source: From Fair Trade Commission, Nihon no Sangyō Shūchū [Japan's Industrial Concentration], Data Table 1.

mitted to the Diet a first draft of a land reform program which would have allowed landlords to retain 5 chō (1 chō = 2.45 acres) of land and obligated them to transfer anything above that amount to the cultivators. But while this bill was being debated, the Occupation forces issued a memorandum on land reform and the bill, though passed by the Diet, was never implemented. Eventually a second draft was prepared under the direction of GHQ, and its content was far more severe than the Agriculture Ministry's proposal. The pro-

Table 2.2. Changes in the Proportion of Tenant Farmers

Region	Total farmland area (1000 chō*)	Proportion of total worked by tenant farmers (%)	
		Novermber 1946	August 1950
Hokkaidō	726	48.7	6.7
Tōhoku	813	48.2	8.4
Kantō	874	50.6	12.5
Hokuriku	426	49.0	9.1
Tōzan	298	43.4	10.3
Tōkai	343	50.5	12.4
Kinki	352	44.9	13.6
Chūgoku	398	40.3	10.2
Shikoku	220	43.5	10.0
Kyūshū	706	41.0	10.3
Total	5,156	45.9	10.1
Total, excluding Hokkaidō	4,430	45.5	10.7

* 1 chō = 2.45 acres.

Source: Kayō Nobufumi, Nihon Nōgyō Kiso Tōkei [Basic Statistics on Japanese Agriculture] (Nōrin Suisangyō Seisansei Kōjō Kaigi, 1958).

gram which was agreed upon after discussions between the Occupation authorities and Japanese officials was a thorough-going reform stipulating that all the land of absentee landlords, and all but one chō (approximately one hectare) of the land belonging to landlords residing in the rural villages, would be bought up by the government for redistribution to the tenant farmers. The government's role as intermediator in the buying and selling of the land was one of the features retained from the Ministry's first draft.

The results of the land reform are shown in Table 2.2. The proportion of total agricultural land area worked by tenant farmers was reduced from nearly 50 percent to about 10 percent. The decrease was particularly notable in the Tōhoku region and in Hokkaidō. Also important is the fact that this stringent reform had the effect of rapidly increasing the productive capacity of rice-growing land in such areas as Hokkaidō, Tōhoku, Hokuriku, and Tōzan—generally the northeast half of Japan—where large landlords had been especially powerful (Table 2.3). After the transfer of property rights, land improvements were carried out on a large scale and combined with the introduction of new rice-growing technology to raise the level of

Table 2.3. Prefectures with Highest and Lowest Rates of Rice Crop Increases per *Tan* in 1951–55*

(%)

Rank order of prefectures with highest percentage increases	Increase over 1930–34	Increase over 1939–43	Rank order of prefectures with lowest percentage increases	Increase over 1930–34	Increase over 1939–43
1. Hokkaidō	74	32	1. Osaka	−11	−10
2. Aomori	57	27	2. Shizuoka	−10	−13
3. Iwate	31	22	3. Nara	−11	−3
4. Akita	29	11	4. Hiroshima	−10	−10
5. Yamagata	28	10	5. Kōchi	−8	7
6. Miyagi	27	15	6. Wakayama	−7	−7
7. Fukushima	26	10	7. Aichi	−6	−10
8. Niigata	23	5	8. Hyōgo	−6	−1
9. Nagano	19	6	9. Kagawa	−4	6
10. Kagoshima	15	21	10. Yamanashi	−3	−11

* 1 *tan* = .245 acres.
Source: Same as for Table 2.2.

agricultural productivity. In terms of the economy as a whole, the technological advances and income increases in rural areas in due course also caused an expansion of domestic markets.

(3) Labor Democratization

Promotion of the labor union movement began with the enactment of three labor laws, the Trade Union Law, the Labor Standards Law, and the Labor Relations Adjustment Law, in accordance with orders of the Occupation forces. The proportion of workers organized into labor unions rose rapidly, from zero in 1945 to nearly 60 percent in 1948–49. This is an extraordinarily high rate in view of the fact that the international average is generally about 30 percent.

As has already been mentioned, the organization of labor unions was able to proceed so rapidly mainly because the wartime Patriotic Industrial Associations were able to convert themselves into company unions and because labor activists who had been in the union movement since before the war immediately started organizing. The latter conducted a violent union campaign, often hauling up company managers before kangaroo courts. Even at that time the company union outlook was strong at the fringes of the union movement, but the two rightist and leftist national labor federations were at the movement's center. At first, the All Japan Congress of Industrial Unions (Sanbetsu), which was linked with the Communist Party, was dominant. It stood in opposition to the Socialist Party's Japan Federation of Labor (Sōdōmei). The Occupation forces were initially sympathetic to the activities of the left-wing unions and sought to allow them full freedom in the name of democratization, but they ordered the cancellation of the planned general strike of February 1, 1947, spearheaded by Sanbetsu. In August 1948 the Occupation authorities issued a political order (No. 201) depriving government employees of the right to strike, and in 1949 matters deteriorated to the point of Occupation acquiescence in political firings—the "Red purge." The long shadow cast by the Cold War, which started so soon after the end of World War II, quickly transformed what had been a liberal policy into one of repression. At the same time, Sanbetsu's dominance began to wane, and in 1950 critical elements within the organization (centered on the League for Democratization—Minshuka Dōmei) formed the Japan General Council of Trade Unions (Sōhyō). Thus the two major currents in the labor movement crystallized in the form of the newly formed Sōhyō, which became increasingly leftist, and the Sōdōmei, which had existed since before the war.

During this process, Japan's union movement was growing strong roots and making rapid gains. The unrest at its center notwithstanding, the movement played an important role in improving working conditions. Early improvements in real wages were spectacular (Figure 2.1), and such results could not have been dreamed of without labor union bargaining power. About this time the unions began to insist on improved working conditions in return for vows of loyalty to the company and compelled management to accept the lifetime employment system with its restrictions on dismissing employees. Such policies gained management's tacit approval in the face of repeated strikes for better working conditions and in opposition to firings and rationalization drives in the 1950s—for example, the coal miners' strike, the Nissan, Amagasaki Steel, and Oji Paper strikes, and, fiercest of all, the Mitsui Miike strike. Whichever side was the technical winner, if a strike were prolonged it would ultimately drive the company into bankruptcy, which meant that both management and labor were the losers. As both sides wanted to avoid such an outcome, the Japanese style of labor–management relations became entrenched, with lifetime employment, the seniority wage systems, and unions organized by each enterprise as its three main tenets. The unions' practice of channeling their energies almost exclusively into an annual spring wage offensive dates from the latter half of the 1950s.

Figure 2.1. Impact of labor democratization, 1945–64
1) Estimated proportion of work force unionized =
      no. of union members
   ——————————————
         no. of employees
2) Number of workdays lost per union member =
      no. of workdays lost due to strikes
   ——————————————
         no. of union members
Source: Ministry of Labour, *Sengo Rōdō Keizaishi* [History of the Postwar Labor Economy], data section.

From the macroeconomic point of view, the improved working conditions, particularly the higher wages, achieved by the labor unions expanded domestic consumption markets and, in combination with increased farm incomes, made a great contribution to the development of the economy. Although managers individually chafed at them, the wage increases were highly significant for the economy as a whole, preparing the way for subsequent growth.

In addition to the above three major reforms, General Headquarters also imposed a variety of other changes on the Japanese economic system. For example, the purge of business leaders hastened the succession of young managers to senior positions. The accumulated effects of all these changes became the foundation of the present-day Japanese economy.

3. *Reconstruction and Stabilization*

Immediately after the defeat, the Allies took the position that they bore no responsibility for the reconstruction of the Japanese economy. That job was incumbent upon the Japanese people themselves, and they were offered only the hope that they would someday be reinstated in the international economy. In addition to the economic setbacks already suffered in war and defeat, the nation was also faced with the exaction of reparations by the Allies. The Pauley Reparations Mission that came to Japan in the autumn of 1945 proposed a stern program (see Table 2.4). All of the aircraft, light metals, and bearing factory facilities, particularly those of the Army and Navy arsenals, were to be removed, along with about half of the equipment in shipbuilding yards, steam-powered electric generating plants, and steel, machine tool, ammonium sulphate, and soda factories. Steel production capacity would be reduced to 2.5 million tons. Japan's industrial level would be set back to the level of 1926–30. If this reparations program had been implemented, economic reconstruction might have taken a very different course.

A further problem was posed by the cancellation of indemnity payments to businesses which suffered losses when, under government order, they had engaged in wartime military production or plant and equipment investment, or had dismantled factories and moved to provincial areas. After the Emergency Financial Measures were implemented in February 1946 in conjunction with the levying of an assets tax in July of that year, the Occupation authorities ordered the suspension of wartime indemnities, despite the Japanese government's public commitment to compensate businesses that had supported the war effort. Burdened by vast sums of bad debts and deprived of gov-

Table 2.4. Changes in Reparations Proposals: Value of Facilities to Be Removed

(¥ millions, 1939 prices)

	Industrial facilities	Military facilities	Total
Nov. 1946 Pauley Report	990	1,476	2,466
March 1948 Strike Report	172	1,476	1,648
April 1948 Johnstone (Draper) Report	102	560	662

Source: Article by Hayashi Yūjirō in *Ekonomisuto*, April 15, 1955, p. 72. Cited in Hayashi Yūjirō and Miyazaki Isamu, *Nihon no Keizai Keikaku* [Japan's Economic Plans] (Tōyō Keizai Shimpōsha, 1957), p. 38.

ernment relief, the companies which had been connected with military production could not turn a profit, nor could the banks and other financial institutions that had lent them money. The sums required for indemnities at that time were ¥53.9 billion for munitions companies, ¥21 billion for general private businesses and individuals, and ¥21 billion for zaibatsu-related firms, for a total of ¥96 billion.

The Japanese government had conceived of the indemnities as a means whereby the firms which received them could repay loans from banks, which in turn could use the funds to liquidate their obligations to the Bank of Japan and other creditors. Thus relieved of financial encumbrances, they would have been ready for a fresh start. When the wartime indemnities were suspended, measures were nonetheless taken for the reconstruction and reorganization of firms and financial institutions. According to the new procedures, both companies and financial institutions consolidated their capital funds and reserves and went into liquidation. With the remaining real capital in the form of production facilities, raw materials, finished goods, etc., they started up new companies and continued production. The formerly liquidated firms were then absorbed into and merged with their new companies. The new enterprises were unstable and did not produce well. They went through a series of ups and downs, and it was not until 1948 or 1949 that rehabilitation was fully on track and they could begin full-scale operations.

Faced with the necessity of proceeding with postwar reconstruction under the double handicap of reparations with suspended indemnities, business and financial institutions needed a system that would supply both material and financial assistance. Prior to this time the government had set up, within the Industrial Bank of Japan, a Reconstruction Finance Department responsible for supplying funds for reconstruction. Now it expanded that department's activities by establishing the Reconstruction Bank, which obtained its funds by issuing bonds accepted by the Bank of Japan.

The first Yoshida Cabinet's (1946) Finance Minister Ishibashi Tanzan, being a "Keynesian," thought along the following lines. The Japanese economy was at that time suffering from a surplus of both labor and production facilities, and prices were rising while production was stagnating. This was not a "true inflation," which in the Keynesian sense meant rising prices under full employment and full capacity utilization. Japan was instead suffering from a deficiency of production, and Ishibashi believed that the government should invest funds in the under-utilized industrial enterprises in order to revive production. Accordingly, he had no qualms about increasing fiscal spending. Based on this conviction of Ishibashi's, the Reconstruction Bank was also expanded as a pipeline for government and Bank of Japan funds being channeled into the industrial sector.

Reconstruction Bank funds also played a key role in the success of the priority production system (*keisha seisan hōshiki*), which aimed at industrial rehabilitation by financing crude oil imports for injection into the coal and steel industries. Since coal was the primary energy source at the time, increased coal production became the key to the revival of industrial production, but coal production had fallen to 21 million tons annually, slightly less than 40 percent of the wartime level. After deducting consumption by the railroads and the Occupation forces, hardly any remained for industrial use. After Prime Minister Yoshida's "heart-to-heart talks" with Occupation authorities in the fall of 1946, crude oil imports were authorized, and under the priority production system, all imported oil was to be injected into the steel industry. The resulting increased steel production would be invested in the coal industry; increased coal production would be reinvested in the steel industry; and so on, so that once steel and coal production had been raised to a certain level by reinvesting the products of these two sectors one in the other, the increased coal production could then be gradually channeled into other basic sectors to produce an overall industrial recovery. The system moved into operation in 1947, and the annual goal of 30 million tons of coal production was with some difficulty attained by investing Reconstruction Bank funds in the coal and steel industries on a top priority basis, by recruiting labor on a large scale, and by rationing food and subsistence commodities as much as possible. Thanks to these measures, from 1948 it became possible to ration coal to electric power, steel, chemical fertilizers, and other key industries, and economic recovery at length ensued.

At the same time, the rehabilitation of industry via the priority production system brought about an expansion of the Reconstruction Bank's funds supply pipeline. Although the aim was to increase production, the immediate result was to accelerate inflation. The supply of goods was increased by the expanded production, but until supply and demand equilibrium was established, the money supply overhang stimulated prices, which were then held down by the Emergency Financial Measures. The consumer price index (including the black market) soared about 40 percent every three months in 1947, and even heading into 1948 it still continued to rise at a stiff 15 percent quarterly (Figure 2.2). It did not settle down until 1949. However, as production began to increase in the latter half of 1948, inflation did

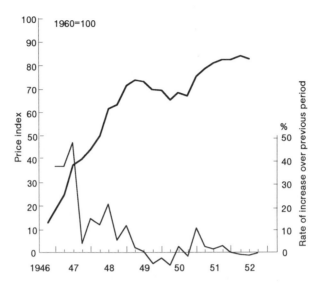

Figure 2.2. The Consumer Price Index and its rates of increase, 1946–52 (1960 = 100)
1) This index includes black market prices.
Source: Statistics Bureau, Office of the Prime Minister, Consumer Price Index.

slack off considerably. This fact has given rise to a debate over whether or not the draconian measures adopted under the Dodge Plan (discussed below) were really indispensable.

The black market was a major problem in the years immediately following the defeat. The ratio of black market to official prices was as high as 7.2 in 1946, and 5.3 in 1947. Even after the enactment of the Emergency Financial Measures, the new yen issue accumulated in the farm villages or in the pockets of black market traders, since people's highest priority was obtaining food. Eliminating the black market economy, conquering inflation, and reviving production were the major tasks confronting the Katayama Cabinet, which was formed by a coalition of the Socialist Party and the Democratic Party in May of 1947.

The Emergency Economic Measures this Cabinet adopted in July of 1947 were a wide-ranging, comprehensive set of policies which, in conjunction with the revival of production via the priority production system, aimed at revising the official price structure and containing inflation. The official prices of basic materials (the so-called stabilization belt goods—steel, coal, fertilizer, soda, gas, electric power, etc.)

in particular were held below production costs, and the government was to provide price-difference subsidies to make up for the resulting deficits. In this way, it would be possible to set low official prices for other goods which used these stabilized materials as their raw inputs, and supposedly this would help to check inflation. The goals of these policies, which assumed that labor productivity was declining relative to what it had been before the war, were to hold down and stabilize prices at 65 times, and wages at 28 times, their respective prewar levels. They proposed to accept a large-scale drop in real wages and to restore supply and demand equilibrium in the economy at this low standard of living. Since the salaries of government employees were set as the standard, the hope was that private business would follow suit.

Inflation continued unchecked, however. By June of 1948 the official price structure could no longer be maintained, and a revision had to be carried out. This time prices and wages were set at 110 and 57 times their prewar levels, respectively. Such was the policy designed to check inflation and revive production. However, when it was pursued, the fiscal burden imposed by the price-difference subsidies for key materials was enormous.[1] Moreover, since the subsidy amounts calculated on the basis of June 1947 costs could not catch up with the increases in prices and wages, deficits in coal mining and other industries mounted and had to be temporarily covered by loans from such institutions as the Reconstruction Bank. (In the end, the government made up these deficits with grant bonds and saw to it that funds from the Reconstruction Bank were repaid.)

These measures succeeded to a certain extent. If the gap between supply and demand is reduced while production increases and official prices are held down, inflation can be curbed. Even given the price movements described above, inflation was being contained. But before the effects of this policy became evident, drastic stabilization policies were adopted under the Occupation-sponsored Dodge Plan.

4. The American Policy Shift and the Dodge Line
As early as autumn of 1946, with the deepening of the Cold War, the Americans began to think in terms of hastening Japan's recovery and using its economic and military strength. Policy toward Japan began to change along these lines during and after the summer of 1947.

For example, consideration was given to amelioration of the reparations called for in the Pauley Report of 1945, and the Strike Committee of Inquiry conducted a full-scale investigation of policies for that purpose when it visited Japan in January 1947. In January of the following year Secretary of the Army Royall stated in a public address that Japan should be a "bulwark against Communism"; and in March Undersecretary of the Army Draper, upon visiting Japan, announced a proposed cut in reparations to one-fourth of the amount proposed in the Pauley Report (see Table 2.4). Then in 1949 the collection of all further reparations was cancelled. The stern anti-monopoly policies adopted with the passage of the Elimination of Excessive Concentration Law in the fall of 1947 also began to be moderated in the spring of the following year; and in the end, as we have seen, only eighteen companies were eventually broken up.

However, the most substantial of these changes was the reopening of private foreign trade in the summer of 1947, allowing private citizens of the Allied countries to come to Japan to conduct business. To take advantage of this opportunity, a credit facility popularly known as the Cotton Revolving Fund was planned by the Americans in order to re-establish the cotton spinning industry, and in 1948 a total of $210 million materialized for the purpose. This provided an important impetus to the recovery of the cotton spinning industry. However, trade at this time was state-managed, and there was not even a fixed exchange rate. The Japanese government set up a special account for trade funds on which it purchased export goods on the domestic economy for an amount of yen, A, and sold abroad for, say, B amount of dollars. The yen/dollar rate for those goods could only be calculated retroactively as one dollar = $(A \div B)$ yen. The process for imports was the reverse. Thus there were complicated exchange rates for each item of trade.

Since, given the situation at the time, the government bought at high prices from domestic producers of export goods and sold these products cheaply overseas, the yen was most often cheap relative to the dollar for export goods, at rates of 500 to 600 yen to the dollar. But for imported goods the yen was for the most part exchanged high, at about 100 yen to the dollar, because the government purchased these commodities on international markets and sold them comparatively cheaply at home. In the end, the special account for trade funds ran a deficit, which was made up from the general account. As a result of this, the government made plans to promote industry by giving trade subsidies (later called "invisible subsidies" by Dodge) to industry. According to some calculations, from 1946 to March of 1949 the government spent about ¥176 billion to support trade, an amount comparable to the total spent for price adjustment and other subsidies in fiscal 1949.

In May 1948 the Five-year Economic Rehabilitation Plan (first

Table 2.5. Five-year Economic Rehabilitation Plan (Targets: FY 1952)

			Actually achieved		
		Target	1951	1952	1953
Mining & manu-	Indexes (1930–34 = 100)	130	127.8	136.4	161.4
facturing	Coal (1000 tons)	44,000	43,312	43,359	43,538
production	Steel products ·(1000 tons)	2,300	4,972	5,099	5,404
Electric power generation	(million kwh)	37,920	47,729	51,645	56,305
Agriculture, forestry, & fisheries production	Indexes (1930–34 = 100) Rice (1000s of *koku*) (1 *koku* = 4.96 bushels)	116 67,921	106 60,278	66,152	54,924
Exports ($millions)		1,647	1,354	1,272	1,156
Imports ($millions)		1,657	1,995	2,028	2,101
Standard of living index (Per-capita income, 1930–34 = 100)		97	82.7	96	109

Source: Same as for Table 2.4.

draft) was drawn up by the Economic Stabilization Board. The central question was, how far could economic recovery progress by fiscal 1952? Table 2.5 presents the plan, which was designed to achieve production and living standards near prewar levels by fiscal 1952, five years away. And since even the Far Eastern Commission had taken the softer attitude that it would be acceptable to sanction an average living standard for the citizenry of about what it had been from 1930 to 1934, the plan was adopted as a goal.

A special feature of this plan was that, although it did not target recovery of the standard of living to prewar levels, production was supposed to surpass those levels. This was particularly true of the heavy and chemical industries, which were planned to far outstrip prewar production. And while the matter was discussed in terms of a return to prewar levels, it was common knowledge that the focus of the economy would have to be shifted away from light industry to the heavy and chemical industries. It can be seen from Table 2.5 that the actual record of achievement followed these lines. However, the path to success was by no means a smooth one: the program had to stand the test of the Dodge Plan.

The Dodge Plan was a broad program of fiscal and monetary policies developed under the guidance of Detroit bank president Joseph Dodge, who visited Japan with the rank of minister from February to April 1949 as financial adviser to the Supreme Commander for the Allied Powers (SCAP). By way of prelude to this program, a mission headed by Ralph Young in the summer of 1948 had, in conjunction with the shift in American policy, recommended that the multiplicity of exchange rates be abolished and a single rate of between 270 and 300 yen to the dollar be established in its place. From another quarter, the possibility of aid to Japan on a large scale (an Asian Marshall Plan) seemed to be growing in 1948. But while in Japan there was a clamor for "foreign capital imports" along with the "interim stability" question, the American Congress that year made sweeping cuts in the aid bill, and the hoped-for program came to nothing.

In October of 1948, however, as it gradually became clear that China's Kuomintang was close to succumbing to the Communist Army and as the significance of Japan's role in the Cold War in Asia was recognized, the U.S. National Security Council adopted Resolution 13/2 concerning Japan. This resolution formalized the major shift in America's basic policy toward Japan, removing many restrictions that had been previously imposed and decreeing that Japanese economic recovery would be expedited. On the basis of this decision, aid to Japan was cut, a Nine-Point Economic Stabilization Program was issued by SCAP in December of 1948 under directions from Washington, and Joseph Dodge came to Japan charged with the task of implementing reconstruction policies.

Dodge, who had drafted the West German currency reform in 1945–46, was an economist of the classical school on fiscal and monetary policy. A believer in the free-market economy, he completely rejected government interference and held that capital accumulation and the rehabilitation of industry could only be made possible by the efforts of the people themselves. He advanced three basic policies for the economy of Japan.

The first was a balanced budget. The issuing of long-term government bonds had already been prohibited by the Finance Act (1947), but the government had been covering its budget deficits by issuing short-term bonds with maturities of less than one year and then continually rolling them over. While calling for complete fiscal balance, not only in the general accounts but in the special accounts as well, the Dodge Plan prescribed an "overbalanced" budget which actually produced fiscal surpluses and redeemed bonds more rapidly than the legally established rate required. Secondly, new loans from the Reconstruction Bank were suspended. This measure was aimed at cutting off at their source the supplies of new currency which were seen as the fundamental cause of inflation. The third policy was the reduction and abolition of subsidies. As a first step, all subsidies which until then had not been made public, such as those to make up deficits in the special account for trade funds, were put into the budget. As a result, the amount for subsidies in the fiscal 1949 budget ended up as quite a large sum, and accordingly the system of economic controls and subsidies was to be abolished as quickly as possible.

Dodge explained that under the above policies, the Japanese were not to look to the United States for aid but must achieve recovery through their own work, economizing, and accumulation of capital. At the same time, Japan's economy should be exposed to international competition. It followed that a single exchange rate should be established, and in April of 1949 the rate was set at 360 yen to the dollar. This pegged the yen slightly lower than the 330 which at the time was widely held to be the appropriate rate. Businesses were forced to come up with rationalization plans so that they could withstand international competition under the new exchange rate. They also came to realize they would have to free themselves from dependence on government subsidies and loss compensation, and become competitive by their own efforts. This was probably the Dodge Plan's most significant consequence.

The Dodge Plan thus was a full-scale deflationary policy ranking with the Matsukata deflation of the early 1880s[2] and the fiscal policies of Finance Minister Inoue Junnosuke, who put Japan back on the gold standard in 1930 with disastrous effects. It was only the authority of the Occupation forces that made its implementation possible. Opinion today is divided as to whether or not the inflation could have been brought under control without the Dodge Plan. In this author's view, the supply-demand gap which was the fundamental reason for the inflation had been closed to a remarkable degree by the fall of 1948 and paved the way for putting a check on inflation. Coming on top of the credit squeeze which had resulted from the stricter enforcement of tax collections and reduced lending since about March or April of 1949 (before the Dodge Plan had been fully set into motion), a stringent tight-money policy would have pushed many firms over the brink into bankruptcy. For this reason, the Ministry of Finance and the Bank of Japan got in touch with the GHQ Economic Scientific Section, which was not on the best of terms with Dodge, and put into effect a Tight Money Neutralizing Measure (Kane Zumari Kanwa Hōsaku) that would channel the fiscal surplus back into private hands. This was to be done by mobilizing banks and

Table 2.6. Financial Conditions from April 1949 to June 1950

(A) Supply of Funds   (¥100 millions)

Funds withdrawn by the government from the private sector	1,289
Increase in deposits at financial institutions	3,825
Total of the above (amount of funds withdrawn from private holders)	5,114
Increase in lending by financial institutions	4,753
Increases in industrial funds supply from other sources	5,574

(B) Major Accounts of Commercial Banks

	Total deposits	Total borrowings	Total lending	Holdings of national bonds	Holdings of corporate bonds
End of March 1949	5,060	534	3,571	799	312
End of June 1950	7,896	1,017	6,815	426	528
Net increase during this period	2,836	483	3,244	-373	216

Sources: (A) Bank of Japan, Research Bureau, Shikin Junkan no Bunseki [Analysis of the Circulation of Funds], No. 5.
(B) Bank of Japan, Honpo Keizai Tōkei [National Economic Statistics], 1950.

other commercial financial institutions to bail out insolvent private businesses by lending them large amounts of money, most of which was to come from the large-scale buying up of bonds held by financial institutions and from Bank of Japan lending. This measure changed the deflationary character of the Dodge Plan into disinflation. The results are shown in Table 2.6. With the re-establishment of the links between firms and financial institutions which had existed since the wartime era and the rise of the financial keiretsu groups, with the advent of the so-called overloan phenomenon whereby increases in commercial bank lending exceeded increases in deposits, and with the attendant strengthening of Bank of Japan control over city banks, the special characteristics of the postwar economy took shape in this period.

In conclusion, a few words about changes in labor policy. As a result of the labor reforms, Japan's labor unions were greatly strengthened, but the left-wing All Japan Congress of Industrial Unions (Sanbetsu) was especially powerful. The at first sympathetic GHQ-SCAP began to take a more oppressive stance after the Yomiuri strike of 1946 and the planned February 1 strike of 1947, which it ordered cancelled. By 1948 SCAP had reached the point of issuing a directive of its own, depriving government employees of the right to strike. This action was for the most part consistent with the shift in Occupation policy. When the national railways and the telegraph and telephone facilities were converted into the self-supporting systems known as Japan National Railways (JNR) and Nippon Telegraph and Telephone Corporation in accordance with the Dodge Plan, employee dismissals were carried out on a large scale: JNR fired just under 100,000 workers while the Post Office and the Telegraph and Telephone Corporation dropped a total of about 220,000 from their payrolls. In the private sector, too, in mining and heavy industry fields such as electric power, electric machinery, automobiles, and coal, there was a move toward rationalization, which included personnel adjustments, in 1949. This provoked a fierce reaction from the labor unions and a succession of strikes, but the unions were ultimately defeated. Dismissals of left-wing activists were openly carried out at that time. With this, "democratization" came to a full stop, and the rebuilding of capitalism began.

5. The Korean War and the Peace Treaty of San Francisco

Even in early 1950, the Dodge Plan was still in force. No relaxation in the monetary situation seemed forthcoming, and a full-scale depression was feared. However, the Korean War began that June, changing the situation completely.

The influence of the Korean War was nothing short of prodigious. The year 1949 was one of worldwide recession, but this state of affairs shifted a full 180 degrees the following year as war sparked a worldwide search for strategic goods. From 1950, when the Korean War began, through 1951, world trade showed an increase of about $19 billion, or 34 percent. Since the volume of exports had increased by little more than 10 percent during this period, most of the dollar value of the increase was due to a 23 percent rise in the unit prices of world exports. This had a tremendous impact on the Japanese economy under the Dodge Plan. Exports jumped in response to the rise in international prices, and along with them production, employment, and business profits all rose rapidly as the economy surged forward into a boom.

As the economic indicators displayed in Table 2.7 show, exports grew by 2.7 times from 1949 to 1951, and production, too, increased by nearly 70 percent. Furthermore, there was a remarkable rise in corporate rates of return due to the rise in prices, particularly wholesale prices, that accompanied production increases. As far as business

Table 2.7. Economic Indicators during and after the Korean War

	1949	1950	1951	1952	1953	1954	1955	1956
Exports (US$ millions)	510	820	1,355	1,273	1,275	1,629	2,011	2,501
Special procurement income (US$ millions)	—	592		824	809	597	557	595
Imports (US$ millions)	905	975	1,995	2,028	2,410	2,399	2,471	3,230
Mining & manufacturing production index	18.2	22.3	30.8	33.0	40.3	43.7	47.0	57.5
Rate of return on gross capital employed (first half — second half, %)		2.8– 5.1	10.6– 6.7	4.8– 4.2	4.2– 4.6	3.2– 2.4	3.0– 3.6	4.1– 4.5
Permanent employment index in manufacturing industries (1960=100)	50.7	48.3	51.9	53.1	55.6	58.7	60.4	66.2
Wholesale price index	59.3	70.1	97.3	99.2	99.9	99.2	97.4	101.7
Consumer price index	72.6	67.6	78.7	82.6	88.0	93.7	92.7	93.0
Nominal wage index for manufacturing industries	33.1	40.2	51.6	60.7	68.1	71.7	74.5	86.4
Real wage index for manufacturing industries	45.6	59.5	65.6	73.5	77.4	76.5	80.5	87.5

For all indexes, 1960 = 100.

Sources: Export and imports data from Ministry of Finance customs clearance statistics. Special procurement figures from Bank of Japan. Production indexes from Ministry of International Trade and Industry. Rates of return from Mitsubishi Economic Research Institute. Consumer price indexes from Statistics Bureau, Office of the Prime Minister. Employment and wage indexes from the Ministry of Labour. All are officially published figures.

firms were concerned, this boom provided a greater boost than anything else to their economic recovery, heavily weighed down as they
were with the burdens of defeat and reconstruction. In addition, as
we will see, the boom prompted a vigorous expansion in plant and
equipment investment.

However, what was most important for the Japanese economy at
this point in time was the foreign exchange income deriving from the
expenditures of the U.S. Army and military personnel—the special
procurements (*tokuju*). Foreign currency from this source reached
gigantic sums for those times: $590 million in 1951 and over $800
million both in 1952 and in 1953. Since exports at the time were
running at approximately $1.3 billion, this enormous level of special
procurement income raised the ceiling on the nation's balance of
payments at a single stroke. That is to say, by means of a combination
of exports and special procurement income, Japan was enabled to
import at the rate of about $2 billion per year. To the Japanese
economy, which had been doing its level best just to import something less than one billion dollars' worth of goods in 1949 and 1950,
$2 billion in imports meant that the key industries which depended
on imports of raw materials could virtually double their scale of production. Freed of balance-of-payments limitations, firms which were
extremely anxious to increase production could obtain the imports
needed to support a much larger scale of activity.

Prior to the war, in the mid-1930s, Japan's imports and exports had
each been about 20 percent of GNP. At the beginning of the 1950s
imports were 10 to 13 percent of GNP, and this ratio remained
unchanged or even slightly declined from that time until the oil crisis
of 1973. Numerous explanations have been offered for the drop in the
rate of import dependence, but the most important reason was the
change in industrial structure. In the textile industry, which had been
of primary importance before the war, the rate of value added was
low. Each dollar's worth of imported raw cotton was processed and
exported as finished goods for no more than two dollars, producing
less than a dollar of foreign exchange income. Thus, even if imports
were 20 percent of GNP, more than half of that would be re-
exported, and the balance left inside the country would not even
amount to 10 percent of GNP. After the war, since the share of value
added in the products of the heavy and chemical industries rose with
progress in those fields, it became possible to cover the foreign
exchange costs of imports needed for domestic consumption even
after deducting more than 10 percent of GNP in imports which were
processed and re-exported as finished goods. In subsequent years the

share of industries with high value added (those involving a high degree of manufacturing, such as the machine industries) grew larger while at the same time Japan's terms of trade improved. Therefore, the ratio of imports to GNP continued to decline, to below 10 percent by the time of the oil crisis of 1973.

The higher ceiling on the balance of payments resulting from U.S. special procurements, as well as the lower ratio of imports to GNP, meant that the upper limit on increases in GNP was raised—that is, a higher rate of growth became possible. If imports are 12 percent of GNP and if they can be financed only from export income, which is a maximum of $1.3 billion, the upper limit on GNP can be no higher than $10.8 billion. However, if the value of imports is raised by $800 million through special procurement income and imports are still 12 percent of GNP, the ceiling on GNP can rise to $17.5 billion.[3] Japan's rapid recovery and growth during the Korean War were made possible in this way.

The Korean War had an invigorating effect on plant and equipment investment and technological innovation, too. Many industries, realizing that they were behind the international competition, imported technology from abroad and set their sights on expanding capacity. Since inadequate capacity in basic industries like electric power, steel, marine transport, and coal was the bottleneck that limited the expansion of production during this period, economic reconstruction was pushed primarily in these four key industries. The figures on plant and equipment investment in Table 2.8 testify to this fact.

It was in 1951 and 1952 that capital accumulation promotion policies for industrial reconstruction were hammered out in quick succession. These became the prototype for Japan's postwar industrial policies. The first of these measures employed national funds to establish the Japan Development Bank, whose mission was to assume the assets and liabilities of the Reconstruction Bank and to supply key industries with low-interest funds for plant and equipment. By priming the pump for finance from commercial banks, by providing security for finance received from abroad, and in other ways, Development Bank financing was highly significant in the long-term capitalization of key industries. The Japan Export-Import Bank, which was established at about the same time, was charged with the promotion of exports by providing financing to exporting firms.

The second area of importance for investment and technological innovation was the tax system. A tax reform had been implemented in accordance with the recommendations of the Shoup Mission, which

Table 2.8. Fluctuations in Plant and Equipment Investment by Industry

(¥100 millions. Figures in parentheses are percentage)

Fiscal year	1951	1952	1953	1954	1955	1956	1957	1958
Steel industry	369	379	396	256	267	625	1,119	1,197
	(8.4)	(7.7)	(6.4)	(4.8)	(4.5)	(6.1)	(8.8)	(9.4)
Marine transport	640	615	465	313	390	741	967	744
	(14.6)	(12.4)	(7.5)	(5.9)	(6.5)	(7.2)	(7.7)	(5.8)
Electric power	553	1,054	1,461	1,422	1,483	2,010	2,437	2,901
	(12.6)	(21.3)	(23.7)	(26.8)	(24.8)	(19.6)	(19.2)	(22.7)
Coal industry	208	202	206	137	143	135	301	338
	(4.8)	(4.1)	(3.3)	(2.6)	(2.4)	(1.3)	(2.4)	(2.5)
Total for these key industries	1,770	2,250	2,528	2,128	2,283	3,511	4,824	5,180
	(40.4)	(45.5)	(40.9)	(40.1)	(38.2)	(34.2)	(38.1)	(40.4)
Total including other industries	4,389	4,955	6,170	5,303	5,989	10,259	12,647	12,789
	(100)	(100)	(100)	(100)	(100)	(100)	(100)	(100)

Source: Japan Development Bank survey.

was in Japan in 1949 and 1950. A proportional corporate tax system
was adopted at that time, placing particular emphasis on special tax
measures for the promotion of plant and equipment investment and
exports. In 1951 a separate tax on interest and dividend income was
instituted, and 1952 saw the abolition of the tax on the reserves of
non-family business firms and the establishment of both a retirement
fund withholding tax and a drought reserve fund for electric power
companies. All were *de facto* tax reductions and exemptions. Moreover, the Enterprise Rationalization Promotion Law, enacted in the
same year, established a special depreciation system for important
machinery with specified machines designated and authorized for
high rates of depreciation. This law played a big role in accelerating
plant and equipment investment since it enabled firms to reduce their
tax burden when they made such investments. In 1953 the exemption
of income from the transfer of securities, tax deductions on export
income, a system of reserves against export losses, a tax exemption
system on key products, the expansion of a bankruptcy reserve fund,
and other such measures for the broadly favorable tax treatment of
business were implemented. Needless to say, these measures promoted capital accumulation, and they became the basis of the subsequent business tax system. Table 2.9 shows how the various industries turned these reforms to account.

The third policy area was the foreign exchange allocation system.
Inaugurated in 1949, this was a system whereby, in an effort to
establish an international payments balance, the government drew up
an import budget for each quarter, made foreign exchange allocations
for each item, and thereby authorized a fixed volume of imports. In
principle it was a system for restricting the total value of imports, but
it turned out that it offered at the same time a splendid means of
protecting industry. For example, it had been a policy objective to
foster the automobile industry since before the war, but by means of
the foreign exchange allocation system, the government took steps to
impose extreme restrictions on automobile imports over the next ten
years or more, steps that were the virtual equivalent of an import ban.
Thus were created the conditions under which the automobile industry was assured of a domestic market for its development. Similarly,
import restrictions on oil were aimed at the protection of the coal
industry. But steps such as increasing crude oil import allocations in
response to the coal shortages that arose from the 63-day-long coal
strike in 1952 were also taken. Furthermore, the attitude toward the
oil industry was such that companies having only domestic capital had
an advantage over joint ventures with foreign capital in obtaining

Table 2.9. Utilization of the Special Tax Measures by Major Corporations

(percentages of gross income)

	A (Mining)	B (Spinning)	C (Chemical fibers)	D (Paper)	E (Fertilizer)	F (Steel)	G (Electric machinery & appliances)	H (Commerce)	I (Electric power)	J (Banking)
Gross income	100	100	100	100	100	100	100	100	100	100
Tax-exempt income from staple products, capital increase, dividends, exports, etc.	0.6	24.1	114.4	3.4	45.1	18.4	4.7	27.1	17.6	4.0
Reserve funds of all kinds	66.8	6.7	−26.4	41.5	0.8	8.5	14.3	14.2	22.0	29.2
Inclusions for expense account losses	−4.2	—	—	−5.3	−5.4	—	—	−1.7	−1.2	−0.9
Special depreciation	4.9	5.7	3.0	—	—	13.2	11.3	—	—	0.3
Taxable income	31.9	63.5	9.0	60.4	59.5	59.9	69.7	60.4	61.6	67.4
Estimated effective tax rate	17.8	31.2	4.4	29.8	29.3	29.5	34.3	29.8	30.4	33.2

Source: Tax Bureau survey. Cited in Morita Minoru, "Shihon Chikuseki to Kokka no Shisaku" [Capital Accumulation and National Policy] (in Aihara Shigeru, ed., *Gendai Nihon no Shihon Chikuseki*)

import allocations. In this way the application of the foreign exchange allocation system played a large role in protecting and fostering domestic industry.

Fourth, foreign technology began to be imported on a large scale during this period. Technology imports via technical cooperation with foreign firms grew rapidly, from 27 agreements in fiscal 1950 to 101 in 1951, 133 in 1952, 103 in 1953, and 82 in 1954. There was at that time a strong inclination among firms when they invested in plant and equipment to attempt to make up for the time they had lost during and after the war by engaging in technical cooperation overseas, and this cooperation was directly protected and encouraged by the Foreign Capital Law and the Foreign Exchange Administration Order. Abroad, this was also the period in which the technology developed during the war was commercialized for general private industry. The electric and electronic machinery, oil refining, and petrochemical industries in particular are representative of the fields in which this occurred.

In attempting to revolutionize industrial technology by bringing in the fruits of two decades of progress at a single stroke, Japan at this time imported much technology that had come into practical use during the 1930s as well as that developed during the war. More will be said in the following chapter about the tremendous effect of this importation process, although there was some imported technology which did not prove to be successful for adaptation to industrial use. It should be noted that the ground had already been prepared for this technology's acceptance in Japan. Many firms had assimilated considerable technology since going into military production, and when they switched back into production for private demand, it was in order to raise productivity and cut costs that they imported foreign technology.

The Peace Treaty of San Francisco and the U.S.–Japan Security Treaty were signed in September 1951, and when they came into effect in April 1952, Japan recovered its independence, even though the latter agreement left American military bases inside the country. Prime Minister Yoshida Shigeru set economic reconstruction and development as the nation's immediate goals while saving on military expenses by leaving defense to the U.S. Army. The first half of the Meiji Restoration motto "strong army, rich country" was a dead letter, but the goal of "rich country" at long last bore fruit in rapid economic growth.

With the coming of independence, revisions of all kinds were made in the policies implemented during the Occupation. Among the industrial policies, the most important of these was the 1953 revision of the Anti-Monopoly Law which authorized depression cartels and rationalization cartels, relaxed restrictions on such things as stock retention by corporations, interlocking directorships, and mergers, and sanctioned retail price maintenance. These changes were in response to the demands of the business world, and the relaxation of the restrictions governing cartel behavior in particular took on great significance thereafter. Moreover, in connection with the revival of cartels, the Ministry of International Trade and Industry (MITI) had begun to engage in administrative guidance in the form of advisory curtailments in 1952, without waiting for revision of the Anti-Monopoly Law. When the textile industry fell into a slump in 1952, MITI evaded the Anti-Monopoly Law regulations and effectively formed a cartel by giving direct counsel to businessmen and contriving to regulate production and shipments in the industry. However, it should be noted that this kind of policy restricting competition did not necessarily permit the immediate control of industries by oligopolistic firms. It meant no more than that firms were able to find some shelter during economic downturns; it never acted as a general restriction on competitive conditions in the markets formed after the war. On the contrary, secure in the knowledge that relief was available, firms adopted bold strategies and competition became all the more vigorous.

In this way, by the time the Korean War ended and the Peace Treaty of San Francisco was concluded, Japan had virtually determined the direction of its subsequent economic policy. The externally imposed Occupation reforms greatly changed the fixed system of the prewar Japanese economy and ended by preparing a rich soil not only for "democratization" but also for economic growth. For example, the rise in both farmers' and workers' incomes and the attendant expansion of consumption capacity, as well as the zaibatsu dissolution and the elimination of excessive concentration, combined to produce the competitive market conditions that were indispensable for this growth. Over and above this, as has been seen in this chapter, policies favoring capital accumulation and the introduction of foreign technology were adopted along with the decision to hold down military expenses and take the "rich country" path, dispensing with the "strong army." In this sense the course of subsequent economic growth had been charted by the early 1950s. Hence I believe it is appropriate to lump together the years from 1951–52 to about 1970 as the period of rapid economic growth.

The economic growth brought about by the Korean War led to an increase in household income and a conspicuous rise in the level of consumption. The common hope, particularly of city dwellers during this time, was to recover the standard of living they had enjoyed in the prewar period, represented by the years 1934–36. As their incomes increased, the first items people purchased were the prewar consumer goods like Japanese-style clothing, rice, miso, and soy sauce. This trend is reflected in the fact that consumption of all these traditional consumer goods peaked in the early 1950s. Lifestyle recovered along with standard of living. The recovery was completed by the mid-1950s, after which living standards continued to rise but accompanied by a move away from the prewar lifestyle and towards a more Western style of living.

Notes

1. The total amount expended for price adjustment subsidies and others in fiscal 1948 was ¥114.1 billion, or 24 percent of general account expenditures. This amount rose in fiscal 1949 to ¥198.8, 27 percent of the general account.

2. Matsukata Masayoshi (1835–1924) was Finance Minister of Japan for an unbroken period of 11 years, from 1881 to 1892, and was chief advocate and executor of the retrenchment policy adopted to cope with the serious inflation that followed the Satsuma Rebellion in 1877.

3. The calculations are as follows. When Imports $\leq$ Exports, then 12% GNP $\leq$ \$1.3 billion. Solving for GNP, $\frac{1.3 \text{ billion}}{.12} \leq$ \$10.8 billion. However, when Imports $\leq$ Exports + Special Procurement, then 12% GNP $\leq$ \$1.3 billion + \$.8 billion $\leq$ \$2.1 billion. Solving for GNP, GNP $\leq$ \$17.5 billion.

3

Rapid Growth

1. A Chronology of Growth and Business Cycles

The rare period of worldwide rapid economic growth from the beginning of the 1950s to the early 1970s was also a period which produced striking changes in Japan's economy, both domestically and in relation to the world economy. These changes were both continuous and quantitative in character. They were results neither of special government policies nor of a few heroic achievements, but were produced by the cumulative efforts of the people. It was only with the "Nixon shock" and the oil crisis of the 1970s that Japan was again visited by events as dramatic as the launching of the Dodge Plan. In order to understand the changes that took place during these years, let us begin by outlining a chronology of the period, supported by quantitative data on growth and cycles.

Figure 3.1 shows real GNP after 1951, real private plant and equipment investment (quarterly data), and the GNE deflator (price-level indicator, three-period moving averages). Figure 3.2 indicates the balance of exports and imports of goods and services (current transactions balance, three-period moving averages) in nominal terms and the ratio of private inventory increases (three-period moving averages, quarterly data) to GNE. Taken together, these two sets of figures show the trends of economic growth and cycles from the Korean War to 1973. The figures also show trends from after the oil crisis, a period which shows markedly different characteristics from the period of high growth, but this will be discussed in the following chapter. Let us summarize a number of facts which can be read from these data for a clearer understanding of the special features of the rapid growth era.

(1) Until the oil shock of 1973, the postwar economy did not change erratically but showed virtually a straight line of economic growth (an average annual growth rate of 10 percent). There were

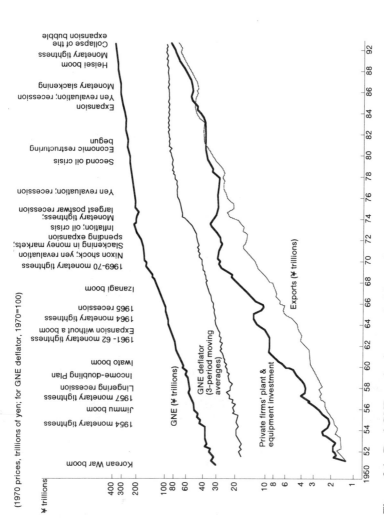

Figure 3.1. Real GNP, real private capital formation, and price changes, 1950–92
Source: Economic Planning Agency, *Kokumin Keizai Tōkei Nenpō* [National Economic Statistics Annual Report].

cycles, but net growth remained positive and relatively strong. A closer look shows that the growth rate was a little lower in the 1950s and a little higher during the 1960s, but it is not particularly necessary to distinguish between the two periods.

(2) During this growth, plant and equipment investment showed large increases, growing at a rate of 22 percent from 1951 to 1973. This was the driving force behind the domestic demand which induced rapid growth. At the same time, it generated a productive capacity commensurate with that growth.

(3) The rise in prices was also comparatively strong. The GNE deflator as an overall price index approximately tripled during this period, growing at 5.2 percent per annum. Like the growth rate, it was also a little lower in the 1950s (4 percent) and somewhat higher from 1961 to 1973 (5.6 percent). Thus it could be termed a mild acceleration of the trend.

(4) The growth process was not a smooth, homogeneous trend. During this period the Japanese economy experienced business upturns and downswings in cycles of slightly more than three years or, at times, two or five years. These fluctuations were systematic, for the most part operating in a definite way. That this mechanism was the inventory cycle (Kitchin cycle) is clear from the fluctuations in the ratio of private inventory increases in Figure 3.2.

(5) The reason for the recurring inventory cycle lay in the fluctuation in the international balance of payments, as shown at the bottom of this same Figure 3.2. In other words, imports increased along with expanded production when, with continued economic growth, internal demand became more brisk, particularly for plant and equipment but also for private consumption, government purchases, and the building up of inventories. But on the other hand, as goods were channeled into internal demand, exports were constrained and the balance of payments went into deficit in the current account.

(6) As a general rule, if foreign currency reserves decline, the monetary authorities are compelled to impose tight-money measures (various types of which are discussed below). Moreover, if there is an excess of imports, money becomes even tighter since the domestic supply of yen funds is soaked up by purchases of foreign currency which must be used to settle the outstanding balance of imports over exports. Then, as internal demand is suppressed in this way, firms are forced to make *unplanned* inventory increases which arise out of the slackness of demand, rather than planned increases arising out of anticipated sales. Then still more funds are required in order to maintain these inventories. In Figure 3.2 rapid increases in the

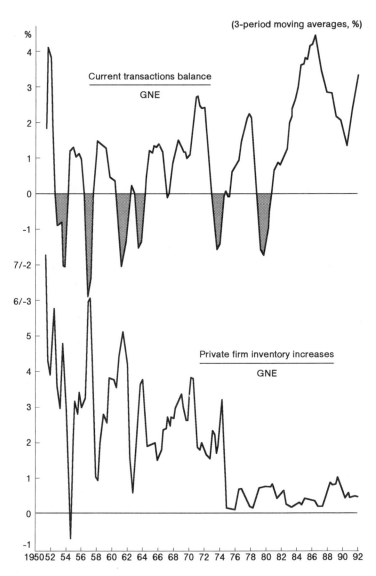

Figure 3.2. Current transactions balance and inventory relative to GNE, 1950–92.

Source: Same as for Figure 3.1.

inventory ratio can be seen in 1957, 1962, 1963–64, 1970, and so on—
years which were preceded by international payments deficits, i.e., an
excess of imports. These were the *unplanned* inventory increases. As
a result, financial conditions grew more and more stringent, plant and
equipment investment was either deferred or brought to a standstill,
hiring was slack, increases in national income were checked, and
consumption was also affected accordingly. Plant and equipment
investment followed the fluctuations of inventories, with a slight lag,
as shown in Figure 3.1. In this way, recessions set in and corporate
profits declined. From the macro point of view, however, since these
slowdowns represented no more than a blunting of the growth rate
during the period of rapid growth, Japan's recessions were, at most,
"growth cycles."

(7) Since, if domestic demand is dull, goods are diverted into
exports and imports are curbed, the international payments current
account will naturally improve and monetary tightness will be
relieved. With the exception of the two-year tight money period from
1973–75, the periods in which monetary stringency was imposed were
all of about twelve months' duration. Japan's tight-money policies
were highly effective, and they took effect rapidly.

(8) After the relaxation of tight money policies, markets did not
immediately revive but instead remained slack or even declined for a
time while businesses were drawing down their unplanned accumu-
lations of inventory. At these times, economic stimuli such as the
easing of financial conditions, expanded fiscal spending, and so on
were applied as countermeasures. As a result, business firms would
resume *planned* inventory increases when they perceived a revival
in demand and would subsequently resume plant and equipment
investment. In this way, business would gradually become brisk again
and head for new growth.

As the figures show, this kind of cycle has been repeated a number
of times. The boom periods in 1951 (Korean War boom), 1953
(investment boom), 1956–57 (the "Jimmu boom"), the plant and
equipment investment expansion of 1959–61 (the "Iwato boom"),
1963 (an expansion without a boom), 1967–69 (the "Izanagi boom"),
1973, and 1989–90, or eight altogether.[1] Monetary restraints were
imposed ten times, in 1951, 1954, 1957–58, 1961–62, 1964, 1967,
1969–70, 1973–75, 1979–80, and 1989–90. Of these, the tight-money
policies of 1967 did not reach the point of causing a recession because
Japan's balance of payments situation improved rapidly with the
business upturn abroad. The monetary stringency of 1969–70 was
implemented in order to check rising prices, not because of a deteri-

oration in the balance of payments. Those of 1973 and 1979–80 were reactions to the two oil crises of the 1970s, and that of 1989–90 was triggered by skyrocketing land and securities prices.

From this overview it can be seen that the economic growth of the 1950s and 1960s was achieved through a succession of short-term business cycles. The balance of payments was the major constraining factor that made these cycles unavoidable. That is, in always trying to achieve maximum growth, Japan expanded production and facilities, and in so doing ran up against the limits of its ability to import, whereupon a reversal of direction was unavoidable. Initially the limit on growth was a growth rate of 10 percent, but this pattern clearly changed near the end of the 1960s. After the 1967 international payments current account deficit was checked before causing a recession, the balance of payments remained in the black, and foreign currency reserves began to show steady increases as growth continued to exceed 10 percent. Since Japan's international competitiveness had been strengthened, the balance of payments—at least at the ¥360/US$1 rate—had ceased to be a constraint on growth. The goal of the monetary stringency of 1969 was to curb the rise in wholesale prices. While this objective was for a time achieved through the suppression of domestic demand, exports grew all the more as imports stagnated and internal demand declined; hence the effect was to increase the balance of payments surplus still further. This in the end led to the upward revaluation of the yen which, along with the subsequent oil crisis, tolled the death knell for the era of rapid growth.

2. The International Environment of Growth

One might enumerate many factors that made rapid growth possible, but in very broad terms they may be divided into the international environment and domestic conditions. Of these two, the influence which the international environment exerted over Japan was extremely important. This issue will be given a rather general treatment here, and domestic conditions will be the subject of the following sections.

According to United Nations statistics, the global gross domestic product (GDP) from 1950 to the mid-1960s grew at a rate of about 5 percent; even when Eastern Europe and the Soviet Union are excluded, the rate is still high, about 4.4 percent. According to Maddison's estimates, the long-term growth rates of Europe and America were only 2.7 percent from 1870 to 1913, and 1.3 percent from 1913 to 1950.[2] Thus, the post-World War II growth rate was far higher than that of the prewar years.

Moreover, again according to United Nations statistics, the volume of world trade tripled between 1955 and 1970, with a growth rate of 7.6 percent, although it grew at 3.5 percent from 1870 to 1913 and at only 1.3 percent from 1913 to 1950.[3] The worldwide increase in this growth rate had an extremely beneficial effect on Japan's growth.

Technological progress and industrial development were of course responsible for the high rate of growth in the world economy. But underlying them was the establishment of the International Monetary Fund (IMF) system to provide infrastructural support for this progress, as well as the worldwide spread of full employment policies buttressed by Keynesian and post-Keynesian macro-economics. The IMF in 1944 conceived the Bretton Woods system, a global arrangement for the management of foreign exchange in place of the international gold standard which had been in use up until that time.[4] It had two main features.

First, in place of gold, which was chronically in short supply, a key currency with convertibility into gold (by default, the American dollar) was to be established. The American dollar was not to be convertible within the United States, but conversion by both domestic and foreign authorities was to be authorized at the rate of $35/ounce. Since the middle of World War II the U.S. had been commonly acknowledged to possess economic strength surpassing that of any other country in the world, and the American dollar was selected as the key currency over objections by John Maynard Keynes that a non-national currency should be established instead. This choice presupposed that, as the key currency country, the United States would contribute to the support of a global monetary system and to the achievement of global full employment—a responsibility which the U.S. did subsequently strive to fulfill.

Second, the system was to establish fixed exchange rates between the key currency and the currency of each member country, with a very narrow band within which each of these rates could fluctuate. These fixed rates were not to be changed except when a fundamental disequilibrium in the international balance of payments arose. In this context, a fundamental disequilibrium meant that the country was burdened with chronic unemployment, regardless of whether domestic business conditions were prosperous or slack, with the implication that an accompanying chronic payments deficit was due to an overvalued currency. Thus, less than ten years after Keynes published his *General Theory of Employment, Money, and Interest* (1936), full employment had been acknowledged as a common policy goal, as was symbolized by the fact that Keynes represented Britain at the 1944 Bretton Woods conference.

In order to fulfill its responsibilities for assisting in the recovery of Europe, the United States distributed dollar funds on a massive scale under the Marshall Plan. An Asian Marshall Plan never materialized, but the United States intervened in the Korean War in order to play its self-appointed role as "defender of the Free World," with the result that a huge volume of dollars was distributed as "special procurement" and in other forms in the Asian region, particularly in Japan (see Chapter 2). Aimed at the developing countries, the Colombo Plan subsequently took shape. Britain, which had led the way in adopting the gold standard in the nineteenth century, had indirectly contributed to the support of that gold standard abroad as its international payments surplus was invested overseas by private business, which received a return on these investments. The United States, however, from the first strove to directly nurture and support the IMF system in the form of Marshall Plan and Colombo Plan aid and special procurements arrangements.

With reconstruction under the Marshall Plan, the countries of Europe, particularly Germany, France, and Italy, adopted full employment as their economic policy objective and aimed primarily for growth rather than stability in the latter half of the 1950s. These policies in due course revived international competitiveness, and in January 1958 six countries on the Continent formed the EEC (European Economic Community, from 1967 reorganized and expanded into the twelve-member EC) in order to compete more effectively against the U.S. Meanwhile, from the beginning of the 1960s America began running a chronic balance of payments deficit, whose major causes were government military and other overseas spending, as well as overseas investments of multinationalizing American firms. By the late 1960s the U.S. trade deficit had become a permanent fixture, and the Vietnam War accelerated America's dollar outflows. The EC and Japan were catching up economically, and this, combined with the situation in Vietnam, began to erode the status America had once enjoyed as the Western superpower even as the U.S. continued to fulfill its role as the key currency country. Turmoil mounted in the IMF system until President Nixon ended the dollar's convertibility into gold in August 1971. This ushered in the era of the Smithsonian Agreement (1971), resulting in the real devaluation of the dollar, and the general float (1973), which are discussed in Chapter 5.

The foregoing is a simple chronology of the IMF system, and it almost completely correlates with changes in Japan from the latter half of the 1960s. Japan re-entered the world economy in 1949, and from the time the ¥360/US$1 rate was established until the upward

Table 3.1 International Comparison of Export Price Indexes, 1950–77

(1958 = 100)

	Japan	U.S.A.	U.K.	W. Germany	France	Italy	World
1950	102.2	81	73	72	61	110	—
55	109.3	92	89	91	71	111	99
60	95.9	99	96	94	95	102	100
65	100.8	104	104	102	105	102	103
				(107)			
70	109.5	121	131	104	126	110	113
			(112)	(119)	(112)		
75	151.6	213	260	137	197	225	241
	(183.9)		(206)	(219)	(217)	(206)	
77	160.3	242	370	142	236	324	268
	(217.0)		(228)	(257)	(240)	(231)	

Figures in parentheses were calculated by multiplying the index for that year by the American dollar exchange rate (base year = 1963).

Source: Calculated from Bank of Japan, *Nihon Keizai o Chūshin to suru Kokusai Hikaku Tōkei* [International Comparative Statistics Focusing on Japan].

yen revaluation in 1971 this rate was consistently maintained. With the ¥360 rate as the standard, Japan's objective during this period was to strengthen its international competitiveness. That this goal was achieved is clear from a comparison of national export price indexes (Table 3.1). Comparing these figures with the U.S. domestic price index adjusted by the exchange rate vis-à-vis the dollar (shown in the table in parentheses), one can observe the process whereby Japan gradually gained an advantage over the other advanced industrial nations. This is how the growth rate gradually rose and is the reason that it was possible to firmly secure a balance of payments surplus by the latter half of the 1960s.

However, the Japanese economy's dependence on the world economy was extremely high. The following simple model may be used to estimate Japan's export function. The model attempts to explain the value of Japan's exports (E_j) in terms of total world imports (M_w) and an index of Japan's export competitiveness (P_j/P_w), where the latter is the ratio of Japan's export price index (P_j) to the world export price index (P_w):

$$E_j = AM_w^{\beta_1} \left(\frac{P_j}{P_w}\right)^{\beta_2}, \qquad (1)$$

where β_2 is the elasticity of Japanese exports.

Excluding the index of Japan's export competitiveness, E can be computed as

$$E_j = AM_w^{\beta_1}. \tag{2}$$

The results are shown in Table 3.2.

The results of the calculation of equation (1) indicate the following with regard to Japan's exports. From the fact that all coefficients have a high degree of significance and the fact that the coefficient of determination R^2 is extremely high, it is clear that the expansion in world trade was the chief factor in the expansion of Japan's exports. However, the exponent β_1 declines from the 1950s to the 1960s and from the 1960s to the 1970s. Significant effects of the competitiveness factor can be discerned through the 1950s and 1960s if this period is taken as a whole. However, if the period is broken down into decades, the exponent β_2 is not significant except in the 1960s, when it scarcely approaches the significant level. If this variable is excluded, high coefficients of determination and exponents with a high degree of significance can also be obtained from equation (2), which explains Japan's exports exclusively in terms of world trade. However, the value of coefficient β_1 declines from the 1950s to the 1960s, and still further by the 1970s.

The exponent β_1, the elasticity of the value of Japan's exports relative to the value of world import, may be written as

$$\left(\eta = \frac{\Delta E_j}{E_j} \bigg/ \frac{\Delta M_w}{M_w} \right).$$

Based on the estimated values for equation (2), elasticity was about 2 throughout the period of the 1950s and 1960s, or 2.7 during the 1950s, 1.8 during the 1960s, and 1.1 in the 1970s. In other words, Japan's exports could expand with a high degree of elasticity in response to the expansion of world trade, but they were particularly responsive to world trade expansion during the 1950s.

The fact that Japan's exports during the period of high growth can be almost entirely explained in terms of trends in world trade means that the Japanese economy was sensitive to the world business cycle. Or, to restate the matter, the Japanese economy did not possess the means to insulate itself from shocks originating in this international cycle. As is shown in Figure 3.3, there is actually a clear correspondence from year to year between the rate of increase in Japanese exports over the previous year and the rate of increase in world imports. Practically all irregularities in this pattern can be traced to Japan's domestic business conditions.

Table 3.2. Estimation of Japan's Export Function, 1951-75

	$E_j = AM_w^{\beta_1}\left(\frac{P_j}{PW}\right)^{\beta_2}$				$E_j = AM_W^{\beta_1}$		
Period	A	β_1	β_2	R^2	A	β_1	R^2
1951–70	2.1445×10^{-6}	1.8165 (24.125)	1.331 (3.6154)	0.9909	2.0672×10^{-3}	2.0281 (33.125)	0.9839
1951–60	4.0495×10^{-6}	2.4384 (10.677)	0.76066 (1.6912)*	0.96864	2.6222×10^{-5}	2.6663 (13.028)	0.9550
1961–70	7.6429×10^{-6}	1.7045 (34.369)	1.7368 (2.2441)†	0.99727	1.3150×10^{-2}	1.7828 (4.1205)	0.9953
1968–75	1.5480	1.1713 (11.929)	-0.48146 (-0.88802)*	0.986722	2.9143	1.1004 (19.615)	0.9846

1) M_W is in US$ 100 millions, E_j in US$ millions. Both are nominal values.
2) World data are from IMF statistics; data for Japan are from customs statistics.
3) P_W is the UN unit price index. P_j is obtained by adjusting the Bank of Japan export price index to 1958 price levels.
4) Figures in parentheses are t-values. Those marked * are not significant for values of $\alpha = 5\%$.
5) Values marked † are extremely low at 5% and not significant.
6) R^2 is the coefficient of determination.

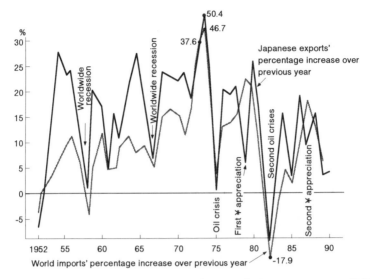

Figure 3.3. World imports and rates of increase in Japanese exports, 1952–90
Source: From Bank of Japan, *Nihon Keizai o Chūshin to suru Kokusai Hikaku Tōkei*
[International Comparative Statistics Focusing on Japan].

This sensitivity to the world business cycle also explains Japan's
monetary policies up to the first half of the 1960s, when the nation
was at last able to accumulate a buffer of foreign exchange reserves.
Since all foreign currency earned from exports was spent on imports
in order to expand production and achieve high growth, there was no
margin left over for the accumulation of foreign currency. Thus, if an
economic downturn occurred overseas, it would set off a chain reaction in which exports would immediately drop off, the balance of
payments would go into deficit, and monetary stringency would be
imposed, in order to immediately dampen spending for imports that
would expend the deficit. In West Germany, by contrast, from the
late 1950s onward productive capacity was high, but firms' behavior
was less expansive, and the balance of payments and foreign currency
reserves were not immediately affected if export growth lagged
because exports were not so directly dependent on imports for inputs.
Thus West Germany was able to pursue a more independent monetary policy. In Japan, however, a trade-off was made in favor of high
growth. Moreover, a large amount of Japan's trade was with the
United States, which had the largest trade volume in the world. From
the latter part of the 1950s, both export and import trade with the
U.S. continuously exceeded 30 percent of Japan's total export and

import trade. Such extensive trade dependence meant that America's business cycles exerted a strong influence on Japan. It was only after Japan began running a sustained surplus in its balance of payments during the latter part of the 1960s that it was able to extricate itself from this kind of dependency.

Since before the war Japan had been developing its strength as a processing trade nation. The postwar results can be clearly seen from a comparison of the structure of its exports and imports with those of the European nations from 1970–75, as shown in Table 3.3. Ever since the 1950s approximately 50 percent of Japan's imports have consisted of raw materials and fuel. If food is added to this, primary products have made up 80 percent, while machinery and other manufactured goods have been less than 20 percent of imports except in 1965 and 1970. This is in marked contrast to the imports of Western Europe, of which 25 to 30 percent were raw materials and fuels and 40 to 60 percent were industrial products. Of course this reflects the composition of exports. In 1955 upwards of 80 percent of Japan's exports were manufactured goods, a figure which had reached 95 percent by the 1970s. In Europe, manufactured goods' share of exports stayed at between 60 and 75 percent. Thus, Europe both exports and imports industrial products, but in Japan the bias has been toward exporting industrial products almost exclusively, while keeping imports of such products extremely low.

A tremendous change in the composition of Japan's industrial exports naturally accompanied heavy and chemical industrialization and economic growth. In 1950 about half of exports consisted of textile products, and this figure was still 37 percent in 1955. But by 1975 it had dropped to 5 percent. On the other hand, steel's share of exports had risen to 34 percent by 1960, but subsequently fell to 10 percent. Machinery and transport equipment, particularly ships and automobiles, replaced steel as the leading exports. These changes should be understood in connection with changes in the domestic industrial structure, but suffice it to say that they were part of the shift toward the export of highly processed, high-value-added goods. The cycle of importing raw materials, processing them, and then exporting them remained unchanged, but the trend was toward raising the level of technology and using low-cost raw material imports to produce higher-value export products.

In this way, Japan succeeded in reducing the proportion of imports used for the processing trade and expanded the scale of imports for domestic consumption, thus lowering its ratio of imports to GNP. However, this did not mean that the importance of imports declined.

Table 3.3. Export and Import Component Ratios of Japan and Western Europe

(A) Imports

(Share of total exports or imports)

	Food		Raw materials		Fuel		Chemical products		Machinery & transport equipment		Other industrial products		Value of imports (US$100 million)	
	Japan	Western Europe	Japan	Western Europe	Japan	Western Europe	Japan	Western Europe	Japan	Western Europe	Japan	Western Europe	Japan	Western Europe
1955	26.4	23.5	50.5	23.6	9.7	11.0	4.7	4.8	5.2	13.1	3.4	24.0	24.7	407.2
60	13.6	20.0	49.5	19.8	14.1	10.0	6.4	6.0	9.0	17.5	7.4	26.7	44.9	571.1
65	19.3	17.9	36.5	14.6	19.0	9.8	5.2	6.7	9.6	21.4	10.3	29.6	84.5	807.9
70	13.6	14.0	35.4	11.1	20.7	9.3	5.3	7.5	11.4	25.1	12.2	31.3	193.2	1405.1
75	15.2	11.4*	20.1	9.9*	44.3	20.3*	3.6	8.5*	6.6	21.0*	9.7	27.9*	557.5	3451.5*
80	10.5	10.7	17.7	7.4	50.1	24.0	4.2	7.9	6.0	21.7	10.8	26.4	1409	8854
85	12.2	10.0	14.5	6.7	43.8	18.7	6.2	9.8	8.3	25.8	13.5	26.5	1295	7388
90	13.6	10.4†	12.9	6.1†	24.8	7.9†	6.6†	10.2†	15.6	33.7†	25.3	30.3†	2348	15667

(B) Exports

	Food		Fuel & raw materials		Chemical products		Machinery & transport equipment		Other industrial products		Value of exports (US$100 mil.)		Share of Japan's total exports	
	Japan	Western Europe	Japan	Western Europe	Japan	Western Europe	Japan	Western Europe	Japan	Western Europe	Japan	Western Europe	Textiles	Steel
1955	6.8	13.5	6.1	16.4	4.7	7.6	12.3	24.7	70.0	36.2	20.1	350.2	37.3	24.0
60	6.7	11.8	4.2	13.1	4.2	8.4	23.2	30.0	62.0	35.4	40.6	515.1	22.8	34.2
65	4.1	11.7	3.3	10.9	6.5	9.2	31.2	31.9	54.3	34.9	84.5	807.9	13.5	15.3

70	3.4	10.2	2.1	9.2	6.4	9.7	40.5	34.3	46.8	35.3	193.2	1405.1	9.0	14.7
75	1.4	10.3	2.0	9.5	7.0	10.5	49.2	35.5	39.2	33.0	557.5	3717.8	5.3	18.3
80	1.2	10.5	1.2	3.5	0.4	8.0	62.8	11.4	58.6	32.7	1298	8095	4.8	11.9
85	0.7	10.0	0.8	3.5	0.3	9.0	71.8	12.7	67.9	33.3	1756	7537	3.5	7.7
90	0.6	9.8	0.7	3.1	0.4	3.7	75.0	12.0	70.8	38.3	2869	15794	2.5	4.4

1) Figures marked * are 1974 data. Those marked † are 1989 data.

2) Western Europe consists of the EC (Germany, France, Italy, Belgium, the Netherlands, Luxemburg, Denmark, Ireland, and Britain), EFTA (Austria, Norway, Portugal, Sweden, and Switzerland) and Greece, and Spain.

3) For 1950, imports were US$974 million, breaking down as follows: food, 30.0%; raw materials, 56.5%; fuel, 5.5%; chemical products, 2.6%; machinery, 0.8%; and other, 1.2%. Exports, valued at US$820 million, consisted of food, 5.9%; chemical products, 2.0%; textile products, 48.7%; and steel, 8.8% (Ministry of International Trade and Industry, ed., *Sengo Nihon no Bōeki 20-nen Shi* [Twenty-Year History of Japan's Postwar Foreign Trade] pp. 39, 50).

Source: Bank of Japan, *Nihon o Chūshin to suru Kokusai Hikaku Tōkei* [International Comparative Statistics Focusing on Japan].

Rather, the effect was to increase still further the level of imports indispensable to the domestic economy, such as ores, textile raw materials, edibles like wheat and domestic animal feeds, and particularly fuels (oil, coking coal). In this respect, too, Japan was favored by the international environment during the period of high economic growth.

A further aspect of the international environment beneficial to Japan was the availability of cheap and stable supplies of the raw materials and energy needed for heavy and chemical industrialization. Production volume of the most important energy source, crude oil, increased rapidly with the large-scale development of the Middle East oil fields in the 1950s. Oil was in a virtually perpetual state of excess supply through the end of the 1960s, and the price was either stable or falling. Prices of primary products, particularly iron ore, were also relatively steady. For this reason, Japan's net terms of trade improved considerably in the latter part of the 1950s, a state of affairs which continued during the 1960s and until the beginning of the 1970s, as is seen in Figure 3.4. Thereafter the terms of trade deteriorated due to the rising prices of primary goods, particularly oil. The improved terms of trade prior to that time, however, were a major element supporting Japan's growth.

3. Growth and Domestic Conditions

The leadership of postwar Japan maintained the Meiji-era emphasis on a "rich country" while abandoning the "strong army" part of the Meiji formula, as we saw in Chapter 2. A number of other domestic conditions which made for rapid growth will be taken up here.

(1) Aggressive Behavior by Firms

With the boom occasioned by the Korean War, business firms made a comeback from the shocks of the zaibatsu dissolution, the elimination of the concentration of production in giant firms, the purge of major companies' top management, and the industrial reorganization which had been forced on them by the postwar "democratization." Important changes began to take place within firms themselves at this time. First of all, there was a complete change of managers. Ever since the Meiji era the trend had been away from owner-managers toward hired professional managers. This trend was accelerated by the dramatic changes during and after the war: many of the remaining owner-managers, who were leaders of the *zaikai* (financial world), were either purged or lost economic power due to inflation, the burdensome assets tax, and so on. The *ōbantō* (chief managers) of zai-

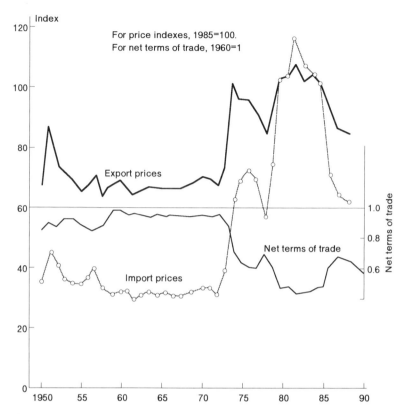

Figure 3.4. Japan's export and import price indexes and net terms of trade, 1950–90

1) Net terms of trade = export price index ÷ import price index. 1960 = 1.
Source: Bank of Japan export-import price indexes.

batsu also lost their positions and were replaced by a new and much younger generation of ordinary directors, factory or branch managers, and section chief. Ridiculed by Genji Keita in his novel *Santō Jūyaku* (Third-rate Executives),[5] this was the class that became responsible for reconstruction and recovery.

The wartime and postwar changes decidedly pushed forward the "separation of ownership and management" in business firms. For example, the Mitsui group of firms had at one time been considered the property of the Mitsui family and had come to be managed along conservative lines with emphasis on reliability and soundness. Despite the fact that they had been expanding, profit-making concerns from the first, after the war these companies were streamlined into an organization of independent firms oriented toward expansion and high profits, and the young "professional managers" strove to achieve these objectives. These men lacked the dignity and authority of their more conservative predecessors, but they aggressively took up the challenge of meeting these new goals, and in many cases they succeeded. However, the reasons for their successes lay wholly in the fact that the forte of these professional managers was "aggressiveness" rather than "soundness" in a changed environment where, for one thing, competition had intensified. For example, fierce competition often raged between companies which had been created out of a single large one under the Elimination of Excessive Concentration Law. This was the case with Yawata Steel and Fuji Steel, the companies into which Nippon Steel was divided;[6] likewise for Sapporo Beer and Asahi Beer, which emerged from the breakup of Dainippon Beer. The *keiretsu* (financial grouping) firms centering on banks competed with firms in other *keiretsu*; there was competition to import technology from abroad, and so on. Thus, there was no lack of opportunity for these aggressive young managers to compete.

In order to expand production and increase sales, advances into new fields were planned unceasingly. As a result, "product-monopoly busting" developed. Among steelmakers this centered on producing special items monopolized by other companies. Fierce competition also developed in the auto industry, where each firm produced a full line of large, medium, and compact cars to market against its competitors. In synthetic fibers, Tōyō Rayon and Nippon Rayon maintained their dominant position in nylon while Teijin and other early producers held their lead in tetron, but the late-coming companies also moved into nylon and then took up the production of polyesters, competing with the original five companies in technology imports. In the petrochemical industry, too, when MITI tried to combine the smaller companies by announcing that they must have a minimum ethylene production capacity of 300,000 tons in order to continue to do business, the companies all announced they would build plants to meet the target, and MITI's efforts ended in failure.

Furthermore, as is seen in Table 3.4, following the postwar reorganization and reconstruction, firms' ratios of equity to gross capital declined to 25 percent from the prewar level of more than 60 percent, instead of recovering from setbacks suffered during the war. Since the proportion of debentures and borrowed funds rose and more burdensome interest payments were unavoidable, there was a great necessity for bold business expansion to increase profits. At that time

Table 3.4. Comparison of Business Firms' Prewar and Postwar Financial Conditions
(All industries; figures in parentheses are totals for manufacturing industries)

	1935 1st half	1950 1st half	1955 1st half	1960 1st half	1965 1st half	1970 1st half
Equity capital as a proportion of gross capital (%)	61	23	39	29	24	19
	(67)	(26)	(41)	(32)	(26)	(21)
Fixed assets as a proportion of gross capital (%)	60	29	54	53	47	43
	(51)	(23)	(42)	(45)	(43)	(42)
Turnover ratio of total liabilities and net worth	0.42	1.64	1.08	1.12	1.03	1.21
	(0.67)	(1.42)	(0.86)	(0.84)	(0.84)	(0.92)
Profit ratio on employed capital (%)	5.7	2.2	2.4	5.8	2.1	2.6
	(7.8)	(2.8)	(5.2)	(7.9)	(2.3)	(2.7)
Profit ratio on paid-up capital (%)	12.1	18.3	21.6	40.5	13.7	25.8
	(16.3)	(23.6)	(40.1)	(50.6)	(13.9)	(25.8)
Corporate debenture borrowings as a proportion of total employed capital (%)	21.1	30.9	33.1	39.1	42.4	39.6
	(13.1)	(28.5)	(28.2)	(35.3)	(40.6)	(38.7)
Depreciation rate on fixed assests (%)	3.9	8.0	8.3	10.1	12.3	13.4
	(5.8)	(6.3)	(10.9)	(13.7)	(14.9)	(15.5)

Source: Mitsubishi Economic Research Institute, Honpō Jigyō Seiseki Bunseki [Analysis of the Nation's Business Performance].

it was strongly asserted that improving the equity capital ratio was
the key to improving the operating base. However, if the ratio was
improved by using only equity capital for plant and equipment investments, rapid expansion would be impossible, profit increases
would be limited, and firms would fall behind other companies in the
industry. In the end, firms abandoned the concept of equity capital
ratios and instead expanded plant and equipment investment on the
basis of borrowed funds, debentures, and other debt capital. Even
though they had high interest and amortization expenses, firms commonly planned on achieving still higher rates of return by maintaining
operating rates at or near 100 percent when they brought new facilities on line. It was thought that if the economy could be relied on to
maintain its high rate of growth, the prospects for the success of these
plans were excellent; and, in fact, in most cases these optimistic plans
were justified. However, as has already been seen, the business cycle
was regularly repeated, and during slumps the burden of interest
payments and amortization costs greatly depressed profit rates. These
cyclical fluctuations are shown in Figure 3.5.

When a business downturn appeared to be becoming rather severe,
a helping hand was extended by the government in the form of cartel
formation, tax reductions or exemptions, and industry-wide plant and
equipment capacity expansion agreements. The latter approach was

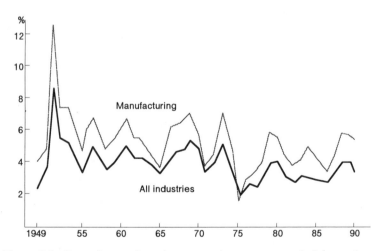

Figure 3.5. Operating profit ratios on gross corporate capital (annual averages), 1949–90
Source: Ministry of Finance statistics.

taken in industries such as iron and steel, in which the industry cartel agreed to make orderly capacity increases in one company per year. While a floor was being maintained under a recession in these ways, business prosperity would begin to revive. As firms became active once more, they launched into their next set of plans. In this sense, the government's industrial policies functioned as a safety valve so that firms could boldly pursue aggressive programs within a secure environment. This aggressive pattern of corporate behavior was successful, and it was repeated without a major rupture until the large-scale drop in profit rates in 1974–75.

A look at firms' investment activity during this period affords the greatest insight into businesses' mode of behavior. From 1952 to 1970 annual private investment increased more than tenfold, and the amount of capital stock in private hands also expanded more than fivefold from the end of 1954 to the end of 1970. What prompted such a rush of investment activity?

The following simple model may clarify the matter. Table 3.5 presents estimates of the investment function

$$I_p = \alpha + \beta_1 K_p + \beta_2 Y_c \tag{3}$$

Table 3.5. Estimation of the Private Plant and Equipment Investment Function ($I_p = \alpha + \beta_1 K_p + \beta_2 Y_c$), 1955–70

Period	α	β_1	β_2	R^2	Durbin-Watson statistic
1956–75	−163.54** (−0.401)	0.05457 (5.115)	0.99765 (10.121)	0.98037	1.4965
1956–70	−587.38** (−0.987)	0.04574* (1.940)	1.25383 (7.990)	0.99472	1.40192
1956–65	−738.68* (−1.114)	0.03136** (1.023)	1.60985 (5.640)	0.97518	2.47395
1966–70	1634.60* (1.382)	0.04801 (3.491)	0.87305 (6.234)	0.94080	1.49657

1) All units are in billions of yen.
2) Figures in parentheses are *t*-values. Values marked * are not significant at 5%. Those marked ** are not significant.
3) R^2 is the coefficient of determination.

Sources: I_p and Y_c are taken from *Kokumin Shotoku Tōkei Nenpō* [National Income Statistics Annual Report], 1976. K_p is from Economic Planning Agency, National Income Bureau, *Minkan Kigyō Soshihon Sutokku, Shōwa 30–50 Nendo* [Gross Capital Stock of Private Firms, FY 1955–57].

where I_p is private plant and equipment investment (1970 prices), K_p is private capital stock at the end of the period (1970 prices), and Y_c is the sum of corporate income and the estimated adjusted value of goods in stock (real values). The coefficient of determination for these estimates is extremely high through the 1960s, so the equation may be considered as a virtually complete explanation of firms' investment behavior. It displays the following characteristics. First, the capital stock coefficient, which is usually negative, is positive and is significant for the 1950s and for the period from 1950 through the 1960s. This was decidedly so in the period from 1950 through the 1960s, as can also be seen from the fact that when I_p is explained solely in terms of K_p, the coefficient of determination for 1956–70 is 0.9831, and for 1956–75 it is 0.9289. In other words, this confirms the existence of conditions under which, contrary to what one would expect, investment was stimulated when the capital stock increased, or, as will be seen later, "investment begat investment."[7]

Secondly, investment behavior was always strongly influenced by firms' income (before taxes and dividends). Investment from year to year sensitively reacted to company profits and was determined by the nominal amount of profit increase. This is indicative of firms' aggressive attitudes; they were unconcerned about increases in borrowed funds or debentures. In fact, companies necessarily experienced large-scale fluctuations in their profit rates due to business cycles, but they attached the greatest importance to profit amounts rather than to profit rates. Why this was so can be seen from the results obtained when the above equation is estimated with the profit rate on gross capital (π_c) substituted for corporate income and inventories (Y_c). Figures in parentheses are t-values:

$$1956\text{–}70 \quad I_p = -9{,}494.30 + 0.23310 K_p + 592.47 \pi_c \quad R^2 = 0.98167$$
$$\phantom{1956\text{–}70 \quad I_p = -9{,}494.30 + } (25.35) (3.14)$$

Both equations have good fit; but it is clear that the amount of profit gives an even better fit. One may conclude that firms preferred high growth to high profit rates.

A further important reason for the firms' success in pursuing aggressive policies was the stability of labor-management relations. As has been seen, the labor union movement revived under "democratization" but was soon thwarted by the Occupation policy shift against labor's leftist leanings as the anti-Communist drive developed. This occurred as early as 1947, when SCAP ordered the February 1 general strike cancelled. Union activity continued to be vigorous into the first half of the 1950s, but after that it gradually subsided. During the postwar period, there were only four years in which the number of workdays lost per union member exceeded one day per year (1946, 1948, 1951, and 1952), and days lost exceeded 0.8 in only five other years (1947, 1950, 1957, 1958, and 1959). These figures are far lower than comparable ones for the United States and England, and they indicate a degree of stability second only to that found in West Germany. Even the comparatively large number of days missed up to 1950 was due not to a large number of strikes overall but to prolonged strikes in the electric machinery, coal mining, automobile, and steel sectors in opposition to personnel reductions that had accompanied rationalization. This is not to discount the major role of Japanese-style industrial relations (management familialism), which revolve around the lifetime employment system and the seniority wage system. Management familialism had been spreading since before World War II, but it became prevalent during the ten years or so following the war. With the defeat firms' scales of operation were necessarily reduced, but the employees and managers who remained united their efforts to rebuild their businesses. The lifetime employment system and the seniority wage system which had taken shape in the years preceding and during the war were tacitly recognized and reinforced as tools for cementing unity between labor and management.

There were large postwar declines in real wages, and wage differences based on length of employment were at first smaller than they had been before the war, but these differences widened beyond their prewar levels in 1954 and expanded still further in 1958, as is shown in Figure 3.6. This meant that Japan's company unions demonstrated their loyalty to their firms by concurring in the use of the seniority wage system and lifetime employment. As related above, there were frequent large-scale dismissals up through the business slump of 1954, but all traces of such practices were eliminated thereafter except in the coal industry, where the energy revolution forced cutbacks. From the standpoint of managers, this meant the establishment of a system whereby they could treat senior employees generously instead of making rash dismissals, and thus could make a strong bid to the workers for their long-term cooperation on company policies. This was the situation by the time business had weathered the post-Korean War recession of 1954.

Bullish behavior on the part of business became the driving force behind economic growth. It overturned the faint-hearted plans and forecasts of the government and of most economists, who held that the rapid growth prior to the 1954 recession had been due to the

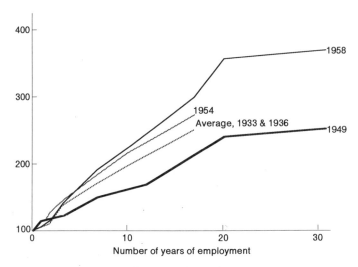

Figure 3.6. Average wage index for male workers
1) For length of employment = 0 years, the wage index = 100.
Source: Ministry of Labour, Statistics Research Bureau, *Sengo Rōdō Undōshi* [History
of the Postwar Labor Movement], analysis section (1968), p. 187. Original
source materials were Cabinet Statistics Bureau, *Rōdō Tōkei Jitchi Chōsa*
[Labor Statistics Field Survey] for prewar data, and for the postwar period,
Ministry of Labour, *Kojin-betsu Chingin Chōsa* [Individual Wage Survey] for
1949–54, and *Chingin Kōzō Kihon Chōsa* [Basic Survey of the Wage Struc-
ture] for 1958.

special circumstances prevailing in the postwar reconstruction period.
It was greatly feared that the growth rate would fall back to prewar
levels and that there would be a labor surplus. In the event, however,
the ensuing astonishing growth rate gave the lie to such pessimistic
forecasts most definitively.

(2) Technological Progress
During World War II a great deal of technology was developed in
Japan for military purposes. Electrical technology and nuclear energy
are the best-known examples, but a range of technology extending
over a much broader spectrum was developed, and its industrial
applications were pursued after the war. In addition, the technology
for such innovations as nylon and continuous rolling equipment in
the steel industry, which had come into use in Europe and the
U.S. before the war, had not yet been introduced in Japan. After
about 1950, when the introduction of foreign technology began, this

prewar and wartime technology began to flow into the country.[8]

Table 3.6 gives an outline of major technological advances in Japan between 1950 and 1975. Let us summarize a few of the special features highlighted by the table and give some examples.

First, at the beginning of the 1950s most of Japan's industries began importing technology from abroad. This not only raised the technological levels of the individual industries, but served to improve technology in related industries as well. For example, the construction of the Sakuma Dam in Aichi Prefecture served its purpose well in introducing the electric power plant technology of the time; but with the importation of large-scale civil engineering and construction equipment for the project, technological progress also began in the construction industry. Cooperating with American firms, Japan's industrial machinery makers launched into the production of construction machinery in the latter half of the 1950s. Plant and equipment investment naturally expanded in order to make this production possible, and in this way economic growth occurred, turning on the axis of such investment.

It should be pointed out that Japan's ability to assimilate this technology was to a great extent shaped by prewar and wartime technological experience. That is, whether in light industries manufacturing radios, television sets, sewing machines, cameras, watches, and so on, or in the assembly industries such as shipbuilding, the technology and skills developed in the wartime industries now formed the basis for the adoption of foreign technology and for success in mass production. The shipbuilding industry's success in establishing itself as an export industry in the mid-1950s and its subsequent meteoric rise to the number one position worldwide is partially attributable to this phenomenon, which facilitated the importation of critical technology for block construction and electric welding.

Still another interesting aspect of the nation's progress in technology is the order in which it developed, beginning with the materials and basic industries such as steel and electric power, then shifting to electric machinery, and finally proceeding to the new assembly industries like automobiles and electronics. Moreover, what Table 3.6 does not show is the transformation wrought by the advent of petrochemicals. The petrochemical industry, which appeared during the latter half of the 1950s and was centered primarily on naptha cracking technology, virtually made over the entire chemical industry, which had existed since before the war and had itself brought in new technology for a time. A whole new system revolving around petrochem-

(*continued on p. 82*)

Table 3.6. Summary of Major Postwar Technological Advances, 1950–75

	1950–54	1955–59	1960–65	After 1965
Steel industry	First Rationalization Plan launched from FY 1951, based on "Outline of Policies for Steel & Coal Industry Rationalization" (Cabinet meeting decision) of June 1950. Blast furnace enlargements, sintering equipment improvements, etc. (20% decrease in proportion of coke). Introduction of continuous rolling equipment (strip mills). Kawasaki Steel opens integrated plant facilities in Chiba; Sumitomo Metals & Kobe Steel also poise for integration.	Second Rationalization Plan promoted, 1955–60. Enlargement of blast furnaces (16% decrease in proportion of coke, new installations of large continuous rolling facilities). Conversion to new installations of LD converters in steel-making process. New, large-scale integrated plants—Yawata Steel (Tobata Works), Kobe Steel (Nadahama), Nippon Kōkan (Mizue), Sumitomo Metals (Wakayama).	New large-scale installations—Yawata (Sakai), Fuji Steel (Nagoya), Kawasaki Steel (Mizushima), etc. Japan becomes possessor of newest & most powerful group of plants in the world.	New installations of large-scale integrated plants—Yawata (Kimitsu), Nippon Kōkan (Fukuyama), Kobe Steel (Kagogawa), Sumitomo Metals (Kashima), Nippon Kōkan (Ōgishima), Nippon Steel Corp. (formed from 1970 merger of Yawata and Fuji Steel) (Oita works), etc. This period concludes a chapter in postwar technological progress. Pollution problems & countermeasures become issues.

Electric power industry	After successful construction of a large hydro-electric power generating dam (Sakuma) using heavy construction equipment, dams at Okutadami Tagokura, Kurobe No. 4, etc., are begun in rapid succession. Large-scale steam-powered generating equipment introduced from America & produced domestically through technological cooperation (increases in heat efficiency, use of fuel oil, automation).	Completion of large generating plants (both steam and hydropowered) begun in previous period. With expanded demand, shift away from the once-prevalent mode "Hydropower first, steam second" to preeminence of steam-powered plants. Research on nuclear power generation begins.	Experiments with nuclear power generation begin. Economies of scale become apparent. In 1963, cost per kW at steam-powered generating plants becomes lowest in the world.	Plant location problems arise as pollution problems become severe.
Shipbuilding industry	Increases in export orders for ships due to adoption of electric welding, block construction method, automatic gas cutters. Ship price reductions via system whereby plant export deficits are covered by special profits on raw sugar imports.	Cost reductions as new shipyards appear in response to demand for bigger & faster ships.	Mitsubishi Nagasaki & Ishikawajima Yokohama No. 2 yards equipped with docks for super-tankers. Advances in welding block construction method. Adoption of precedent-setting methods for fittings.	Advent of 200,000-ton-plus super-tankers, development of combination carriers, demonstration model ships (standard models). Development of new products such as automated ships, bulk car carriers, container ships. New docks and yards for 1-million-ton tankers at Mitsubishi's Kōyagi yards.

Table 3.6. (*continued*)

	1950–54	1955–59	1960–65	After 1965
Electrical machinery industry	Technology for such things as large-scale generators & electronics introduced; Sony, Hayakawa (Sharp), etc., go into business; Sony produces transistors domestically in 1953. Matsushita, Sanyo, etc., begin producing household electrical appliances such as washing machines, TVs, & vacuum cleaners. Large electrical machinery makers enter into competition in this area.	Spread of household electrical appliances such as TVs, transistor radios, tape recorders, & refrigerators. Trend emulated by heavy electrical machinery makers. Sony develops transistor radios as export product.	Further growth with spread of household electrical appliances & exports. Growth in large electrical machinery, introduction of atomic power generating technology, development of computer technology.	Mass production of color television sets. Development of air conditioners & other large household appliances; development of pocket calculators & further progress in computer technology.
Sewing machines, cameras, watches, etc.	Taking advantage of wartime technology, optical equipment makers switch to production of cameras, binoculars, etc.; machinery (weapons) makers to sewing machines. With standardization of sewing machine parts & successful conversion to mass production, production for export is undertaken.	Both sectors advance in mass production technology. With progress in production of high-quality products comes success in mass production of wristwatches & in production for export.	Cameras surpass those of Germany in both quality & quantity of production. Progress in labor-saving mass production technology in automatic lathes, transfer machines.	Digital clocks, development of completely automated assembly technology. Establishment of worldwide position as producer of high-quality products.

Automobiles	Nissan, Isuzu & Hino, in technical cooperation with Austin, Hillman of the Rootes Group & Renault, respectively, and Toyota & Prince on their own, all grapple with developing passenger automobiles. Toyota succeeds in semiautomating the production process.	After announcement of Toyota Crown & Prince Skyline and development of the Nissan Datsun about 1955, all companies announce passenger car lines—Bluebird, Corona, Gloria, etc., and the motorization era begins.	With expanded demand & falling prices, coping with auto import liberalization becomes a possibility. Honda & other late-comers enter the field. Production expands, rapidly approaching European & American levels.	Firm establishment as export industry. Expanded scale of production. Air pollution caused by exhaust gas becomes a problem, and makers develop new technologies to combat it.
Petrochemicals		Nippon Petrochemical, Mitsui Petrochemical & Mitsubishi Yūka established and develop polyethylene & polystyrene production by the naphtha cracking process. These materials are developed as raw materials for synthetic fibers, plastics.	Technological competition begins between original four firms & five later entrants. Notable are advances in rationalization by using ethylene, enlarging scale of operations; development of synthetic resins. Succession of petrochemical complexes appears.	Shift to mass production & rationalization through enlargement of plant continues. Pollution problems.
Synthetic fibers	Using in-house technology, Kurashiki Rayon produces vinylon on a commercial basis, with carbide as a raw material. Tōyō Rayon purchases nylon technology from DuPont.	In 1955 Nippon Rayon enters production of nylon; firms begin development of acrylic fibers. Polyester fiber technology introduced (Tōyō Rayon, Teijin).	Marked expansion in synthetic fiber demand, industry closes down cotton yarn as export industry. Intensification of industry competition.	Earlier-developing firms cut costs by supplying own raw materials.

icals was created, and new product uses were also developed. For example, the plastic forms processing industry had begun by using mainly vinyl-chloride and urea resins in the manufacturing process, but when petrochemicals developed, this industry retooled to use polyethylene as a raw material. In addition, the uses of plastic forms expanded from small containers to a whole spectrum of products ranging from kitchenware and plastic hothouses for agriculture to automobile and electrical parts, and to construction materials as well. In this example, as in many others, the center of technological progress shifted by turns from industries that primarily produce materials to processing industries. As new materials appeared, previously produced materials were improved, their uses were expanded as a result, and new products were born. It was as a result of technological progress in the casting of parts that Japan's automobile manufacturers, too, grew into an industry for the first time able to compete in international markets.

It used to be argued that Japan produced very little technology of its own. Certainly, in the 1950s and 1960s, little that is epoch-making was independently developed in Japan. There was Kurashiki Rayon's vinyl chloride and Sony's transistors (the Esaki semi-conductor), but not much else. Japan's achievement during this period, however, was the combining of numerous imported technologies to create low-cost mass production systems. Steel plant design is a prime example of this. The plants were built along the seacoast to save the costs of shipping imported raw materials inland and finished products back to the coast for export, and Japanese steelmakers developed a new plant construction technology for this purpose. Moreover, the production line was laid out as a continuous process from raw materials staging areas for coal and iron ore to a new type of Japanese-made furnace to rolling production, and the plants were built using the latest technologies for each of these steps. Such systematic use of technology only becomes possible when there is large-scale plant and equipment investment, and this was facilitated by the investment boom of the late 1950s and 1960s. This combination of synthesizing technology and heavily investing produced the facelift undergone by many industries such as steel, shipbuilding, and automobiles within the space of about ten years.

Such were the reasons for Japanese firms' aggressive behavior, and such were the secrets of their success as well. Industries exerted a mutual influence on each other as they developed, and one after another they were caught up in a spiral of development. Representative of this phenomenon are the machinery and installation industries that were the object of plant and equipment investment. The machine tool industry, for example, stagnated until the end of the 1950s due to a surplus produced during the war. It was during the so-called Iwato investment boom of around 1960 that the industry revived and began to expand its production volume by importing new technology and tackling the production of high-grade machinery. The advanced equipment produced was quickly snapped up by industrial machinery producers and the producers of integrated plants, both of which were lines of business catering to industries that used huge installations, particularly the chemical and petrochemical industries.

Technological progress extended into still broader fields. Construction, transportation, and communications number among those which were transformed as new products were developed. Construction techniques underwent a technology-induced metamorphosis. The appearance of various new building materials such as plywood, synthetic resin products, and aluminum sashes completely transformed both the materials and (in response to that change) the construction methods for everything from mammoth skyscrapers to private residences. In transportation, Japan's Bullet Train (the Shinkansen) appeared, combining the results of progress in electrical machinery and electronic engineering. The life of the individual consumer, too, was revolutionized by household appliances and the passenger car. Surrounded by such accoutrements, consumers soon found the practice of dining on instant and frozen foods—also fruits of the new technology—crowding in on them as well.

Technological progress was not made without sacrifices. The greatest of these occurred in conjunction with the so-called "energy revolution." It was based on the large-scale decrease in international crude oil prices that resulted from the discovery of oil in the Middle East. Until the 1950s Japan's major energy source had been coal, but oil abruptly took its place from the mid-1950s on. As is shown in Table 3.7, imported oil became Japan's major energy source virtually overnight, and oil constituted approximately 90 percent of energy imports by the beginning of the 1970s. Table 3.8 shows the downward trend in the price of crude oil which began in the mid-1950s. Although the price shot up at the time of the Suez crisis in 1956–57, it soon resumed its decline as a result of increased Middle East production. The difference between the price of crude oil and that of coal became particularly noticeable at the end of the 1950s. However, the switch from coal to crude oil had begun prior to this time, and a number of measures had been taken in an attempt to counteract this trend. Inefficient coal mines were bought up from 1954 onward; the Coal

Table 3.7. Primary Energy Supply
(A) FY 1935–60 (Units are millions of tons of coal equivalent)

Fiscal year	Hydro-electric power	Coal (and % imported)	Lignite	Oil (and % imported)	Natural gas	Fire-wood	Charcoal	Total (millions of tons)	Imported energy as % of total
1935	18.3	61.7 (9.2)	0.1	10.4 (8.0)	0.1	5.9	3.7	62.8	18.8
40	16.2	66.1 (12.0)	0.2	7.0 (6.5)	0.1	7.0	3.7	90.7	18.2
47	35.5	45.9 (0.2)	2.8	3.7 (3.2)	0.1	8.3	3.6	50.5	3.3
50	32.7	51.2 (1.6)	0.9	6.3 (5.5)	0.1	6.2	2.7	69.4	7.1
55	30.5	44.0 (3.7)	0.7	17.9 (17.4)	0.3	4.4	2.2	95.5	21.1
60	22.7	38.1 (6.2)	0.4	34.7 (34.1)	0.7	2.3	1.0	154.5	40.3

(B) FY 1953–91 (Units are percentages except for column 1)

Primary energy sources (in trillion kcal)	Coal	Oil	Natural gas, LNG	Electricity			New energy sources
				Hydro	Atomic	Thermal	
1953	61.6	47.7	15.3	0.2	29.0	—	—	7.8
58	73.9	44.1	24.2	0.7	24.7	—	—	6.3
63	136.6	31.6	52.6	1.5	12.1	—	—	2.1
68	243.2	23.6	67.1	1.0	7.0	0.1	0	1.2
73	385.4	15.5	77.4	1.5	4.1	0.6	0	0.9
78	386.5	13.3	73.3	4.7	4.3	3.5	0	0.9
83	383.6	18.0	61.5	7.5	5.1	6.7	0.1	1.2
88	445.5	18.1	57.3	9.6	4.7	9.0	0.1	1.3
91	479.5	17.3	56.1	10.9	4.7	10.0	0.1	1.3

(C) Coal Production and Volume of Oil Imports (Units: Millions of tons, millions of kiloliters)

Fiscal year	1953	1958	1963	1968	1973	1978	1983	1988	1991
Coal production (million tons)	46.5	51.3	54.9	50.5	21.7	19.3	18.4	12.8	7.9
Crude oil imports (million kl)	7.4	16.3	59.3	140.5	286.7	270.2	207.8	193.9	238.6

Sources: Tsūshō Sangyō Daijin Kanbō Chōsa-ka, ed., Enerugi Tōkei Shū [Energy Statistics]; Shigen Enerugi-chō Kanbō Sōmuka, ed., Sōgō Enerugi Tōkei [Comprehensive Energy Statistics], both selected years.

Table 3.8. Per-kilocalorie Unit Price Comparison of Coal and Crude Oil (Tokyo, 1955–65)

Year	Coal		Crude oil		Ratio of crude oil price per 10 kcal to price of coal
	¥/ton	¥/10 kcal	¥/kl	¥/10 kcal	
1955	4,065	0.754	9,677	0.982	1.30
56	4,426	0.847	12,160	1.233	1.46
57	5,167	1.003	11,281	1.144	1.14
58	4,501	0.871	8,566	0.865	0.99
59	4,106	0.811	8,368	0.845	1.04
60	3,887	0.777	7,480	0.755	0.97
61	3,708	0.732	6,523	0.658	0.90
62	3,638	0.708	6,191	0.627	0.89
63	3,582	0.682	6,199	0.628	0.92
64	3,546	0.686	6,048	0.611	0.89
65	3,757	0.730	5,913	0.600	0.80

Sources: Japan Energy Economics Research Institute, ed., Sengo Enerugi Sangyōshi [History of the Postwar Energy Industry], Tōyō Keizai Shimpōsha, 1986. Primary materials from Electric Industry Association, Denki Jigyō Benran [Electric Industry Handbook]. Supplemental materials to the Provisional Measures for Coal Mining Industry Rationalization (June 1955) indicate that, in view of oil's greater convenience of usability, crude oil prices should be viewed as viewed as 80% of the figures shown in order to make valid comparisions with coal prices.

Industry Rationalization Law, authorizing the opening of new coal mines only of superior quality, and the Crude Oil Boiler Installation Regulatory Law, designed to control conversions to crude oil use, were both enacted; and a customs levy on crude oil imports was also established. But in the face of such sizeable crude oil price decreases, these efforts were like trying to empty the ocean with a bucket. The coal industry subsequently made three drastic rationalization moves —firings, the closing of inefficient mines, and a clamp-down on labor agitation—but in the end it could not fight the trend of the times. The situation turned into a tangle of social problems. All the coal companies went heavily into the red, high rates of unemployment appeared in the coal-producing regions, and there was an overall decline in the affected areas as a whole. For industry in general, the switch to crude oil, which was both cheap and easy to handle, did constitute technological progress in the broad sense. One may also take the view that change in the industrial structure was necessary for growth. However, the other side of the coin of technological

progress was that it had to be achieved at the cost of the collapse of
the coal industry.

From another angle, technological progress in the heavy and
chemical industries caused pollution and damage to the environment.
In the industrial belts, river and sea water was fouled, sulphate and
nitrate air pollutants from factory smoke increased, foul odors and
noise pollution mounted, and residents of these areas suffered men-
tally and physically. Exhaust fumes increased with the spread of the
automobile. Pollution-related diseases like Minamata disease and
Yokkaichi asthma attracted wide attention. Criticism of this kind of
pollution grew vehement in the latter part of the 1960s and turned
into criticism of the industrial technology which was entirely lacking
in countermeasures to deal with such problems. In response, the
principle of compensation by the firms responsible for the pollution
was worked out and then strengthened with the passage of the
Environmental Pollution Prevention Act in 1970, about which more
will be said in Section 4 of this chapter. In these ways technological
progress for the sake of industrial development reached a turning
point at the same time that rapid growth was coming to an end.

(3) Economic Policy and Economic Planning
It was primarily the efforts of the people, mainly in industry, which
produced economic growth. However, this is not to say that economic
policy played no role in the process. It is a fact that the economic
policy-making authorities at first underestimated growth capacity, but
it is also a fact that once growth had begun, they made every effort to
sustain it and strove to remove obstacles to it.

The Cabinets of the era of rapid growth were headed by Yoshida
Shigeru, Hatoyama Ichirō, Ishibashi Tanzan, Kishi Nobusuke, Ikeda
Hayato, and Satō Eisaku, succeeded in the early 1970s by Tanaka
Kakuei. (See the Appendix for a table of Cabinets and major events.)
All were LDP (Liberal Democratic Party) Cabinets, and insofar as
they all made it a policy to protect the capitalistic economic system in
the broad sense, they were all cut from the same mold. However, it is
clear that there were differences in the nuances of their policies.

The man who took the most activist road to growth was Ikeda
Hayato, who had been Finance Minister in the third Yoshida Cabinet
and in the Ishibashi and Kishi Cabinets before he became Prime
Minister in 1960. Inasmuch as he was quick to recognize the significance of economic growth and was aggressive in his pursuit of it
under the banner of his Income-doubling Plan, Ikeda was the single
most important figure in Japan's rapid growth. He will be remem-

bered as the man who pulled together a national consensus for economic growth and who strove unceasingly for the realization of that goal—so much so that Charles DeGaulle, with his classical "great power" view of the world, condescendingly dubbed him the "transistor radio salesman." In the 1970s, Ikeda's one-time Finance Minister Tanaka Kakuei was still pursuing Ikeda's dream when he published his grandiose *Building a New Japan: A Plan for Remodeling the Japanese Archipelago*, in which he quixotically ignored the fact of Japan's straitened circumstances in the changing times.

In contrast to this was the anti-growth view espoused by Prime Minister Hatoyama's Finance Minister Ichimada Hisato (1954–56), formerly Governor of the Bank of Japan, who in the mid-1950s adhered to a policy that attempted to fix the national budget at the level of one trillion yen, harking back nostalgically to classical economic policies. Later on, Prime Ministers Satō Eisaku in the late 1960s and Fukuda Takeo (Satō's Finance Minister) in the years following the 1973 oil crisis espoused stable growth and made an issue of curbing growth-induced inflation, although in reality neither had any choice but to follow the growth path marked out by Ikeda. Fukuda, who was also Finance Minister in the second Tanaka Cabinet at the end of the high growth period, and who promoted a stable growth policy as head of the Economic Planning Agency in the Miki Cabinet (1974–76), continued to press for "stable growth" after he succeeded Miki as prime minister and took control of post-oil-crisis economic policy. But, as we will see, by an ironic turn of events it was this same Fukuda who, as prime minister in 1978, embarked on a major economic growth policy in response to American demands. In the post-oil-shock 1970s and through the 1980s there has been an overall weakening of this pro-growth line due to mounting fiscal deficits, but it was revived briefly during the high-yen recessions of 1978 and 1986–87.

The above summary shows that even in the midst of rapid growth, economic policy was guided by alternating sets of aggressive and conservative programs. From a broader perspective, however, Japan consistently adhered to elder statesman Yoshida Shigeru's view that armaments should be curbed and military spending suppressed while all efforts were concentrated on the reconstruction of the economy. The fact that even at the end of the 1980s military spending was less than one percent of GNP bears witness to this more than anything else.

Now let us examine some more specific policies—policies that primarily promoted industry, which is central to growth. A series of policies for the protection and fostering of industry had been established before economic growth began. This policy system was subsequently maintained while at the same time the government remained in extremely close contact with industry, to which it dispensed administrative guidance (*gyōsei shidō*). Let us single out one or two examples of these high-growth period policies for closer scrutiny.

During the latter half of the 1950s the world was caught up in a wave of trade liberalization as the reconstructed European nations moved toward dismantling import restrictions. Japan, which was just at that time improving its position as an exporter of industrial goods, also faced rising demands for trade liberalization and for the abolition of the foreign capital budgeting system. In 1960 the Japanese government decided in principle to proceed with liberalization. It switched from the previous policy of applying general import restrictions and announced instead a list of items for "nonliberalization," with the result that 90 percent of imports, in value terms, were liberalized by 1962. However, farm products and the products of some strategic industries were treated as exceptions. Passenger cars, for example, were not removed from the "nonliberalization" list until 1965, and electronic calculators remained on it until 1973. The principle of protecting industry has been followed even when it was known to be disadvantageous to consumers, right up to the liberalization of beef and oranges in 1991. Aiming at "greater industrial efficiency" in order to improve international competitiveness in the chemical and heavy industries, the Ministry of International Trade and Industry (MITI) in March of 1962 submitted to the Diet a bill for a Designated Industries Temporary Measures Act. This law specified such industries as automobiles, automobile tires, petrochemicals, and machinery as "designated" industries, and stipulated measures for promoting their development (standardization, specialization of production, establishment of joint capital enterprises, the organization of industrial complexes, rationalization of plant and equipment investment, mergers, the conversion of businesses to other fields of activity in line with the reorganization of industrial structure, and so on). The bill would have obliged businessmen to comply with these programs while the government devised the requisite monetary and tax measures and made exceptions to the Anti-Monopoly Law as necessary, and while the banks supplied the funds. This bill was defeated by the opposition of the financial institutions which would have been compelled to fund the programs. After another two years it was resubmitted to the Diet in a different form; and although it never actually passed into law, it suffices to give a general idea of MITI's posture at that time toward industry protection and the strengthening of competitiveness.[9]

In the synthetic fibers industry, a Five-year Plan for Fostering the Synthetic Fibers Industry was decided upon at a vice ministers' meeting in 1953, and measures for the preferential treatment of nylon, vinylon, and vinylidene chloride were implemented with a goal of 100 million pounds of annual synthetic fiber production in fiscal 1957. Under the plan steps were taken to stimulate a wide variety of demand, such as that for fishnet line, and particularly government demand, which was expected to amount to 16 million pounds per annum. It further provided for capital funding, favorable tax treatment, priority allocation of electric power, research subsidies, and so on.[10]

In 1957 the Electronics Industry Promotion Temporary Measures Act was passed. Its main purposes were to specify "type, of machinery that would accelerate research and development," "types of machinery that would open up industrial production," and "types of machinery that would hasten the rationalization of production," all of which became the objectives of the "promotion measures" of MITI's newly established Electronics Industries Section. The results were "the establishment of unified public and private research and development objectives for research equipment," "priority grants for experimental research subsidies" (totalling ¥3.64 billion from 1957 to 1968), the provision of "long-term low-interest loan funds from the Japan Development Bank for production rationalization machinery" (a total of ¥7.36 billion for the same period), and the wide application of special depreciation standards based on the Enterprise Rationalization Promotion Law. Among the items specified as targets for research and development at that time were electronic calculators and industrial instruments for use in automation, with outstanding results. In particular, three firms in the electronic calculator business were granted four-year subsidies of ¥350 million in 1962.[11]

All of this brings to mind the cliché of "Japan, Inc.," coined by the U.S. State Department, or the lines written by the London *Economist*'s Norman Macrae, that the Japanese economy is "the most intelligently *dirigiste* system in the world" and that "the ultimate responsibility for industrial planning, for deciding in which new directions Japan's burgeoning industrial effort should try to go, and for fostering and protecting business as it moves in those directions, lies with the government."[12] The government also extended protection and relief to the declining coal and textile industries, attracting wide attention thereby. But nothing further need be said of that here. If

Macrae's remarks require any comment, it simply comes down to this: the attitude on the part of both government and business that such guidance and protection is not strange but quite natural had been taking shape for a considerable period of time, ever since the days of wartime controls.[13]

Nevertheless, Japan does espouse a free enterprise system. Naturally firms should act on their own initiative. If, under government guidance, they adopt policies which do not produce results, the government does not guarantee them against losses. The most it can do is act as a mediator in obtaining low-interest funds for their relief. Since the government engages in administrative guidance but not in direct planning *per se*, there have been instances in which new entrants have overwhelmed promising fields of industry. The ensuing fierce competition has given rise to a production surplus, with the result that the bottom has fallen out of prices. Incapable of permitting matters to take their own course, the government has repeatedly come to the rescue through "administrative guidance." In the absence of real planning, a series of relief policies becomes necessary instead. But during the high growth period it was precisely because firms could cling to the hope of just such relief that they were able to make daring investments in plant and equipment. So, clearly, it was industry that was the driving force behind economic growth. Since the end of the high growth period, firms have accumulated more equity capital and have increasingly resisted administrative guidance. The "planned economy" and "Japan, Inc." views, therefore, tend to exaggerate the importance of only one aspect of the Japanese economy.

What function did the government's economic plans fulfill with respect to all this? Between 1955, when the government first began to formally set economic plans, and 1992, twelve plans were adopted. Most were five-year plans, but the average lifespan of a plan has been about two and a half years. It is an undeniable fact that new plans were often put together in an effort to build up a new Cabinet's image when there was a change of Prime Minister. In addition to this, however, actual economic growth has continually exceeded prior planned estimates, so that the figures and the thrust of economic plans have repeatedly been outstripped by reality. The plans are summarized in Table 3.9.

Japan's economic plans possess three basic characteristics. First, they indicate the "desired direction of economic and social development"; second, they indicate the policy direction the government should take in order to achieve these ends; and third, they indicate behavior guidelines for the people and for businesses. While the

Table 3.9 Summary of Government Economic Plans

Name of plan	Five-year Economic Self-support Plan	New Long-range Economic Plan	National Income-doubling Plan	Medium-term Economic Plan	Economic & Social Development Plan	New Economic & Social Development Plan
Date adopted	December 1955	December 1957	December 1960	January 1965	March 1967	May 1970
Cabinet	Hatoyama	Kishi	Ikeda	Satō	Satō	Satō
Plan Period (years)	FY 1955–60 (5 years)	FY 1958–62 (5 years)	FY 1961–70 (10 years)	FY 1964–68 (5 years)	FY 1967–71 (5 years)	FY 1970–75 (6 years)
Objectives	Economic independence; full employment	Maximum growth; higher living standard; full employment	Maximum stable growth for full employment and higher living standards	Correction of distortions	Development for a balanced & rich economy & society	Building a livable Japan through balanced economic development
Real GNP growth rate						
Planned	4.9%	6.5%	7.8%	8.1%	8.2%	10.6%
Achieved	8.8%	9.7%	10.0%	10.1%	9.8%	5.1%
Nominal GNP growth rate						
Planned	—	—	—	10.6%	11.3%	14.7%
Achieved	14.1%	15.0%	16.3%	15.9%	15.9%	15.3%
Unemployment rate	(Last year of plan period)					
Planned	1.0%	—	—	—	—	—
Actual	1.5%	1.3%	1.2%	1.1%	1.3%	1.9%
Rate of increase in consumer goods prices						
Avg. planned	—	—	—	ca. 2.5%	ca. 3%	ca. 3%
Avg. actual	1.8%	3.4%	5.7%	5.0%	5.7%	11.1%
Balance on current account, last FY of plan						
Planned	<$100 million	$150 million	$180 million	<$100 million	$1.45 billion	$3.5 billion
Actual	– $10 million	– $20 million	$2.35 billion	$1.47 billion	$6.32 billion	$130 million

Notes: 1. Achieved growth rates are based one the new SNA database (base year = 1985).
    2. Rate of increase in consumer goods prices in based on the general price index.
Source: ESP, August 1992.

Basic Economic & Social Development Plan	Economic Plan for the Latter Half of the 1970s	Seven-year Plan for the New Economic Society	Outlook and Guidelines for the Economic Society of the 1980s	Five-year Plan for the Economic Management of Japan	Five-year Plan for a Quality-of-Life-Superpower
February 1973	May 1976	August 1979	August 1983	May 1988	June 1992
Tanaka	Miki	Ohira	Nakasone	Takeshita	Miyazawa
FY 1973–77 (5 years)	FY 1976–80 (5 years)	FY 1979–85 (7 years)	FY 1983–90 (8 years)	FY 1988–92 (5 years)	FY 1992–96 (5 years)
Simultaneous achievement of improved national welfare & promotion of international cooperation	Extrication from recession & movement toward new growth path; counter-measures to reduced growth rate	Movement toward a stable growth path; improvement in the national welfare; effort to develop the international economy	Establishment of stable international relations; formation of a vital economic society; securing a rich national life	Correction of trade imbalance; improving people's quality of life; developing a regionally balanced economic society	Achieving quality of life, harmony with the rest of the world, and stable international development
9.4% 3.5%	6% 4.5%	ca. 5.7% 3.9%	ca. 4.0% 4.5%	ca. 3.75% 4.9% (FY 1988–91)	ca. 3.5% —
14.3% 14.5%	13% 10%	ca. 10.3% 6.5%	6–7% 6.0%	ca. 4.75% 6.6% (FY 1988–91)	ca. 5% —
— 2.1%	(Last year of plan period) 1.3% 2.1%	(Last year of plan period) <1.7% 2.6%	(Last year of plan period) ca. 2% 2.1%	(Last year of plan period) ca. 2.5% 2.1% (FY 1991)	(Last year of plan period) ca. 2% —
ca. 4% 12.9%	<6% 6.4%	ca. 5% 3.6%	ca. 3% 1.6%	ca. 1.5% 2.4% (FY 1988–91)	ca. 2% —
		Adjusted to internationally acceptable level	Achieve external balance at internationally acceptable levels	Reduce surplus: GNP ratio to internationally acceptable levels within plan period	Achieve external balance at internationally acceptable levels
$3.5 billion $14 billion (surplus)	$4 billion –$7.1 billion (deficit)	$55.02 billion (surplus)	$33.72 billion (surplus)	$90.08 billion (surplus, FY1991)	—

government is to a certain extent restricted to fairly well-defined levels in its figures on public investment, social security, and the like, the planned figures for such things as private plant and equipment investment and consumption spending are very much in the nature of forecasts. On the whole, the plan figures are somewhere between predictions and guidelines. What this has meant for economic growth may be elucidated by a closer look at the plans.

The postwar economic plans can be broadly grouped into three time periods. The first, up to and including the Income-doubling Plan of 1960, was the period in which the Japanese economy's capacity for rapid growth was gradually being recognized and the achievement of economic independence (an international payments surplus) and full employment were the leading issues. The most important plan during this period was the Income-doubling Plan, which for the first time generally recognized the economy's capacity for rapid growth, forecast a rosy future, and imbued business and the public with hope for that future. As examples of its influence, one may cite the great expansion in plant and equipment investment in 1961, following as it did the investment boom of 1960 and itself causing an unprecedented boom; or again, the extensive wage increase obtained by the labor movement's spring offensive in March of 1961, whereby average wages rose by 13.8% at one stroke, compared with 8.7% the previous year. This plan was not very elaborate technically, but it was potent.

Employing econometric models, subsequent plans made abundant use of the refined techniques of economic forecasting and measurements of policy effects. In the second period, from the Medium-term Economic Plan of 1965 to the New Economic and Social Development Plan of 1970, efforts were made to cope with a new problem— mild inflation under full employment—using these methods. Since they were contrived so as to deal with this problem (1) by "correcting distortions" and avoiding the rapid growth which had already demonstrated that actually a generalized latent growth capacity existed in Japan, and (2) by holding the inflation rate to a low level, the first two plans during this period wound up somewhat divorced from reality, as growth continued unabated and prices continued to rise. Then, immediately after the rapid growth pattern of the 1960s was finally recognized in the 1970 plan, the economy was engulfed by the new environment of the 1970s. Tanaka Kakuei's Basic Economic and Social Plan, pledging to "rebuild the Japanese archipelago," was the banner under which the Tanaka Cabinet attempted to sustain rapid growth while dispersing industry to the less developed parts of the country and constructing a high-speed transportation network to facilitate this process. But the plan collapsed under the high rate of inflation and the oil crisis.

The third period includes five plans, from the Miki Cabinet's "Economic Plan for the Latter Half of the Seventies" to the Miyazawa Cabinet's "Five-year Plan for a Quality-of-Life Superpower" in 1992. More than their predecessors, they tend to present an "outlook" for the economy, setting only approximate numerical targets for economic growth, for example, and limiting their scope to the administrative aspect of government. Second, the plans tend to define policy goals in terms like "achieving harmony with the rest of the world" and improving the people's quality of life," rather than purely in terms of economic growth. This change reflects Japan's new stance in the "post-high growth period," which is examined in Chapter 4.

It seems undeniable that, of all the plans, the Income-doubling Plan was preeminent in its far-reaching effects. Until the latter half of the 1950s most people did not see growth as long-term or stable. However, after the announcement of the Income-doubling Plan and the achievement of large-scale pay increases, the public, too, began to take it for granted that rapid growth and what went with it—rising incomes and living standards—had come to stay. It should be added that, even though they erred in their assumed growth rates and inflation rates, the later plans, too, became guidelines for numerous aspects of the economy, particularly government policy management. They also set policy standards for social capital.

4. Higher Living Standards and Pollution

What did economic growth produce? As has been seen, growth brought great strides in the development of Japan's industry, achieved full employment, and raised the material standard of living as the economy expanded.

This rise in the living standard and some of the ways in which it changed are summarized in Figure 3.7. First, over a period of nearly thirty years, consumption in urban households virtually quadrupled. This is far lower than the GNP growth rate, but even at that, it is a startling increase. A particularly straightforward indicator of the nature of this increase is the decline in the Engel coefficient (the share of total consumption expenditure devoted to food). The reverse of this, the proportion of total spending for miscellaneous discretionary items (grooming and hygiene, transportation and communication, education, culture and recreation, and entertainment) rose sharply. The reversal of the proportions of these two measures of consumption in the latter half of the 1960s and the continuing gradual widen-

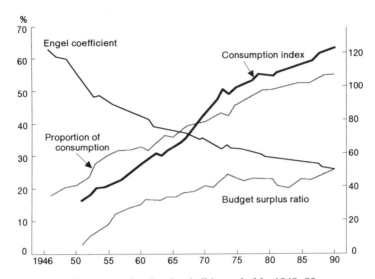

Figure 3.7. Real consumption levels of all households, 1948–90

Source: Statistics Bureau, Office of the Prime Minister, *Kakei Chōsa* [Household Budget Survey] data. Budget surplus ratio is working household income ÷ disposable income.

ing of the difference between the two testify to the fact that, even though housing problems still remained, at least the population's basic demands with respect to food and clothing were being satisfied, and varied consumption in response to individual tastes had become possible. It is noteworthy that, as reflected in increases in spending on miscellaneous items, consumption of services, such as culture, recreation, and entertainment, has expanded rapidly (see Table 3.10). Furthermore, the consumption of goods is moving increasingly towards items, such as pre-cooked meals and lunchboxes, that incorporate services to save time in the household.

In the area of housing, where standards have been slowest to rise, major improvements have been made, but serious problems remain. The number of residences increased by over 60 percent during the period of rapid growth while the number of persons per household declined sharply, reflecting the trend toward the nuclear family (see Table 3.11 and Figure 3.8). The proportion of homeowners dropped, but this can be seen as indicative of the fact that large numbers of urban workers moved into rented homes. The striking increase in the amount of floor space per person shows that the number of overcrowded households was diminishing. Despite all this, the housing

Table 3.10. Goods and Services as Proportions of Consumption Spending, 1971–1991

(%)

	Totals for goods	Goods			Services
		Durables	Semi-durables	Non-durables	
1971	73.1	8.6	16.0	49.3	26.9
74	71.8	8.2	16.1	47.4	28.2
77	69.3	7.0	14.9	47.4	30.7
80	67.3	6.1	14.3	47.0	32.7
83	66.1	6.4	13.3	46.3	33.9
86	64.5	6.4	13.1	45.0	35.5
89	63.3	7.1	13.6	42.5	36.7
91	62.7	6.8	13.5	42.4	37.3

Source: Statistics Bureau, Office of the Prime Minister, *Kakei Chōsa Nenpō* [Household Budget Survey], 1985, 1991.

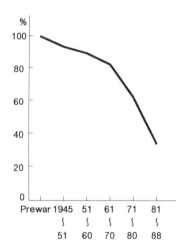

Figure 3.8. Period-by-period residential construction totals
Source: Statistics Bureau, Office of the Prime Minister.

problem has been a major social issue because land prices rose so phenomenally in the 1970s and 1980s that it became impossible to purchase land and build a home on an ordinary income (see Table 3.12). There are a number of reasons for the rise in land prices, but

Table 3.11. Changes in the Housing Situation

	Number of residences (1000s)	Persons per residence	Composition of housing by type of proprietary relationship (%)					Composition of housing by number of tatami mats per person (%)					
			Total	Owned home	Rental from publicly managed or owned corporation	Rented from private owner	Company-provided housing	Total	2.9 tatami or less	3–4.9	5–6.9	7–9.9	10+
1958	17,432	5.26	100.0	71.2	3.5	18.6	6.7	100.0	31.6	45.3	17.1	9.4	6.7
63	20,372	4.72	100.0	64.3	4.6	24.1	7.0	100.0	22.2	35.3	20.3	12.5	9.8
68	24,198	4.19	100.0	60.3	5.8	27.0	6.9	100.0	14.2	33.9	23.5	15.6	12.9
73	28,731	3.78	100.0	59.2	6.9	27.5	6.4	100.0	7.5	26.8	25.0	20.5	20.2
78	32,189	3.58	100.0	60.4	7.6	26.1	5.7	100.0	3.8	19.0	23.0	24.1	29.8
83	34,705	3.44	100.0	62.4	7.6	24.5	5.2	100.0	2.5	14.0	21.4	24.5	37.3
88	37,413	3.28	100.0	61.3	7.5	25.8	4.1	100.0	1.5	10.1	18.5	24.2	44.5

Note: One *tatami* mat = 1.67 square meters.
Sources: Ministry of Construction, Housing Bureau, *Jūtaku Taisaku Yōran* [Housing Policy Handbook]; Office of the Prime Minister, Statistics Bureau; Kokumin Seikatsu Sentā, *Kokumin Seikatsu Tōkei Nenpō* [Annual Report of Statistics on National Life].

Table 3.12. Urban Land Price Increases
(A) Comparison with prewar levels (Sept. 1, 1936 = 1)

	Commercial property	Residential property	Industrial property	Average (A)	Bank of Japan wholesale price index (B)	A/B
1945	1.63	5.99	5.31	5.01	3.02	1.66
55	366.5	291.6	263.1	310.6	331.3	0.94
65	2,607.8	2,067.4	2,404.5	2,384.8	343.3	6.95
75	8,607.8	8,664.3	7,286.8	8,346.7	593.9	14.1
85	12,312.35	15,993.0	10,008.1	12,955.9	801.2	16.2
90	19,990.2	22,020.9	13,826.2	20,350.7	743.4	27.4

(B) Increases from 1970 to 1992 (1970 = 100)

	National land price averages (A)	Six major urban centers		Average (B)	Bank of Japan wholesale price index (C)	A/C	B/C
		Commercial property	Residential property				
1975	193	160	210	187	157	1.23	1.19
80	231	195	319	242	207	1.12	1.17
85	299	299	427	332	206	1.45	1.61
90	437	1,170	1,077	987	184	2.34	5.28
91	483	1,208	1,113	1,016	186	2.60	5.46
Sept. 1992	461	896	816	779	183	2.52	4.26

Source: Statistics from Japan Real Estate Research Institute.

the major one is that the extremely heavy concentration of population in the urban belt along the Pacific Coast has tremendously
increased the demand for land. The supply of land is limited in any
event, and now that it has been divided up into "urbanization adjustment zones" and the like, where industrial and residential builders
must obtain building permits from municipal authorities, there are
now areas in which needed residential construction is restricted. And
inevitably land prices rise still higher when, in anticipation of further
price increases, landholders such as owners of small farm plots in the
suburbs are reluctant to sell. In addition, while of course realtors and
other businessmen do buy up land for development purposes, they
frequently buy it for speculative purposes, too. The cumulative effect
of all this has been soaring land prices. A prohibitive tax on profits
from the sale or transfer of land was levied under the national Land-
Use Planning Law (National Land Law) in 1974, but land prices had
already risen greatly by that time. Prices continued to rise after the
end of the high-growth period, culminating in the abnormal housing
prices of 1989–90. This is considered in detail in the next chapter.

A few words should be added about the abrupt Westernization of
the national lifestyle. As is shown in Figure 3.9, with the spread of the
Western way of life throughout the 1960s and early 1970s, nearly half
of all households became owners of dining room sets and automobiles, and over 80 percent had telephones. The spread of household
electrical appliances was remarkable: all kinds of items which had still
been rare at the end of the 1950s had become necessities in every
home by the mid-1970s. There is some truth in the view that this was
artificially induced or forced consumption brought about through
advertising by durable consumer goods makers; but for whatever
reason, lifestyles undeniably underwent a complete change. This
included eating habits. Bread began to compete with rice as a staple
food while spending on all staples as well as traditional foods and
seasonings declined and the consumption of side dishes, animal pro-
tein, and salad vegetables increased. As a result of changes in diet,
the Japanese physique was transformed (Table 3.13). The height and
weight of young people increased conspicuously beginning in the
1920s and 1930s when urbanization was in progress and changed
decisively during the postwar period of high economic growth. In a
word, the changes in people's personal lives during this growth period
were stunning indeed. They might even be called revolutionary, but
they seemed to occur uneventfully, in the course of everyday life.

The level of consumption spending did rise, bringing about a
change in lifestyles, but individual families were extremely frugal, and

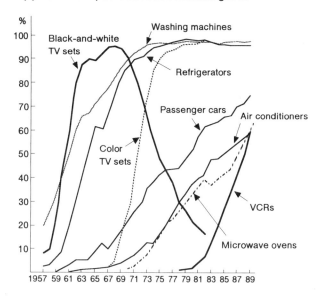

(1) Household possession of consumer goods

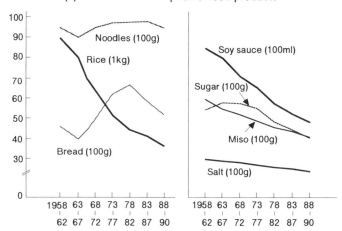

(2) Individual consumption of food products

Figure 3.9. Changes in national consumption patterns

Source: Economic Planning Agency, *Kakei Shōhi no Dōkō* [Household Consumption
Trends], various years.

Table 3.13. Heights and Weights of Young People

	6 years of age				17 years of age			
	Height (cm)		Weight (kg)		Height (cm)		Weight (kg)	
	Male	Female	Male	Female	Male	Female	Male	Female
1900	107.0	104.8	17.0	17.0	157.9	147.0	50.0	47.0
05	106.4	105.2	17.5	16.8	159.1	147.9	50.3	46.7
10	107.0	105.8	17.5	17.0	159.1	148.8	51.4	46.8
15	107.0	105.5	17.5	17.1	159.7	149.1	51.7	47.1
20	107.0	105.8	17.6	17.0	160.0	149.7	51.8	47.4
25	107.6	106.1	17.7	17.3	160.6	150.3	52.4	47.3
30	108.1	106.9	17.9	17.3	161.0	150.7	53.0	48.1
35	108.9	108.0	18.1	17.5	161.8	151.2	53.7	48.5
40	—	—	—	—	—	—	—	—
45	—	—	—	—	—	—	—	—
50	108.6	107.8	18.5	17.9	161.8	152.7	52.6	49.1
55	110.3	109.3	18.7	18.1	163.4	153.2	54.5	49.8
60	111.7	110.6	19.1	18.5	165.0	153.7	56.1	50.4
65	113.4	112.5	19.7	19.2	166.8	154.8	57.5	51.3
70	114.5	113.6	20.1	19.5	167.8	155.6	58.7	52.1
75	115.1	114.4	20.5	20.1	168.8	156.3	59.2	52.2
80	115.8	114.9	20.8	20.3	169.7	157.0	60.6	52.1
85	116.4	115.7	21.2	20.7	170.2	157.6	61.5	52.8
90	116.8	116.0	21.5	21.1	170.4	157.9	62.0	52.8

According to prewar data from physical examinations for conscription, the average height of 20-year-old males was 156.3 cm in 1891, 157.3 cm in 1902, 157.9 cm in 1910, 158.8 cm in 1920, and 159.4 cm in 1925, less than the heights shown above for 17-year-old males in the same years. Since the figures in the table are for students attending middle school, their physiques may be considered to have been better than the average.
Sources: Ministry of Education, Mombushō Nenpō [Ministry of Education Annual Report].

the result of their thrift was a simultaneous increase in savings. Data on the rate of savings derived from several indicators (Figure 3.10) show an extraordinarily steep rise after the war. An international comparison of national income statistics on the proportion of personal savings to private disposable income in 1976 reveals that, in contrast to Japan's 24.9 percent in 1976, this ratio was 7.9 percent for the U.S., 11.2 percent for England, 14.5 percent for West Germany, 12.3 percent for France, and 19.4 percent (1973) for Italy.[14]

What produced this high rate of savings? As a result of the sustained efforts of numerous researchers to obtain an answer to that question, it has become possible to make rough distinctions among

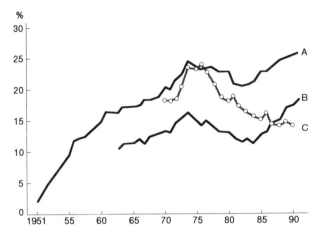

Figure 3.10. Changes in the rate of personal savings, 1952–75

A = personal savings divided by disposable personal income, from national income statistics

B = net rate of increase of savings in workers' household budgets, from Household Budget Survey data

C = SNA model of savings as a proportion of household budgets

the many possible factors as to which bear virtually no relation to the high rate of saving and which are closely related.[15]

Of the many hypotheses which have been advanced, Shōji Nobuo[16] identifies the following two as virtually insupportable because they yield no results whatever from statistical verification procedures:

(1) Japan's social security is inadequate, and compensatory savings for old age and emergencies boost the Japanese savings rate.

(2) Many people now living in rented houses or rooms are saving to buy or build homes.

Two factors are recognized as having some influence but cannot be considered major:

(3) Customarily, even when the rate of increase in real income over the previous period is high, it is difficult for consumers to radically depart from their previous consumption habits, and the savings rate, rather than the rate of consumption, rises as a result.

(4) The decline in the number of family members per household resulted in a decline in per-household consumption spending.

This leaves the following two factors as the most powerful in explaining Japan's high rate of saving:

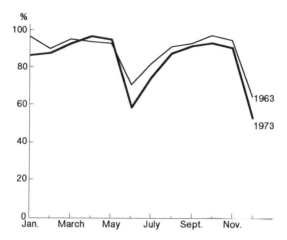

Figure 3.11. Month-by-month average propensities to consume for workers'
household budgets (as proportion of disposable income), 1963 and 1973
Source: Statistics Bureau, Office of the Prime Minister, Household Budget Survey
        data.

(5) Increases in real income which accompanied Japan's high rate
of growth; and

(6) Increases in the proportion of bonuses and other temporary
income.

Of these, the former is an unsophisticated Keynesian consumption
function and requires no explanation here. The latter may be
explained as follows: As is shown in Figure 3.11, the ratio of consumption spending to disposable income (the average propensity to
consume) in the household budgets of Japan's workers comes to
about 90 percent except in the bonus months of June–July and
December, and the average monthly savings rate is thus not particularly high. Komiya Ryūtarō interprets this as having resulted from the
fact that "the income increases over and above what was expected
and which accompanied economic growth took the form of increases
in the proportion of bonuses in household budgets, for which reason
they were accompanied by considerable lags in the rise of consumption levels; moreover, these lags widened."[17] It can be seen from the
high values of the coefficients of determination in Table 3.14 that this
variable has great explanatory power, as of course does real income,
which shows an R^2 as high as 0.9. For these reasons, the bulk of the
high savings rate is considered to be explained by these two factors
alone.

Table 3.14. Regression Formulae $(Y = \alpha + \beta X)$ and Coefficients of Determination Ratio of Household Head's Temporary Income to Fixed Periodic Income (X) and for the Average Propensity to Consume (Y)

Period	α	β (Figures in parentheses are t-values)	Coefficient of determination R^2
1952–75	−2.801	0.5017 (14.45)	0.9047
1952–62	−5.722	0.6571 (6.20)	0.8103
1963–75	0.3699	0.4212 (5.82)	0.7548

Source: Calculated from data in Statistics Bureau, Office of the Prime Minister, *Shōwa 38-nen-50-nen no Kakei—Kakei Chōsa* [Household Budgets 1963–75—Household Budgets Survey], 1977, using time series data for workers' household budgets in cities with populations of 50,000 or more.

Certainly, people did experience greater satisfaction with their lives as they both raised consumption levels and increased their savings. But as lifestyles changed in accordance with the rise in average consumption levels in each social class, there also arose the burdensome compulsion to "keep up with the Joneses." People would think, for example, that without a television set their children could not keep up in conversations with their friends at school; that the children were becoming accustomed to meals of bread, meat, and milk in school lunches and change the menus at home accordingly; or that since everybody else was remodeling, failure to modernize their own home would be humiliating. In a society which had become "information-oriented" and where income levels were equalized, Duesenberry's "relative income hypothesis" took on key significance.

However, if one accepts this interpretation, one can also be persuaded that the rise in the standard of living did not mean an immediate improvement in levels of satisfaction either for individuals or for the society. This is because an increase in dissatisfaction is immediately linked to increases in a society's standard of living if such increases cannot be duplicated or sustained; and even if they can be, all that can be done is to maintain previous levels of satisfaction. It is also understandable that, as incomes and living standards continued to rise under rapid growth, a critical attitude toward this growth emerged. Once the rising standard of living accompanying growth came to be taken for granted, such things as "human alienation" and "the distortions of growth" became issues. Ideology and social thought are beyond the scope of this book, so here we will simply touch on the "distortions" controversy as represented by pollution.

An awareness of the "industrial pollution" problem goes back as far as the pollution incidents connected with the Ashio and Besshi copper mines in the early decades of the twentieth century, and the foul odors, polluted effluents, and noise pollution of factory districts are as old as modern industry. Their effects were not all that conspicuous in those early days, or it may be that even though they were conspicuous, they were ignored; in any case, it was not until about 1960 that pollution began to be seen as an important issue. From the 1950s to the beginning of the 1960s "Minamata disease" and "Yokkaichi asthma" began to be raised as serious issues. It was also at about this time that the extraordinary water pollution in the Arakawa and Tama rivers in Tokyo, the Kanzaki and Neya rivers between Osaka and Kobe, and the sludge at Tagonoura Bay in Shizuoka Prefecture became social problems while the cadmium poisoning rice became an issue in connection with the *itai-itai* ("It hurts! It hurts!") disease in the area of Toyama and around Annaka in Gunma Prefecture.[18] In 1964, the residents of Mishima City in Shizuoka Prefecture mounted a campaign in opposition to plans for building an industrial complex in the environs of nearby Numazu, and firms which had expected to locate there were forced to revise their plans. Here, for the first time, developed open opposition to the factories for which the various regions had until then competed in enticements for locating in their respective areas. The Japanese word for environmental pollution, *kōgai*, came into use at the beginning of the 1960s, and from that time on the subject became firmly entrenched as a social issue.

There are many kinds of environmental pollution: many sources, such as industry, automobiles, cities, and agricultural chemicals; and a variety of damage, waste disposal problems, and destruction to the natural environment from air pollution, befouling of water, noise and vibrations, land sinkage, foul odors, soil pollution, and farm pesticides. Pollution primarily originating in industry began to be pronounced in the early 1960s, and in the latter half of the decade measures for dealing with the problem became key policy issues. An Environmental Pollution Section was established in the Ministry of Health and Welfare in 1964, and 1965 saw the establishment of public facilities for the elimination and prevention of pollution and the designation of industrial sites to which large numbers of factories were to be moved. The Pollution Prevention Association (Kōgai Bōshi Jigyō Dan) was also launched that year. In 1966 restrictions on exhaust gases in new-model cars were implemented. In 1967 the Basic Environmental Pollution Prevention Law went into effect, and in 1970 it was revised and strengthened. In the 1967 law, "protection of the people's health" and "preservation of the living environment" were set forth as goals. The legislation's declaration that it would undertake to achieve "harmony" between the preservation of the living environment and "the healthy development of the economy" attracted criticism, but the enactment of this law established that the burden of compensation for losses due to environmental pollution would be borne by the polluting firms. Laws stipulating measures for the prevention of air, water, and noise pollution were passed, and in 1971 the Environment Agency was inaugurated. A 1970 amendment to the Basic Law deleted the "harmony with economic development" clause, clarified the goal of preventing environmental pollution, and strengthened the regulations overall. The situation as a whole took a turn for the better, as Figure 3.12 shows.

There is no doubt that the sudden increase in environmental pollution was a concomitant of economic growth, particularly of chemical and heavy industrialization and the spread of the automobile. It is also understandable that regulation became necessary as a result of the prominence which the problem assumed as the 1960s began and

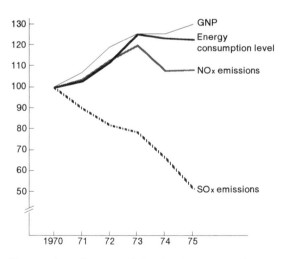

Figure 3.12. Changes in pollutant emission levels, 1970–75 (FY 1970 = 100)
Source: Environment Agency, *Kankyō Hakusho* [Environmental White Paper], 1977.

the serious nature of pollution diseases was brought to light. At the same time, the achievement of full employment and higher standards of living via economic growth required a shift in emphasis away from the primacy of growth in the direction of greater attention to other values. Thus, both the positive and negative effects of economic growth have demonstrated that they have sufficient power to bring about changes in the posture of national economic policy as well. At work in this process was the phenomenon known as the pluralization of values.

Notes

1. The terms "Jimmu boom," "Iwato boom," and "Izanagi boom" were originated by journalists who were wryly referring to these periods of prosperity as the most remarkable in Japanese history since the legendary days of the Emperor Jimmu (supposed to have ascended the throne in 660 B.C.), or the even more ancient era when the Sun Goddess Amaterasu Omikami was lured out of her sullen seclusion in a cave (Iwato). Of still greater antiquity is the god Izanagi (progenitor of the Sun Goddess) who with his sister Izanami in legend gave birth to the islands of Japan.

2. Angus Maddison, *Economic Growth in the West: Comparative Experience in Europe and North America* (Twentieth Century Fund, 1964).

3. Maddison, *op. cit.*

4. In the first part of his book *Gendai Nihon Keizai Ron—Sekai Keizai no Henbō to Nihon* (Tōyō Keizai Shimpōsha, 1977), Yoshitomi Masaru gives an extensive treatment of the gold standard as it related to the Japanese economy.

5. Genji is a modern novelist whose works deal with the lives of white-collar workers in present-day Japan. *Santō Jūyaku* is his best-known novel.

6. Ironically, these two companies were amalgamated again in 1968, and became Shin Nihon Seitetsu (New Japan Steel).

7. This had already been pointed out by Uchida Tadao in 1960.

8. This period is considered to be the fourth period of rapid technological development in the world economy in modern times. It corresponds to a fourth peak in the approximately 55-year-long Kondratyev cycle, whose peaks occur in conjunction with the pace of technological progress.

9. Ministry of International Trade and Industry, *Tsūshō Sangyō-shō Nijū-nen Shi* [Twenty-Year History of the Ministry of International Trade and Industry], 1969, pp. 29–31.

10. MITI, *op. cit.*, pp. 80–81.

11. MITI, *op. cit.*, pp. 62–66.

12. *The Economist* (London) May 27 – June 2, 1967, Special Report, "The Risen Sun; Japan—Seven Keys to the Sun."

13. Such practices go back even further for the steel and shipbuilding industries, to the beginning of the twentieth century.

14. Bank of Japan, *Nihon Keizai o Chūshin to suru Kokusai Hikaku Tōkei* [International Comparative Statistics Focusing on Japan], 1977.

15. See, for example, Komiya Ryūtarō, "Kojin Chochiku no Kyōkyu" [The Supply of Personal Savings], *Gendai Nihon Keizai Kenkyū* (University of Tokyo Press, 1975; Mizoguchi Toshiyuki, *Shōhi Kansū no Tōkeiteki Bunseki* [Statistical Analysis of Consumption Functions] (Iwanami Shoten, 1964), and "Nihon no Shōhi Kansū no Tenbō" [Observations on Japanese Consumption Functions], *Keizai Kenkyū* [Economic Research], vol. 39, no. 3 (1988). Most exhaustive is Shōji Nobuo, "Kojin Shōhi to sono Patān" [Patterns of Private Consumption] in Japan Economic Research Center, *Chūki Antei Seichō Jitsugen no tame ni* [For the Achievement of Medium-term Stable Growth].

16. Shōji Nobuo, *op. cit.*

17. Komiya Ryūtarō, *op. cit.*

18. Minamata disease refers to the mercury poisoning that occurred in the city of Minamata in Kyūshū. Yokkaichi, on the Ise Bay near Nagoya, is the site of the largest of Japan's first petrochemical complexes. Itai-itai disease, resulting from cadmium poisoning, produces a brittleness in the bones that results in painful splintering and fractures.

Part II

Ways and Means of Rapid Growth

4

The Mechanism and Policies of Growth

1. The Growth Mechanism

Preparatory to a consideration of the structure of the Japanese economy, let us first summarize the growth mechanism.

(1) First we shall establish the ceiling for growth in the 1950s and 1960s. It is assumed that the imports Japan requires are covered by its exports. The price elasticity of Japan's exports relative to world imports (η), as calculated in Chapter 3, was 2.7 in the 1950s and 1.8 in the 1960s. On the other hand, the growth rate of world trade was 4.4 percent from 1951 to 1960 and 10 percent from 1961 to 1970. Therefore, the maximum growth rate for Japan's exports equals the product of the two, which was 11.9 percent in the 1950s and 18 percent in the 1960s. If these figures are calculated for the entire period, their product is 14 percent since the growth rate of world imports was 7 percent and the elasticity was 2. Imports could grow at a rate corresponding to the growth rate of exports. While Japan's ratio of imports to GNP was a little unstable in the 1950s, fluctuating at between 10 and 15 percent, it was 12 percent on average and then stabilized at 10 percent in the 1960s as a result of a decline in the import price of raw materials. If this ratio is considered fixed, the ceiling on the import growth rate may be regarded as the upper limit of the GNP (nominal) growth rate. Thus, the conditions existed for a possible nominal growth rate of 12 percent in the 1950s, a nominal 18 percent in the 1960s, and an average of 14 percent for these twenty years.

When price rises of 4 percent in the 1950s and 4.6 percent in the 1960s—4.5 percent for the entire period—are deducted from the nominal figures, it can be seen that growth rates of 8 percent, somewhat more than 13 percent, and 9.5 percent were possible in the 1950s, the 1960s, and the entire period, respectively. The actual growth rate of real GNP was 8.3 percent in the 1950s and 10.5 percent in the 1960s, averaging out to 9.6 percent for the entire period. In other words, growth exceeding the limits imposed by the balance of payments was achieved during the 1950s because of dollar income from the special procurements, while it was contained within the balance of payment limits during the 1960s. For this reason, Japan was able to achieve a steady balance of payments surplus in the latter half of the 1960s.

(2) This makes a very interesting comparison with the postwar experience of West Germany, where growth was held in check within the confines of the balance of payments constraint beginning in the 1950s. This was the result of West Germany's postwar economic policies and the cautious behavior of firms, and it led to the achievement of a balance of payments surplus by the end of the 1950s and to the West German government's adoption of policies that attempted to prevent imported inflation by revaluing the mark in 1961. If the government and firms in Japan had had an attitude like that of the Germans, the balance of payments surplus and the upward revaluation of the yen might have been achieved nearly ten years earlier than they in fact were. The pattern of Japan's economic growth following the two successive oil crises drew distinctly closer to that of West Germany. Both nations adopted policies of strict monetary restraint, brought inflation under control, withstood massive revaluations of their currencies, rationalized industry, and increased the level of overseas investment. In addition, they both chose not to become military powers but to limit themselves to the economic arena. From the 1970s onward, as the economic power of the U.S. declined, their currencies increasingly came to support the U.S. dollar as pivotal world currencies.

(3) In order to attain 10 percent growth in the economy, a 10 percent per annum increment in goods and services must be supplied. Otherwise, the real growth rate will be confined to the level at which it is possible to supply additional goods and services. Moreover, even if a 10 percent increment in supply is achieved, there will be excess capacity if a 10 percent increment in demand is not created. How was this problem resolved? First, aggressive action on the part of firms during the period of high economic growth expanded the capacity for additional supply. As Table 4.1 shows, gross private capital stock increased approximately fivefold from 1955–1970 while real GNE more than quadrupled, a growth rate more or less the same as real GNP during this period. This means that Japan's average capital coefficient was low, with a value close to its marginal capital coefficient. However, from the mid-1970s onwards growth in GNE slowed relative to growth in capital stock, and we see a clear increase in the

Table 4.1. Changes in Capital Coefficients

(1985 prices, ¥ billions)

	Private capital stock (K)	Real GNE (Y)	Average capital coefficient (K/Y)	Increase in K (ΔK)	Increase in Y (ΔY)	Marginal capital coefficient (ΔK/ΔY)
1955	30,813	42,943	0.72	—	—	—
60	45,665	65,145	0.70	14,852	22,202	0.67
65	81,196	100,821	0.81	35,531	35,676	1.00
70	151,001	171,293	0.88	69,805	70,472	0.99
75	251,548	212,876	1.18	100,547	41,583	2.42
80	347,800	266,634	1.30	96,252	53,758	1.79
85	493,131	321,532	1.53	145,331	54,898	2.65
90	690,396	383,448	1.80	197,265	61,916	3.19

Sources: Y is calculated from *Chōki Sokyū Shuyō Keiretsu Kokumin Keizai Keisan Hōkoku* [Long-term Retroactive National Economic Accounts for Principal Business Groups] 1955–1989, and *Kokumin Keizai Keisan Nenpō* [National Economic Accounts Annual] 1992. K is calculated from *Shōwa 60-nen Kijun Minkan Kigyō Shihon Sutokku* [Capital Stock of Private Businesses, 1985 base] 1955–1970 and 1965–1990 editions, both published by the Economic Planning Agency.

capital coefficient. There was an overall decline in the productivity of capital, and this is one factor that dictated the growth rate ceiling since the 1980s.

(4) During the high growth period domestic demand alone set the stage for 10 percent growth, with the private sector accounting for 75 percent and government demand for 25 percent, while exports and imports roughly cancelled each other. From 1975 to 1985, however, approximately one fourth of economic growth was sustained by overseas demand. From 1985 onward overseas demand made a minus contribution to growth, but this seems to have been a temporary trend due to the rapid appreciation of the yen. From 1990 onward there is once again a clear excess of export-based over import-based demand in both real and nominal terms.

(5) During the extraordinary appreciation of the yen that began in 1985, Japan stuck to a low interest rate policy for three years. This was because the general price index remained steady, held down by the drop in the price of imports. But the policy invited a sudden rise in the value of asset stock, particularly land and stock prices, and created the conditions for the "bubble economy." This abnormal situation, which arose due to the appreciation of asset stock in the broad

sense, demonstrated the need to look at asset prices, and not just the prices of goods and services, as indicators of inflation. This indicates that the economy took on a different character in the mid-1980s.

(6) Next, let us consider the problems of income distribution and inflation. The distribution of the income increases arising out of economic growth to the various classes of the population was achieved via the market mechanism and through labor unions and other groups or institutions.

As will be elaborated in Chapter 5, the labor force in postwar Japan shifted from a condition of surplus to one of shortage, and for this reason there was a general rise in wage levels in the labor market. The labor unions were quite successful in promptly translating these advantageous labor market conditions into the reality of pay increases. With the pressure of the labor shortage in the background, the "spring wage offensives" conducted each year by the labor unions functioned as a system for distributing the previous year's increase in GNP to the workers. When the salaries of government employees were reviewed on advice from the National Personnel Authority, the market wage-levels determined by that year's "spring offensive" were taken as standards. And the rates and levels of "spring offensive" wage rises were also used as a reference by firms without labor unions.

These wage increases did not just mean income increases for workers who received wages, but came to carry the weight of a shadow price—a target income level for the entire labor force. Farmers, the self-employed, family workers—all hoped that their incomes would rise in tandem with those of the unionized workers, and strove to effect those increases. For example, farmers' groups demanded that the government raise its buying price for rice, had the rice price computation formula changed from the parity formula to a production cost income compensation formula, and succeeded in gearing the wages of workers employed at home to those in the industrial labor market. But the costs of general agricultural commodities, of the industrial products of small and medium-sized firms, and of services (the prices of haircuts and permanents or of a cup of coffee, room charges in hotels, designers' fees, etc.) also soared. This was due to the fact that since these were, generally speaking, goods and services for which there was little possibility of raising labor productivity by means of plant and equipment investment, the only way to increase incomes was to raise the labor expense included in costs.

In general, if the rate of increase in labor productivity is high, it may be that the supply curve will not shift upward at all (and may

Table 4.2. Special Group Consumer Price Indexes

	1990 (1970 = 100)	Average annual rate of increase (%)
Total	289.8	5.5
commodities	257.2	4.8
Agricultural & marine products	276.9	5.2
Grains	276.9	5.2
Perishable foods	278.0	5.3
Industrial products	249.5	4.7
Food & beverages	276.3	5.2
Products of large firms	192.7	3.3
Products of small medium-sized firms	310.5	5.8
Textiles	286.1	5.4
Durable consumer goods	124.4	1.1
Other manufactured goods	246.8	4.6
Utilities	221.8	4.1
Publishing	348.7	6.4
Services	347.1	6.4
Rent on private land & structures	281.7	5.3
Public utilities service charges	338.3	6.3
Service charges to individuals	406.1	7.3
Dining out	344.1	6.4

Source: Calculated from Statistics Bureau, Office of the Prime Minister, Consumer Price Indexes Annual.

even shift downward), even if labor costs spiral. Or if an upward shift does occur, it will be only minor. The general validity of the above discussion is borne out by Table 4.2.

Writers who have taken note of the above phenomenon have characterized the inflation of the 1950s and 1960s as a "productivity differential inflation."[1]

(7) In one respect it was, broadly speaking, a mechanism for comparatively evening out income distribution among the various classes of the population. As is shown in Table 4.3, income distribution was in fact equalized during the 1960s. Whether one looks at the family income differences among the quintile classes given by the Household Budget Survey or the interquartile variations for individual wages given by a private survey, all showed striking declines. The degree of dispersion in the Household Budget Survey shows a tendency to

Table 4.3. Interquartile Variations in Average Wages of All Male Workers

(¥ 1000s)

	1st quartile	Median	3rd quartile	Interquartile variation (%)
1948	4.6	6.7	9.4	0.72
54	10.4	15.1	21.3	0.73
58	11.5	17.3	27.1	0.90
64	20.8	29.1	39.5	0.64
73	67.7	87.0	113.4	0.52
80	142.9	185.3	233.2	0.49
91	210.2	277.2	363.9	0.55

Interquartile variation $= \dfrac{\text{3rd quartile} - \text{1st quartile}}{\text{median}}$

Source: Ministry of Labour, *Kojin-betsu Chingin Chōsa* [Survey of Individuals' Wages].
Others from Ministry of Labour, *Chingin Kōzō Kihon Chōsa* [Basic Survey of the Wage Structure].

decline sharply between 1963 and about 1970, as shown in Figure 4.1. Moreover, interquartile variations in male wages, which are completely comparable throughout the period and which had been widening up through 1958, drastically contracted thereafter. High economic growth encouraged a leveling of income distribution. Household income differentials widened temporarily at the time of the first oil crisis, but subsequently narrowed again, and although real income differentials widened slightly at the beginning of the 1980s the distribution of disposable incomes—after subtraction of tax and social insurance—has remained almost as level as it was at the beginning of the 1970s.

(8) The equalization of income distribution produced among 95 percent of the people a sense that they were members of the middle class.[2] As consumption patterns changed in favor of Westernization, they produced the lifestyle of contemporary Japan: people eat bread and meat, acquire color television sets, refrigerators, and the full spectrum of household electrical appliances, own automobiles, enjoy their leisure, have a taste for travel, and are very fashion-conscious. Another manifestation of this change is the fact that 90 percent of junior-high graduates go on to high school, and nearly half of all high-school graduates advance to universities or junior colleges. The leveling of lifestyles may be the greatest change of all wrought by rapid growth.

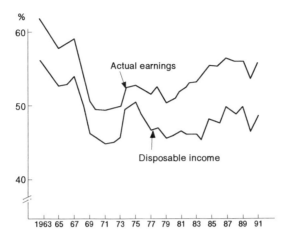

Figure 4.1. Index of workers' household income distribution, 1963–91
Source: Statistics Bureau, Office of the Prime Minister, *Annual Survey of Household Incomes.*

Of course, this was not all. During the growth decades, households in Japan had extremely high rates of saving, with rates for urban workers which had been 5.2 percent in 1955 climbing to 9.3 percent in 1960, 11.1 percent in 1965, 12.9 percent in 1970, and 14.5 percent in 1975.[3] Moreover, the in-the-black ratios (*kuroji-ritsu*) of household budgets (the ratio of the household budget balance of disposable income, less consumption expenditure, to disposable income) for the years noted above showed remarkable increases of 9.2 percent, 14.9 percent, 17.8 percent, 19.9 percent, and 22.6 percent, respectively. This is indicative of households' patterns of sound budget behavior. As we have seen, these kinds of changes may have lost some of their vigor as high growth came to an end, but the trends begun in the high-growth period became irreversible.

Doubts about growth were repeatedly voiced. Ryū Shintarō's *Hanami-zake no Keizai*[4] (Asahi Shimbunsha), a representative work on the subject, raised fundamental questions about the growth mechanism. From the mid-1960s onward there was a growing awareness of environmental pollution as yet another evil produced by growth. It was this same period that saw a transition from the era when economic development was aggressively supported by regional centers, which offered enticements to attract factories to locate in their areas, to a time when residents' opposition to development intensified.

However, the reality was that the objectors did not possess the power to directly challenge the growth mechanism. The government's fundamental policy was that coping with environmental pollution through legislation such as the Basic Pollution Prevention Law and the Air Pollution Prevention Law would suffice. What shook the growth mechanism to its foundations, as we will see in Part III, was the impact of the international events of 1971 and thereafter. The economy was rocked by these events in the short term, as they led to the inflation and economic crises of the early 1970s, but by the early 1980s it had overcome them and was ready to embark on a new phase.

2. Chemical and Heavy Industrialization
It is well known that chemical and heavy industrialization was the prime mover behind growth. An "investment begets investment" mechanism was also at work in this process. Let us consider this phenomenon in a little more detail.

While chemical and heavy industrialization itself produced a huge investment demand, it also had a far greater impact than ever before in terms of the derived demand it generated. One might say that this mechanism was the unseen driving force behind rapid growth. Indeed, the chemical and heavy industries occupied a pivotal position in the economy's cyclical process. This fact may be confirmed by means of input–output analysis. Perhaps the power of dispersion coefficient and the sensitivity of dispersion coefficient used in this type of analysis first require some explanation. The former indicates the total volume of production required from each sector throughout the entire economy per unit increase in final demand for a specific industry, while the latter shows the magnitude of output which a specified sector must produce given a one-unit increase in final demand in each sector of the economy. If the value of the power of dispersion coefficient is greater than one, the specified sector exerts considerable influence on other sectors, and if the sensitivity of dispersion coefficient is greater than one, the specified sector is heavily influenced by other sectors.[5]

The following breakdown classifies Japan's industries according to the size of their power of dispersion and sensitivity of dispersion indexes according to the 1960 Industrial Linkage Table (Administrative Management Agency). The position of the heavy and chemical industries in input–output relations is clear from this breakdown. And if we look at subsequent Industrial Linkage Tables we find there is no significant change in this basic pattern. That is, the following patterns emerge among the various industries:

(1) Industries for which both the power of dispersion and the sensitivity of dispersion were high—pig iron and crude steel, primary steel products, basic chemical products, pulp and paper, general machinery, electrical machinery, other food products not listed elsewhere, cloth and other textile products, lumber and wood products.

(2) Industries for which only the power of dispersion index was high—seafood, furniture, rubber products, butchering, meat and dairy products, spinning of chemical fibers, wearing apparel, leather and leather products.

(3) Industries for which only the sensitivity of dispersion was high—industrial crops, food crops, forestry, commerce, transportation, finance and insurance, electrical power.

Clearly, for the secondary industries and particularly for the heavy and chemical industries, both the power of dispersion index, which derives from final demand for those industries' products, and the sensitivity of dispersion index, which derives from these industries' final demands for the products of other industries, are high. Moreover, these industries characteristically are expanding and they sensitively reflect increases in demand, particularly investment demand. For most light industries, however, the power of dispersion index is high but the sensitivity of dispersion index is low. For most tertiary industries, only the sensitivity of dispersion index is high. For this reason, chemical and heavy industrialization extended its effects throughout the economy and brought about a mutually reinforcing expansion in demand, particularly in the heavy and chemical industries. Thus, the ease with which it brought on investment booms was in the nature of the chemical and heavy industrialization process. The formation of this kind of industrial structure meant that, compared to the situation in the prewar era of an industrial structure centered on light industry, it had become easier for derived demand to arise within the economy, and it was easier to stimulate growth internally.

Moreover, the expansion of plant and equipment investment spurred the economy's heavy and chemical industrialization. Table 4.4 indicates the additional production in each sector generated by one unit of fixed capital formation. In 1960, ranking next after construction and civil engineering, where each unit of fixed capital formation induced an increase in production by a factor of approximately 0.3, production increments for the machinery and steel products sectors were 0.2 and 0.15. It is immediately clear that with such a structure, if

Table 4.4. Induced Production Coefficients for Fixed Capital Formation, 1960–70

	1960	1965	1970
Construction	0.33718	0.38771	0.36478
Civil engineering	0.29099	0.23987	0.20929
General machinery	0.23605	0.19902	0.22474
Primary steel products	0.20264	0.14030	0.14411
Transportation equipment	0.16301	0.16726	0.15409
Electrical equipment	0.15865	0.13572	0.15362
Iron & steel materials	0.12029	0.07460	0.07611
Commerce	0.11498	0.12655	0.16055
Lumber & wood products	0.08159	0.07025	0.05929
Forestry	0.07548	0.04613	0.02573
Metal products	0.07175	0.08041	0.08048
Ceramic, earthen & stone products	0.07155	0.06956	0.06924
Transport	0.06457	0.06565	0.04623
Primary non-ferrous metal products	0.03764	0.02760	0.03144
Basic chemical products	0.03109	0.02654	0.02249
Petroleum products	0.03022	0.03081	0.02658

Calculated as $(I - (I - \bar{M}) A)^{-1} X (I - \bar{M}) Y + E)$, where $\bar{M}$ is the diagonal matrix of non-competitive import coefficients and E is the vector of export coefficients.
Source: Administrative Management Agency, *Shōwa 35-40-45-nen Setsuzoku Sangyō Renkanhyō* [Linked Input-Output Tables for 1960-1965-1970], Data Section 1.

fixed capital formation increases sharply, there will be marked production increases in the capital goods sectors, and these sectors themselves will also have to invest in order to expand capacity. The inevitability of this kind of induced investment also gives some idea of the "investment begets investment" mechanism of around 1960.

How had Japanese industry changed by the time the heavy and chemical industrialization of the 1960s was more or less complete? Let us summarize the shape of things around 1970 in a few figures.

As shown by Tables 4.5 and 4.6, both private capital stock and total production increased dramatically after 1955. Here, let us look at the rate of increase in total production and existing volume of stock for the two periods 1955–73 and 1973–90. Since the first period is eighteen years and the second seventeen, they ought to bear direct comparison. We find there is a good correspondence between the two periods, and there is no significant rise in the capital coefficient. The problem lies not so much in the total figures, however, as in the discrepancy in rates of growth between different sectors. During the period of high growth there was striking expansion in the secondary

Table 4.5. Increases in Private Capital Stock (run-on base)

(1985 prices, ¥ trillion)

	Actual amounts			Growth rates	
	1955	1973	1990	1973/1955	1990/1973
All industries	31.18	217.74	705.76	7.0	3.2
Agriculture, forestry & fisheries	6.77	34.32	92.66	5.0	2.7
Mining	0.62	1.54	2.40	2.5	1.6
Construction	0.38	7.59	25.49	20.0	3.4
Manufacturing	10.81	96.68	257.72	8.9	2.7
Light industry	4.23	38.86	73.19	9.2	1.9
Materials industry	2.22	34.96	99.17	15.8	2.8
Machinery	1.37	22.87	85.36	16.7	3.7
Wholesale & retail trades	4.26	21.94	74.12	5.2	3.4
Finance & insurance	0.68	5.35	15.37	7.9	2.9
Real estate	0.17	5.55	20.08	32.7	3.6
Transportation & communication	2.06	14.76	72.89	7.2	4.9
Electric gas & water utilities	3.90	19.35	56.60	5.0	2.9
Service industries	1.52	10.66	88.45	7.0	8.3
Primary industries	6.77	34.32	92.66	5.1	2.7
Secondary industries	11.82	105.82	285.61	9.0	2.7
Tertiary industries	12.51	77.60	327.50	6.2	4.2

Source: National Income Department, Economic Research Institute, Economic Planning Agency, *Minkan Kigyō Sōshihon Sutokku—Shōwa 30–40 Nendo, Shōwa 40-Heisei 2 Nendo* [Gross Capital Stock of Private Business, FY 1955–65 and FY 1965–1990].

industries, particularly the heavy and chemical industries, where both production and capital stock showed record rates of growth. Next came the tertiary industries like commerce, finance and insurance, and real estate. From 1973–90, however, the position was reversed, and growth rates in the secondary industries fell below those in the tertiary sector (Table 4.5). And while capital stock in the primary industries rose more or less in step with rates of growth, this reflects the rapid rise in labor productivity made possible by mechanization and energy-saving measures. In the high-growth period we find all industry undergoing a rapid transformation, led by the heavy and chemical industries. After the oil crisis these dramatic changes are no longer visible.

Table 4.6 shows that the labor productivity of industry as a whole increased by a factor of 3.2 during the period of high growth, from 1955–73. The rate of increase was highest in the materials and

Table 4.6. Numbers of Employees and Per-capita Production in Key Industries

(1985 prices, 10,000 people, ratio)

	Value of production by type of economic activity (¥ billions)			No. of employees			Gross value of production		No. of employees		Per-capita gross value of production	
	1955	1973	1990	1955	1973	1990	1973/1955	1990/1973	1973/1955	1990/1973	1973/1955	1990/1973
Agriculture, forestry and fisheries	8,633	10,431	10,482	1,680	903	599	1.21	1.00	0.54	0.66	2.25	1.51
Mining	292	1,061	957	48	19	10	3.63	0.90	0.40	0.53	9.18	1.71
Manufacturing	6,032	54,785	125,205	747	1,522	1,549	9.08	2.29	2.04	1.02	4.46	2.25
Light industry	4,429	22,678	34,001	421	679	655	5.12	1.50	1.61	0.96	3.17	1.55
Materials	1,134	19,167	31,974	158	339	294	16.90	1.67	2.15	0.87	7.88	1.92
Machinery	468	12,940	59,231	168	503	600	27.65	4.58	2.99	1.19	9.23	3.84
Construction	3,797	24,228	35,212	217	521	607	6.38	1.45	2.40	1.17	2.66	1.25
Electric, gas & water utilities	1,074	6,720	14,512	22	41	51	6.26	2.16	1.86	1.24	3.36	1.74
Wholesale and retail	1,937	24,247	55,301	498	932	1,180	12.52	2.28	1.87	1.27	6.69	1.80
Finance and insurance	895	8,564	25,328	64	146	230	9.57	2.96	2.28	1.58	4.19	1.95
Real estate	5,387	19,749	40,070	5	43	85	3.67	2.03	8.60	1.98	0.43	1.03
Transportation and communication	2,277	14,679	25,761	180	323	369	6.45	1.75	1.79	1.14	3.59	1.54
Service industries	12,453	38,947	75,992	507	992	1,720	3.13	1.95	1.96	1.73	1.60	1.13
Public service	4,911	9,617	14,747	102	194	209	1.96	1.53	1.90	1.08	1.03	1.42
Total	47,688	213,030	423,558	4,068	5,635	6,608	4.47	1.99	1.39	1.17	3.22	1.70
Import tax	120	2,231	2,505									
Imputed interest	-922	-8,035	-23,606									
GDP	46,886	207,126	402,456									

Data calculated from Economic Planning Agency, *Chōki Sokyū Shuyō Keiretsu Kokumin Keizai Keisan Hōkoku* [Long-term Retroactive National Economic Accounts for Principal Business Groups] 1955–1989 and *Kokumin Keizai Keisan Nenpō* [National Economic Accounts Annual] 1992.

machinery industries, followed by commerce, finance, and insurance. The rate of increase in productivity slowed down after 1973, to an average 1.7 times for industry as a whole, and 3.8 times even in the machinery industry. But the machinery industry showed particularly high growth in production, and labor productivity rose much faster than in other industries. Machinery was followed by finance and insurance, wholesale and retail sales, electric, gas and water utilities, and real estate, all of them tertiary industries. But the changes in the economy as a whole that began under the high-growth period completely transformed the Japanese economy. The point of departure for economic growth was chemical and heavy industrialization, but it can be seen from the above discussion that the entire economy possessed a latent capacity for flexible adaptation that allowed it to adjust to the changes entailed in the growth process.

3. The Functions of Fiscal Policy

As we have seen, the government and its related institutions played a major role in rapid growth. How did fiscal and monetary policy, which are supposed to constitute the core of economic policy, function in this regard? Let us first review fiscal policy.

The Finance Act, passed in 1947, clearly set forth the principle of a balanced budget, including a clause prohibiting the issue of long-term national bond debt. This law incorporated the lessons drawn from the inflation brought on by the wartime overissue of public bonds and the Finance Ministry's desire to maintain fiscal "neutrality" in the face of political pressures. The 1949 Dodge Plan even disallowed the previously sanctioned short-term Finance Ministry securities with maturities of one year or less, and thenceforward the administration of Japan's public finances was predicated on the principle of maintaining strict fiscal balance. At the time of the 1965 recession, the Finance Act had to be amended and its restrictions relaxed. This marked a watershed beyond which fiscal policy underwent great changes, and it became possible to adopt strong policies for dealing with business fluctuations. However, since the foregoing is limited to the realm of national finances while the picture is quite different if one includes local finances and the resumption of the issuing of bonds by local governments in the latter half of the 1950s, it may be argued that exaggerated importance should not be attached to the "fiscal balance" imperative. Nevertheless, in view of the tremendous relative importance of national finances, these changes cannot be ignored.

With the foregoing in mind, let us consider Japan's national finances after the Peace Treaty, beginning with the relationship between economic growth and the scale of the budget. Clearly, the postwar era can be divided into five periods. The first is that of Ichimada Hisato's fiscal policies, from 1954 to 1956. In order to hold down the balance of payments deficits and price increases which were occurring just at that time, Ichimada, Finance Minister in the Hatoyama Cabinet, adhered to a "One-Trillion-Yen Budget" for three years while at the same time reducing taxes, primarily on incomes. This was, most likely, a bid to reinstate classical policies aiming for "low-cost government."

During the second period, under the Ishibashi Cabinet (1956–57), Prime Minister Ishibashi and Finance Minister Ikeda Hayato switched to growth-promoting policies. Although they were diluted somewhat under the Kishi Cabinet with Finance Ministers Ichimada and Satō Eisaku, policies favoring growth once more became predominant when Ikeda became Prime Minister in 1960 and his Cabinet made "income doubling" its major policy thrust. A special feature of this period is the strikingly large budget expansion. The tremendous rate of annual increase, in excess of 25 percent during the high-growth period at the beginning of the 1960s, particularly accelerated growth.

Several factors made possible the budgetary expansion of this period. Since the fiscal authorities consistently underestimated both the economic growth rate and the growth in tax revenues when they drew up the budgets, subsequent tax revenues would then exceed expectations when the actual growth rate climbed higher than was foreseen. As a result, supplementary budgets would be drawn up in the second half of the fiscal year, and spending increased. This is why the percentage increases over the previous year in the post-revision budgets for 1959 and 1960 were conspicuously higher than similar percentages for the original budgets in those years. It can be seen that the fiscal spending increases accompanying rising prosperity added still more fuel to the "Iwato boom." If the desideratum is counter-cyclical management of the economy such that fiscal policy is rather inhibitory in prosperous times and somewhat expansionary during economic downturns, the fiscal policies of this period reversed this principle and instead were themselves a major factor amplifying business fluctuations. The very progressive income tax levied during this period worked as a "built-in stabilizer" whereby the growth rate of tax revenue exceeded the growth rate of national income in times of prosperity and declined in times of recession, but this effect was not strong enough to inhibit fluctuations in the business cycle.

The counter-cyclical function was left entirely to financial policy. This was manifest as well in the boomerang effect produced when, in conjunction with sagging corporate profits from 1963 to 1965 and a slackening of tax revenue increases, fiscal spending increases also fell off, causing still further deepening of the business recession. When tax revenues fell below the original budget, as in the period of monetary stringency in 1964, the rate of expansion in the supplementary budget was all the more sharply curtailed. This is why the rate of increase in the original budget for the recession year of 1965 was the lowest of any for the immediately preceding and following years. Moreover, in June of that year the fiscal authorities, expecting a leveling off of tax revenues, made plans for further expenditure reductions even beyond those called for in the original budget. No sooner had they done so, however, than Yamaichi Securities, which at the time was Japan's second largest securities firm, reached the brink of disaster when a stock market crash touched off a run on that company. The Bank of Japan had no choice but to announce unlimited credit for the firm in order to avert panic, so under Finance Minister Tanaka Kakuei a decision was reached to amend the Finance Act and to issue public debt funding. Thus, an increase in the supplementary budget's rate of expansion became possible.

The third period, from 1966 to 1973, is characterized by the government's ability to get by with only small-scale supplemental budgets during the course of each fiscal year. This was a result of the fact that it had become possible to issue national bonds, thereby facilitating the adoption for the first time of counter-cyclical fiscal policies, and the fact that high growth rates and large-scale tax revenue increases were anticipated from the outset when the budgets were drawn up. Actually, during the latter half of the 1960s it was decided that national bond issues would be held down, and a stable 15 to 20 percent rate of fiscal spending increases was established.

The fourth period lasted from 1974 to the late 1980s, coming after the monetary tightness of 1970–71 and the yen revaluation shock which immediately followed it. The fiscal authorities strove to revive prosperity by issuing national bonds and expanding fiscal spending on a large scale. Just after that the inflation and the oil crisis of the seventies suddenly erupted, tax revenues declined and the rate of dependence on government bonds rose, and spending was curbed due to recession (see Figure 4.2). As shown in Figure 4.2(a), however, this resulted in the expansion of the abnormal fiscal deficit and a rapid increase in bond issues and the level of dependence on deficit bonds. Meanwhile, despite the increase in nominal income that

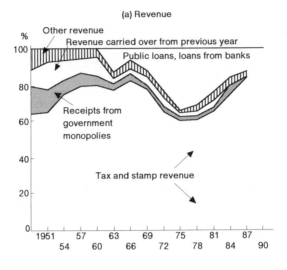

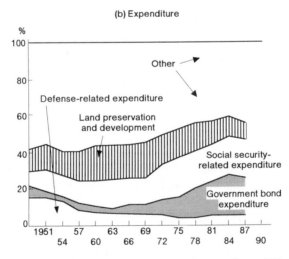

Figure 4.2. Composition ration of revenue and expenditure (%)
Source: Ministry of Finance data.

accompanied inflation, there was a rapid increase in the tax burden
because tax rates for income and other taxes had been left
unchanged. The situation was critical; pressure mounted for reconstruction and, as we have seen, an Emergency Administrative Commission of Inquiry embarked on a course it proclaimed as "fiscal

reconstruction without tax increases." The reining in of government spending during the early 1980s, when the growth rate was declining, meant government spending could no longer contribute to the flotation of the economy.

The fifth period starts with the increase in tax revenues due to the boom of the late 1980s, and the achievement of what was thought to be a nearly impossible goal—stopping the issue of deficit-financing bonds. By 1992, although government bonds in circulation still totaled more than 190 trillion yen, finances had recovered their mobility to the point where it was possible to compile a 7 trillion yen supplementary budget as a pump priming measure. On the other hand, however, increases in direct taxation had reached their limits and in 1989 the government both reduced income taxes and introduced a new consumption tax. There is now a need for a thorough review of the financial structure and an overhaul of the whole tax system.

The composition of government spending is highly significant in terms of the functioning of public finance. Figure 4.2(b) shows trends in the composition of government spending. Land preservation and development expenditure centered on public investment began to account for a larger percentage of government spending in the early 1960s, and large amounts of so-called social capital were built up during the period of growth-directed policies, in the form of roads, harbors, and the high-speed rail network, which created an external economy for industry. Table 4.7 summarizes changes in the level and composition of public investment. From the 1950s into the 1960s the emphasis was on flood control and damage restoration, but from the 1960s it shifted on to roads, and from the 1970s onward more spending was directed to housing and sewerage systems. It is clear from Table 4.8 that automobiles gradually became the most important means of domestic transportation. From the late 1960s on, government spending was increasingly directed to social security, particularly to pensions and health insurance. But social security spending is now proving a heavy burden on the public purse due to shortfalls in fiscal revenue and the aging of the population, and there seems no alternative to raising the pension-qualifying age to 65. Another item that will continue to account for a large proportion of spending is the increased government bond expenditure due to the servicing of deficit bonds. The government bond expenditure burden will inevitably limit the future mobility of public finance.

Let us now turn to the income redistribution effects of the social security system. The system was expanded in the 1970s and covers pensions, social insurance, and income support. People receive a wide

Table 4.7. Trends in Public Works Expenditure (5-year average values)

(Total figures in ¥ billion; other figures expressed as % of total)

	Total	Flood control	Road improvements	Harbors and airports	Housing	Sewerage systems and environmental hygiene	Agricultural infrastructure	Forestry roads, irrigation	Damage restoration	Other expenditure
1955	153	24.1	25.1				18.1	0.5	31.9	0.3
60	316	19.7	34.2	7.2	[4.7]	[8.6]	12.9	2.8	23.0	0.4
65	750	16.8	42.1	7.6	5.4*	2.3*	12.6	3.6	12.0	0.6
70	1,640	16.5	39.9	8.2	6.6	5.8	12.9	2.4	7.4	0.5
75	3,581	15.8	32.0	7.7	9.2	10.3	12.3	2.4	9.9	0.3
80	6,709	16.1	28.1	7.6	11.4	14.0	13.0	2.6	6.9	0.2
85	7,081	15.9	26.7	7.5	13.1	14.2	12.8	2.5	7.3	0.2
90	7,851	16.2	26.8	7.5	13.9	14.7	12.7	2.4	5.7	0.1

Figures in brackets are estimates; *figures include estimated figures equivalent to 2.4% and 0.7%, respectively.
Source: Ministry of Finance, "Financial Statistics."

Table 4.8. Road Extensions and Freight Transportation Volume

	Road extensions		Freight transport volume (billion ton/k.)	
	Paved road extensions (1000 km)	Expressway extensions (km)	Rail	Road
1955	14.0*	—	43	10
60	29.8	—	55	21
65	73.4	190	47	48
70	186.6	710	63	136
75	370.8	2,022	47	130
80	535.7	3,010	38	179
85	674.9	3,910	22	206

*1953 figure.
Source: Ministry of Transport survey.

range of social insurance benefits in exchange for the taxes and social insurance contributions they pay. In that high earners bear a heavier cost burden than low earners, who therefore receive greater benefits, the system effectively redistributes income by transferring it from higher to lower-income bands.

Figure 4.3 shows the Lorenz curves representing income before the deduction of contributions and the payment of benefits, and after redistribution, for the year 1989. It is clear from the figure that income inequalities are substantially ironed out by the redistribution of income to lower-income groups. By looking at the Gini coefficients for 1981 to 1989, and the income redistribution improvements summarized in Table 4.9, we can determine that initial income inequalities expanded through the decade but, as a result of redistribution, the Gini coefficient did not significantly worsen. The widening disparity of initial incomes was a general feature of the 1980s and reflects the growth in incomes among the young and middle-aged. Again, due to income tax reductions in the latter part of the decade, the degree of correction of income inequalities through direct taxation declines in 1989. On the other hand the degree of correction due to social security shows a clear increase in the second half of the 1980s, reflecting the aging of the population. From Figure 4.4, which charts tax and social security payments against receipts in each income band for initial incomes in 1989, we see that the gap between payments and receipts is a plus figure for incomes up to ¥4.5 million

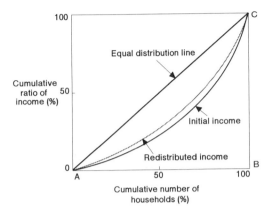

Figure 4.3. Lorenz curves for 1989

Income distribution and redistribution can be illustrated by means of a Lorenz curve plotted against a vertical axis representing the cumulative ratio of incomes and a horizontal axis representing the cumulative number of households, with households arranged in order of lowness of income. If income is distributed completely evenly, the Lorenz curve will correspond to the 45°-angle equal distribution line; the more unequal the distribution, the more it will deviate from that line. In a completely unequal situation, where one household monopolized the income and others and zero income, the Lorenz curve would correspond to the line ABC.

Source: Ministry of Welfare, Minister's Secretariat, *Heisei 2-nen Shotoku Saibunpai Chōsa Kekka* [Survey of Income Redistribution, 1990].

but switches to a minus value for incomes in excess of that amount. In today's society households are guaranteed an income of around ¥2 million. But maintaining present conditions for an increasingly aging population without increasing the tax and social security burden on the people remains a problem for the future.

Additionally, in connection with the question of public finance, treasury investments and loans must be mentioned. The lending of national funds accumulated through the various national financial institutions, postal savings, the welfare and national pension funds, and post office life insurance premiums, was institutionalized at the beginning of the 1950s and gradually expanded to play a large role in economic growth as a "secondary budget." Table 4.10 summarizes the sources and uses of these funds. From the very first, the amounts involved here increased as a proportion of GNP as long as economic growth continued, from around 3 percent in the 1950s to 8 percent in the 1980s, reaching almost half the value of the general account. The major shifts in the investment of funds, also of great interest, are clearly shown by the component ratios of the various uses of funds. In

Table 4.9. Corrective Effect of Income Redistribution on Income Inquality (Gini Coefficient)

	Initial income	Redistributed income		Income redistributed through tax (Initial income−Tax)		Income redistributed through social security (Initial income + Medical expenses + Social security benefits–Social security contributions)	
	Gini Coefficient	Gini Coefficient	Level of improvement (%)	Gini Coefficient	Level of improvement (%)	Gini Coefficient	Level of improvement (%)
1980	0.3491	0.3143	10.0	0.3301	5.4	0.3317	5.0
1983	0.3975	0.3426	13.8	0.3824	3.8	0.3584	9.8
1986	0.4049	0.3382	16.5	0.3879	4.2	0.3564	12.0
1989	0.4334	0.3643	15.9	0.4207	2.9	0.3791	12.5

The Gini Coefficient expresses the level of equality of distribution, in terms of the ratio between the area enclosed by the Lorenz curve and the line of equal distribution, and the triangular area below the line of equal distribution, in Fig. 4.3. The Gini Coefficient can therefore have a value from 0 to 1, income distribution being more equal the closer it is to 0 and more unequal the closer it is to 1.

$$\text{Gini Coefficient level of correction (\%)} = \frac{\text{Gini Coefficient for Initial Income} - \text{Gini Coefficient for Redistributed Income}}{\text{Gini Coefficient for Initial Income}}$$

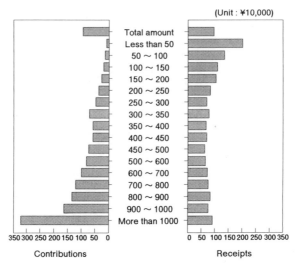

Figure 4.4. Redistributed income per household by initial income band, 1989
Source: Same as for Figure 4.3.

Table 4.10. Trends in Treasury Investments and Loans

	1953	1955	1965	1975	1985	1990
Total fiscal resources	337	298	1,776	11,344	29,432	36,572
General account	46	11	—	—	—	—
Industrial investment special account	57	34	43	66	31	64
Operating funds	175	153	1,187	9,800	23,642	28,453
Postal savings	81	82	465	5,050	8,739	7,200
Welfare & national pensions	16	31	370	2,132	5,325	5,540
Collected loans etc.	77	39	353	2,618	9,577	15,713
Postal insurance funds	20	48	109	1,014	2,577	6,055
Government guaranteed bonds	38	52	437	464	3,182	2,000
Total expenditure	323	322	1,621	9,310	20,858	34,572
Public welfare, housing and education	123	146	856	5,972	14,566	19,208
Roads, transport and communications, regional development	106	103	516	2,345	4,674	6,015
Industry, technology, trade, economic cooperation	94	73	248	992	1,718	2,400
Loans	—	—	—	—	—	6,950

the 1950s funds were directed mainly to the basic industries, followed by housing, small business, and transportation and communication. Thus, aside from housing, the items heading the list were industry and social capital for industry. However, as they moved into the 1960s, the basic industries became self-sustaining, their need to be shored up financially waned, and the relative importance of this use of funds declined. The emphasis shifted to housing, the maintenance of the living environment, education, small business, transport and communication, trade and economic cooperation. In the latter half of the 1960s, housing and environmental maintenance led other items and reached still higher levels with the coming of the 1970s. This development testifies to the fact that the main target of public investment and loan policy was shifting away from growth to welfare.

Nevertheless, a distinguishing feature of Japanese fiscal spending was its small scale relative to that of spending in other countries. Moreover, it was low as a proportion of GNP. This was due both to the fact that military spending was held down to below one percent of GNP—it reached 3 to 5 percent in Europe and the U.S.—and to the fact that the traditional posture of avoiding tax increases was maintained. But since the late 1970s changes have been forced in this posture and policy has shifted in the direction of "high welfare, high tax burden." Finding the limitations of this policy remains a problem for the future.

4. The Monetary Mechanism and Policies

The monetary system and controls of the wartime and immediate postwar periods, as described in Part I of this book, undeniably exerted a great influence on postwar finance. This may be summarized as follows. In the first place, before the war the Bank of Japan had preserved a relatively independent position vis-à-vis the Ministry of Finance; and in turn, the powerful city banks such as the zaibatsu banks, priding themselves on sound management based solely on equity funds, had maintained relative independence from the Bank of Japan. However, all this changed in the period during and following the war: the Bank of Japan found itself in a situation in which it had no choice but to accept Finance Ministry controls, while the city banks likewise fell into a similar position relative to the Bank of Japan. Secondly, while financial policy was aimed at military production during the war and economic recovery after the war, and supplied the requisite funds to fulfill these aims, it was also forced to impose strict controls since it was charged with the difficult task of keeping down runaway inflation. Even after the 1950s, when funds were needed for the expansion of key industries, government funds were channeled in this direction to attract additional private funding. Thirdly, as we have seen, since it was difficult to stimulate the economy out of recession or restrain the economy to deal with the international balance of payments deficit, by means of fiscal policy, measures to revive the economy became the preserve of monetary policy.

The reorganization of the financial system which had prevailed since the war days was more or less completed by about 1951. This was the result of a large-scale reform of the system in accordance with Occupation policies and, subsequently, further adjustments in order to adapt the reforms to Japanese conditions. Let us summarize the results.

(1) Reorganization of the Financial System
As a result of Occupation reforms, first, institutions connected with colonial and occupied areas, such as the Bank of Korea, the Bank of Taiwan, and the Southern Development Bank, were closed in October of 1945. Then in 1950 the Hypothec Bank of Japan, the Industrial Bank of Japan, the Yokohama Specie Bank (which became the Bank of Tokyo), and the Hokkaido Development Bank were converted into commercial banks. The Industrial Bank of Japan would be reconverted in 1952 into a bond-issuing long-term trust bank, but, with the exception of the Bank of Japan, government-related special financial institutions predating the war were liquidated at this time. Japan's financial institutions seemed to have been broken down into an undifferentiated system of commercial banks. However, these reforms had to be modified yet again. Particularly after the Korean War began and prospects for the conclusion of the Treaty of San Francisco were at last in sight, the tempo of change quickened. In 1951, the Japan Development Bank and the Japan Export Bank (later renamed the Japan Export-Import Bank) were established with national treasury funds. The two banks were set up with the goal of "supplementing the financing done by ordinary financial institutions" (Development Bank Law, Article 1) in the provision of long-term funds to industry and in export finance (particularly plant export and foreign investment, and later including plant imports), respectively. In actuality, these two special banks did not stop at assuming the risks of private financial institutions, and the Development Bank in particular performed the function of a pilot for the funds advances of private financial institutions, which fell into the practice of taking their cues from this bank's funds advances. Furthermore, in 1952 the Long-term Credit Bank Law was passed, doing away with the prob-

lems which had until than been caused by private bank funds being tied up in long-term lending. This law also attempted to liquidate overloans, a goal which was not achieved. But long-term credit banks were established as private firms, and the Industrial Bank of Japan began issuing bonds and got a fresh start as a debenture-issuing bank.

The prewar trust companies, which had been operating as ordinary banks during the war years, had no choicc but to make a fresh start since the trust deposit business was stagnating under the postwar inflation and they were not authorized to simultaneously engage in the securities business. In 1952 the Loan Trust Law was passed, authorizing these companies to absorb the general public's long-term stable funds and to channel them into "critical industries." This gave the trust banks the motive power behind which they were able to engineer their recovery. Thus, the long-term trust system, which for a time had been done away with, made a new beginning with the end of the Occupation and later took on a central role in the expansion of plant and equipment investment.

Yet another change was the opening of specialized financial institutions. Following the Banking Law reforms of 1927, the liquidation of the smaller banks proceeded apace, while the mutual aid finance companies and trust associations were weak. The predominance of the big banks was thus assured. However, under these conditions a tendency gradually developed to try to fill in the gaps left by the smaller institutions through the use of specialized financial institutions. The first move in this direction was the formation of a set of financial institutions in the agriculture industry, sparked by the launching of the agricultural cooperative association system in 1947, after which the system of agricultural cooperatives, prefectural associations, and the Central Bank for Agriculture and Forestry (Nōrin Chūō Kinko) was reorganized. The surplus cash of these organizations came to play a key role in the whole financial system. Second, specialized financial institutions for small businesses appeared in rapid succession. As a result of the prewar concentration of banks, small business finance had become one of the most neglected fields in the industry. The Central Bank for Commercial and Industrial Associations (Shōkō Chūō Kinko), the People's Bank (Shomin Kinko), and so on had been created during the war years to make up for this deficiency, but they were still inadequate. They were organized, and the People's Bank was converted into the People's Finance Corporation, while the Small Business Finance Corporation (1953) was established for firms of an intermediate size between the large firms which were the object of the Japan Development Bank's activities

Table 4.11. Capital Resources and Loan Investments of Financial Institutions

		All banks nationwide		Mutual savings banks	Credit associations	Shōkō Chūō Kinko Bank	Nōrin Chūō Kinko Bank	Agricultural cooperatives
		Bank accounts	Trust accounts					
1960	(A)	51.8	7.6	5.8	5.1	0.9	1.5	4.4
	(B)	51.4	4.5	6.0	4.9	1.1	1.4	2.1
	(C)	47.9	18.1	2.1	2.6	0.1	1.6	0.4
1970	(A)	42.7	6.7	5.9	7.2	1.1	2.1	5.7
	(B)	43.3	5.7	5.8	7.3	1.3	1.8	3.4
	(C)	40.3	7.8	3.1	3.6	0.1	3.0	1.3
1980	(A)	35.0	7.2	5.5	6.9	1.1	2.5	6.1
	(B)	35.4	4.6	5.6	6.8	1.4	1.6	2.9
	(C)	33.2	11.4	3.1	4.7	0.3	4.6	1.7
1988	(A)	33.4	7.2	4.5	6.0	1.0	2.4	4.3
	(B)	42.7	3.4	4.9	5.9	1.2	1.4	1.6
	(C)	26.0	15.8	2.6	3.0	0.5	3.3	0.6

Source: Statistics Department, Bank of Japan, *Keizai Tōkei Nenpō* [Economics Statistics Annual], various years.

and the petty businesses served by the People's Finance Corporation. On the other hand, in an effort to fully provide for small business finance, the government reorganized the mutual aid finance companies and urban credit cooperative associations into mutual savings banks (Sōgō Ginkō) and credit associations (Shin'yō Kinko), and allowed them to engage in ordinary banking. As they played their roles in small business finance, these businesses gradually expanded in scale.

The Housing Loan Corporation began operations in 1949, opening the way for government-funded housing finance. Subsequently established were the Agriculture, Forestry, and Fishery Finance Corporation in 1952, the Hokkaidō Development Corporation in 1956 (Hokkaidō and Tōhoku Development Corporation as of 1957), the Finance Corporation for Local Public Enterprise in 1957, the Small Business Credit Insurance Corporation in 1958, the Medical Care Facilities Finance Corporation and the Overseas Economic Cooperation Fund in 1960, and the Environmental Finance Corporation in 1967. In the field of foreign exchange, the former Yokohama Specie Bank was revitalized as a commercial bank, the Bank of Tokyo. As foreign trade became an important part of the economy, this bank and other commercial city banks established foreign exchange departments and cornered part of the nation's foreign exchange business.

In this fashion, a virtual reorganization of Japan's financial system

(A = Deposits and securities; B = Loaned-out funds; C = Negotiable securities; Percentages of total inc. other)

Life & other insurance companies	Gov't. financial institutions	Investment capital	Postal life insurance, and pensions	Total, including Other (¥ trillions)	Double-counting (¥ trillions)	Net total (¥ trillions)
4.6	—	10.3	3.7	18.82	2.11	16.71
6.0	9.5	9.6	3.3	15.91	1.16	14.75
8.0	0.4	13.2	1.8	3.19	0.82	2.37
6.2	—	12.7	2.2	107.88	12.11	95.78
4.4	8.6	11.4	1.6	91.12	7.73	83.39
9.6	0.2	19.4	3.8	17.76	3.49	14.27
7.1	—	22.0	3.4	499.30	54.58	447.72
4.4	12.5	22.3	2.0	385.51	39.35	346.16
8.5	0.3	17.4	5.4	119.82	11.82	108.01
9.9	—	19.2	3.7	1,094.26	151.54	942.71
4.7	9.8	18.7	1.9	779.72	65.80	713.93
15.2	0.2	18.4	5.6	338.58	282.23	310.35

was completed at about the time the Occupation ended. It is clear from Table 4.11 that there was a major change after the 1960s. The relative importance of institutions in the agricultural cooperative system and of those involved with small business gradually increased, and the relative importance of the banks declined as postal savings accounts and postal life insurance policies raised their interest rates and drew in ordinary deposits. Recently mutual savings banks have been permitted to reconstitute themselves as ordinary banks, and most have already made the switch.

(2) The Functions and Application of Monetary Policy
Economic growth began in the 1950s, and during the high growth period facilitating a smooth supply of funds has been the greatest task of monetary policy. As is widely known, lending from financial institutions has come to be the major channel of supply for funds. The trend is illustrated by Figure 4.5, which expresses the financial surplus and deficit in the five sectors of individual, government, public corporation and local government, corporation, and overseas funds as a percentage of GNP. From the period of high growth until the beginning of the late 1970s public corporations and local government showed a relatively small shortage whereas the corporate sector showed an extremely large deficit, and this was made up by the sur-

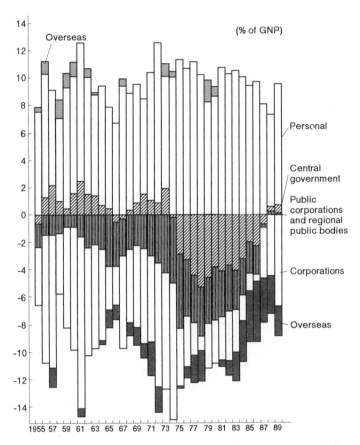

Figure 4.5. Financial surpluses and deficits in different sectors of the economy, 1955–89

Source: Calculated based on data from Bank of Japan, *Shikin Junkan Kanjō* [Flow of Funds], and Economic Planning Agency, *Chōki Sokyū Shuyō Keiretsu Kokumin Keizai Hōkoku* [Long-term National Economic Statistics for Important Economic Sectors].

plus in the individual sector. Financial institutions played the role of intermediaries, on the one hand absorbing surplus household funds in the form of deposits, and then supplying them to firms by loaning them out. This method of fund supply is known as "indirect finance."

As a result, financial institutions competed fiercely to attract deposits and supplied funds to *keiretsu* firms. Under these conditions, as long as the banks remained dependent on loans, there was no change in the dominating position of the Bank of Japan, which retained its grip on the final pipeline of fund supply. The system consistently upheld the Bank of Japan's power of control. During periods of economic growth the Bank of Japan was bold in supplying funds through loans and buying operations. On the other hand, especially during the high growth period, economic booms gave rise to balance of payments deficits and there was a need to suppress domestic demand and promote exports to wipe out those deficits. Monetary policy therefore had to address the regulation of the economy. From the mid-1960s, when the government was allowed to issue deficit-covering bonds, fiscal policy was also given a certain amount of leeway to act, but up to that time responsibility for countercyclical measures rested almost entirely on finance. This may be the reason why Japan's financial policy since the war has not been able to stay within the normally adopted framework of market mechanisms and merely fiddle with interest rates and the reserve ratio against deposits, but has always resorted to means close to direct control, such as "window regulation" (*madoguchi kisei*). Such policies were able to function effectively because in times of economic growth Japanese firms and financial institutions generally lacked funds on hand and were not therefore strong enough to resist policy control. Hence financial policy in the period of high growth swung violently back and forth all the time in a "stop-and-go" fashion.

From the mid-1960s, and after the balance of payments surplus became a permanent feature of the economy, the main role of financial policy turned to domestic anti-inflationary and countercyclical measures. However, the monetary restraint aimed at controlling the spread of overseas inflation from 1969 further expanded the international balance of payments surplus, inviting the so-called Nixon shocks and leading to the revaluation of the yen. As a counter-measure, in 1971–72, the government promoted a policy of expanding domestic demand, but this only stoked inflation and led to abnormal monetary expansion which, as we have seen, triggered the rampant inflation in the wake of the first oil crisis. With this past experience, and in the prevailing atmosphere of hostility to Keynesian economics, the annual rate of growth in the money supply came to be seen as the primary indicator for financial policy. It was on the basis of this rate that financial policy came to be adjusted. Since $M_2 = kY$, we can derive a relationship whereby the growth rate M_2 equals the growth rates of real GNP, the GNP deflator and k. We know that k is increasing over the long term. Hence, a reasonable level for the M_2 growth rate is taken to be the nominal GNP growth rate (the sum of real GNP and the deflator growth rate) plus some 2 percent (the growth rate of k). After the introduction of certificates of deposit (CDs) in 1979, $M_2 = CD$ was adopted as the main money supply indicator.

However, as we can see from Figure 4.5, from the mid-1970s to the mid-1980s the central government deficit expanded, and at the same time, since firms held back from equipment investment, personal sector funds were indirectly channeled into the absorption of government bonds. The increase in government bonds gave rise to financial liberalization. And as the shortage of treasury funds began to be alleviated there was an increasing outflow of funds overseas.

It became increasingly difficult to steer financial policy as the factors to consider both increased in number and grew more complex with the deregulation and internationalization of the economy. Not only import prices but ordinary prices are affected by fluctuations in the exchange rate. The deregulation of international capital movements means that firms are now left to make their own decisions, on the basis of interest arbitration, as to whether they procure and invest funds at home or whether they look overseas. As we will see in Part III, the so-called bubble economy of inflated land and stock prices was an asset inflation that came about against a background of ordinary price stability, due to the appreciation of the yen. With the hike in interest rates in 1990, funds invested overseas were suddenly channeled back into the country. These kinds of problems did not exist during the period of high growth, when there was a fixed exchange rate and overseas capital transactions were regulated. Under the deregulation and liberalization since the 1980s, financial policy has been forced to come up with new responses. Noting that the movements of a free market that takes interest rates as an indicator have come to play a more decisive role than heretofore, we can conclude that policy will now have no option but to take overseas as well as domestic factors into consideration. The Bank of Japan abandoned its policy of "window guidance" regulation after the July–September 1991 quarter, a move which symbolizes the fact that these kinds of quantitative controls are now losing their effectiveness in the tide of deregulation and internationalization.

Notes

1. Takasuga Yoshihiro, *Gendai Nihon no Bukka Mondai (Shinban)* [Price Problems of Contemporary Japan (New Edition)] (Shin Hyōron, 1975).

2. Statistics Bureau, Office of the Prime Minister, *Kokumin Seikatsu ni kansuru Yoron Chōsa* [Public Opinion Survey on National Life], 1960s.

3. Bureau of Statistics, Office of the Prime Minister, *Kakei Chōsa* [Household Budget Survey], annual.

4. This title might be translated as something like "The Economy of the Sakè Merchants Who Went Cherry-blossom Viewing." The allusion is to an old comic story (*rakugo*) about two sakè merchants who went out at cherry-blossom time to sell some of their brew to the people who came to admire the flowers and celebrate the arrival of spring. Before either one had made a sale, however, each decided he would like to have a taste of the sakè himself before selling it all. Having a coin, one of the merchants thereupon offered it to the other in return for a drink. The other reciprocated by buying a drink from his companion with the coin he had just received. One drink led to another, each buying in turn from his companion with the same solitary coin, until they had both managed to sell all their sakè—a very brisk day's business!

5. Letting X, Y, and A stand, respectively, for the gross product vector, the final demand vector, and the input coefficient matrix, while I stands for the identity matrix, then

$$X = AX + Y, \text{ and since}$$

$$Y = (I - A)X, \text{ then}$$

$$X = (I - A)^{-1}Y.$$

Here, if the elements of the identity matrix $(I - A)$ are b and if n is the number of sectors, then the power of dispersion coefficient V and the sensitivity of dispersion coefficient V, respectively, may be expressed as follows:

$$V_j = \frac{\displaystyle\sum_{i=1}^{n} b_{ij}}{\dfrac{1}{n}\displaystyle\sum_{i=1}^{n}\sum_{j=1}^{n} b_{ij}}$$

$$V_i = \frac{\displaystyle\sum_{j=1}^{n} b_{ij}}{\dfrac{1}{n}\displaystyle\sum_{i=1}^{n}\sum_{j=1}^{n} b_{ij}}.$$

A value of one for either of these coefficients indicates equivalence with the average for all sectors. Accordingly, the extent to which a coefficient exceeds the value of one indicates the extent to which the sector's power of dispersion or sensitivity of dispersion exceeds the average for all sectors.

5

The Dual Structure:
Labor, Small Business, and Agriculture

1. The Composition of Employment and the Supply and Demand for Labor

Both in the Shōwa depression at the beginning of the 1930s and in the immediate aftermath of the Pacific War, around 1950, the number of unemployed and the unemployment rate were much lower than might have been expected. According to the national census of 1950, those reporting themselves as repatriated from abroad numbered 4,820,000, or nearly 6 percent of the total population of 83,200,000, which indicates that tremendous population pressure did actually exist. However, according to the same census, the number of employed persons among the repatriates was 3,070,000, while 76,000 were unemployed, and the rest were not included in the labor force. This gives an unemployment rate among those repatriated of no more than 2.5 percent. Of the total labor force of 36,310,000, about 730,000 were unemployed, for an overall unemployment rate of somewhat over 2 percent.

According to the results of the Labor Force Surveys conducted annually from 1947 onward, the unemployment rate has hardly ever risen above 2 percent. However, this does not mean that there were no employment problems, for there were a great number of employed persons on extremely low incomes who were at that time referred to as "latent unemployed" (the term used later was "under-employed"), and the rectification of this situation became an important policy issue. To put it another way, the people of this period had no choice but to find some kind of employment, however poor the conditions, since they could not live with no source of income. This situation can be called "total employment" to distinguish it from "full employment."

By tracing in the data in Table 5.1 the changes that took place following the shock of the defeat and during the process of rapid growth thereafter, one can gain an understanding of why large-scale unemployment did not occur, where the "latent unemployed" concen-

145

Table 5.1. Composition of the Employed Population (1940–90)

(1000s of persons)

	Totals for all sectors				Agriculture, forestry & fisheries				All other industries			
	Total	Self-employed (A)	Family workers (B)	Hired employees (C)	Total	A	B	C	Total	A	B	C
1940	32,230	8,455	10,268	13,508	14,193	4,890	8,610	693	18,037	3,567	1,658	12,815
47	33,329	8,216	12,974	12,139	17,812	5,329	11,562	921	15,517	2,887	1,412	11,218
50	35,575	9,297	12,248	13,967	17,224	5,666	10,537	1,019	18,351	3,631	1,711	12,984
60	43,691	9,687	10,509	23,490	14,346	5,231	8,329	785	29,344	4,456	2,180	22,705
70	52,235	10,151	8,536	33,544	10,075	4,246	5,336	492	42,161	5,905	3,201	33,053
80	55,811	9,543	6,495	39,764	6,111	2,728	2,927	455	49,700	6,815	3,568	39,309
90	61,682	8,305	4,764	48,607	4,391	2,028	1,955	406	57,291	6,277	2,809	48,201

Note: Those who were unclassifiable are included in the all-sector totals and in the totals for "all other industries." Therefore, the A-, B-, and C-values shown under "all sectors" and "all other industries" are smaller than the figures in the totals columns.

Sources: Results of the national census. Compiled from Statistics Bureau, Office of the Prime Minister, *Kokusei Chōsa Saishū Hōkokusho* [Final Report on the National Census], 1950; and *Nihon no Jinkō* [The Population of Japan], 1960, 1970 and 1980; and *Kokusei chōsa Hōkoku* [National Census Report], 1990.

trated, and where outmigrations took place. Based on national census figures from 1940 to 1990, this table shows fluctuations in the employed population, dividing industry into two categories consisting of agriculture, forestry, and fisheries on the one hand, and all other industries—that is, the secondary and tertiary sectors—on the other. Of those industries in the latter category, data for manufacturing and construction and for commerce and services are displayed separately. Then the employment status of persons in each of these industrial categories is classified as one of three types: (A) self-employed, including those working at side jobs, (B) family workers, and (C) hired employees.

First, let us compare 1947 with 1940. Here we find about 17,800,000 people in the primary sector (agriculture, forestry, and fisheries) in 1947; since 1940 there had been an influx of over 3,600,000 employed persons, about 3 million of whom were family workers. This took place at a time when the total employed population increased by about 1,100,000 persons. On the other hand, the non-primary industries lost about 2,500,000 people, with hired persons constituting 1,600,000 of the decrease. The major share of these decreases was in construction and manufacturing and in commerce and the service industries. The absorption of such a huge labor force by the farm villages caused a large-scale decrease in the marginal productivity of the agricultural and forestry industries due to the law of diminishing returns. Nevertheless, the farm villages had to take in this labor force because the marginal productivity of other sectors had fallen even below that of agriculture, or at least to a corresponding level. Such were the straitened circumstances to which the economy was reduced immediately following the defeat.

Accordingly, when the economy showed even meager signs of recovery in the period from 1947 to 1950, the marginal productivity of the non-primary industries improved, and the labor which had once been absorbed by the farm villages turned into an offsetting outflow. On the other hand, the number of "self-employed" in agriculture and forestry increased up until 1950 as new land was brought under cultivation and as second and third sons who had become family workers established separate households. These may be considered the reasons for the large decrease in the number of family workers from 1947 to 1950 while the total employed population in agriculture and forestry showed only a minor decline. In the cities, which received an influx of population from the farm villages as well as of young people new to the labor force, employment in the secondary and tertiary industries once again began to grow.

Table 5.2. Increases in Number of Employed Persons in Manufacturing
(1000s of persons)

	Total	Textile industry	Machinery industry	Other industries
1955	6,902	1,543	1,603	3,756
60	9,495	1,804	2,814	4,877
65	11,510	2,015	3,748	5,474
70	13,541	2,157	5,143	6,241

Machinery industry includes metal products manufacturing; textile industry includes garment manufacturing.
Source: Kokusei Chōsa Hōkoku [National Census Report].

From 1950 to 1955, the foundations for economic growth were being laid and a rapid recovery got under way following the Korean War. More than 1,100,000 people left agriculture and forestry, and the working population in non-primary industries increased by 4,800,000 people.

In about 1955, a large-scale exodus from agriculture and forestry began. These people went first of all into construction and manufacturing. The developing chemical and heavy industries, particularly the machinery industry, showed a tremendous absorptive capacity. The machinery industry expanded precipitously during investment booms and was, moreover, extremely labor-intensive. As is seen in Table 5.2, more than half of the increases in number of employed persons in manufacturing between 1955 and 1970 occurred in the machinery industry. The main thrust of the "Iwato boom" which began in 1959 was in investment, but such items as household electrical appliances and light machinery for export also expanded during this period. Along with this, the cry of "labor shortage" suddenly began to be taken seriously. The situation may be grasped with the help of the several indicators shown in Table 5.3.

The transition to a "labor shortage" did not occur overnight. The difference between the supply and the demand for labor had been rapidly shrinking all through the 1950s. In other words, even if the Employment Security Bureau's effective ratio of openings to applicants,[1] which indicates the supply of and demand for workers other than new school graduates, unmistakably shows an excess supply, the ratio began to rise steeply from the latter half of the 1950s. With regard to new graduates in particular, the proportion of employed middle-school graduates working in agriculture and forestry (almost all of whom were agricultural family workers) began to fall off sharply

Table 5.3. Labor Market Trends from the Latter Half of the 1950s Onward
(A)

	(1) Employment Security Bureau ratio of job offers to applicants*	(2) Proportion of middle-school graduates taking jobs in primary industries	(3) Ratio of job offers to applicants for new graduates**		(4) Farm, forestry & fishing labor force
			Middle-school graduates	High-school graduates	
	Ratio	%	Ratio	Ratio	1000s
1955	0.22	31.9	1.1	0.7	
60	0.59	13.8	1.9	1.5	14,542
65	0.64	7.4	3.7	3.5	11,514
70	1.41	5.2	5.8	7.1	10,252
75	0.61	3.7	5.9	3.4	7,907
80	0.75	2.5	2.8	1.9	6,973
85	0.68	1.9	1.8	1.8	6,363
90	1.40	1.7	3.0	2.6	5,653

Sources: (1) and (3) from Ministry of Labor's Employment Security Service Statistics;
(2) from Ministry of Education's Basic Survey of Schools;
(4) from Ministry of Agriculture and Forestry's Survey of Job Placement Trends among Farmers, Fishermen, and Those Engaged in Forestry. (Only farmers were surveyed from 1963 on. The survey was re-named Survey of Job Placement Trends among Farmers.)
 * Effective number of job offers ÷ Effective number of job applicants.
 ** Number of job offers ÷ Number of job applicants.

(B) Figures for the first half of the 1950s are as follows:

	Proportion of middle-school graduates taking jobs in primary industries	Ratio of job offers to applicats for middle-school graduates	Ratio of job offers to applicants for high-school graduates
	%		
1950	61.5	0.6	—
1951	52.4	0.8	0.5
1952	48.4	0.9	0.5
1953	36.1	1.1	0.7
1954	33.1	1.2	0.7

in the first half of the 1950s. Meanwhile, the ratio of job offers to applicants for middle-school graduates exceeded one in 1953, indicating a shift to an excess demand situation, and the ratio for high-school graduates had also exceeded one by 1957. The supply of young labor was already exhibiting a trend toward shortage in the latter half of the 1950s. Thereupon, the sudden increase in the demand for labor, primarily in the machines industry, brought the shift to excess labor demand to the surface in one swift stroke. The exodus of labor from farm villages also intensified from this period onward.

Japan had experienced a shift from labor surplus to labor shortage on two previous occasions. The first was during and after World War I (1917–19), and the second was during the period from the Sino-Japanese conflict in the 1930s to the end of World War II. Both of these were brought on by sudden developments. The former was reversed by the conclusion of World War I and the postwar depression, while the latter was truncated by the military defeat of Japan. In the postwar growth era, however, the supply–demand relationship for the first time exhibited excess demand over a long period. It is more or less established opinion that the turning point for this change was the beginning of the 1960s.[2] During the period of adjustment from the late 1970s to the early 1980s the labor market slackened and the ratio of job offers to applicants fell to around 0.6 or 0.7. However, it was still a sellers' market for younger workers, and there was no change in the underlying excess of demand.

The composition of the employed population underwent a further change from the late 1960s. The basic trends of outmigration from the primary industries and an increase in hired workers remain unchanged, but the major sector absorbing this population shifts from construction and manufacturing to the tertiary industries, primarily commerce and the service trades. Secondary industry has instead become labor-saving. In the tertiary industries, on the other hand, along with expanding volume, commerce and the services are extending into new fields. The data clearly show these trends continuing from the oil crisis down to the present day.

How did such changes as the above modify the labor market mechanism, and in what ways did they influence agriculture, the traditional industries, and small business?

2. The Labor Market and the Wage Structure

Drastic changes occurred in the agricultural population as tremendous numbers first flowed into the farm labor force (fed by the surplus labor supply resulting from the military defeat) and then,

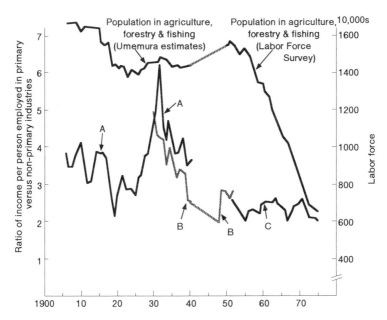

Figure 5.1. Ratio of income per person employed in primary versus non-primary industries, and population in primary industries, 1906–75

Income ratio = $\dfrac{\text{Income per person employed in non-primary industries}}{\text{Income per person employed in primary industries}}$.

Sources: National income data: Data for 1906–40 from Ohkawa Kazushi et al., *Koku-min Shotoku* [National Income] (Tōyō Keizai Shimpō-sha, 1974); for 1930–51 from old estimates by the Economic Planning Agency; for 1952–75 from new EPA estimates. Data on the employed population: to 1940, from Umemura Mataji, "Changes in Employment by Industry 1880–1940: Summary Findings from New Estimates" (*Keizai Kenkyū*, vol. 24, no. 2); postwar data, from the Ministry of Labour's Labor Force Survey. However, figures for 1951–54 were estimated by regression using old and new Labor Force Survey data.

reversing their direction, flowed out of that sector into the secondary and tertiary industries in the course of rapid economic growth, dramatically reducing the farm population. Underlying this phenomenon, however, was the simple principle of the equalization of marginal productivities among the sectors, as has been seen above.

Let us begin with a comparison of urban and rural incomes. Before the war, a striking income differential existed between the cities and the agricultural villages. Figure 5.1 has been drawn by linking Ohkawa Kazushi's prewar national income data and Umemura Mataji's prewar figures on the employed population with official statistics for the postwar period. A comparison of prewar and postwar relative incomes using this graph reveals the following. The relative income ratio (the ratio of per-capita income in the non-primary industries to per-capital income in the primary industries) averaged between 3 and 4 prior to World War II. The ratio was lowest at the zenith of the World War I boom (2.16) and highest at the trough of the Great Depression in 1931 (6.25). In general, the ratio was low during prosperous times and rose during periods of economic downturn. This phenomenon may be thought of in terms of the following economic mechanism. During prosperous times, the prices of agricultural commodities rose, earnings from side jobs expanded, and incomes increased, while at the same time the employed population was absorbed into the non-primary industries, leaving a smaller number of employed persons in agriculture among whom to divide up farm income. Of course, the total amount of income in the non-primary industries also grew, but, as a result of the increase in the employed population in that sector, per-capita income grew more slowly there than in primary industry. But this poses a problem in terms of economic theory. This is because, although it is natural to think that the desire of people in the primary industries to move into the non-primary industries would be stronger when the relative income ratio is high and less compelling when the ratio is low, the changes here indicate that the trend is for outflows to increase when the ratio falls but to cease when the ratio rises. This can be attributed to the fact that before the war, labor demand in the non-primary industries, which rose in prosperous times and fell off during economic slowdowns, decidedly predominated, while labor supply factors were overshadowed. The outflows of the late 1950s and 1960s were also the result of strong demand factors. In addition, farming became increasingly mechanized during this period, in particular the rice cultivation system, and there was a rapid decline in the amount of labor required by agriculture. In this period, therefore, conditions were already in place for farming communities to supply their excess labor to other industries.

On the other hand, in the cities, where population was becoming concentrated, the labor force seeking employment opportunities was growing. There is an empirical law called the Douglas-Arisawa effect, which runs as follows. Household finance is the principal factor determining labor supply, and the head of the household works in order to support the family. But if the income of the household head falls, the other members of the family must also go out to work in order to obtain income. Accordingly, the lower the income of the

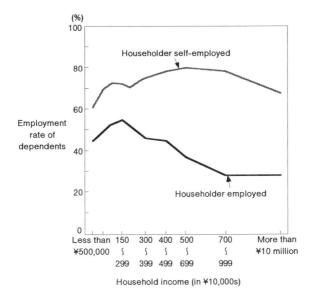

Figure 5.2. Employment rate for female dependents by householder's income and employment status, 1982

Source: Statistics Bureau, General Affairs Agency, "Basic Survey of the Employment Structure."

head of the household, the higher the employment rate of the family. (For farmers, "agricultural income" may be substituted for "income of household head" and "rate of side-job employment for household members" for "the employment rate of the family.") Figure 5.2 plainly shows that this trend was evident both in the 1950s and much more recently, in the 1980s. The employment rate for female dependents (Table 5.4) consistently rose through the 1970s and 1980s, apart from the brief period of the oil crisis. This testifies to the fact that as employment opportunities increased in tandem with economic growth, new workers, primarily women, were entering the labor market. According to the Ministry of Labor's Survey of Employment Trends, women part-time workers, nearly all of whom are housewives, numbered about 700,000, or about 3 percent of the corporate work force in 1975, but this had risen to 4.67 million, or more than 12 percent of the work force, by 1991. The Household Budget Survey also reveals that whereas "wives' incomes" comprised approximately 3 percent of real household income in mid-1965, it

Table 5.4. Trends in Rate of Female Employment by Dependent Status

(%)

	Total	Unmarried	Dependent	Widowed, divorced or separated
1968	47.5	57.0	45.1	40.2
71	46.5	57.6	44.0	38.5
74	44.0	54.0	42.5	35.4
77	45.3	52.6	45.3	35.2
79	45.6	50.6	46.6	34.3
82	48.5	52.1	50.8	34.5
87	48.1	51.3	51.0	32.6

Source: From "Basic Survey of the Employment Structure," General Affairs Agency, Statistics Bureau.

approached 6 percent in the late 1970s and stood at 8.5 percent in 1990. The increasing participation of dependent women in the labor force is a phenomenon common to all the industrialized nations, not only Japan, but in Japan the trend began suddenly in the 1960s and continues to the present.

The data on the labor participation rate for men and women by age group in Figure 5.3 are impressive as indications of the mobilization process. Calculated as the ratio of labor force population (total of employed and completely unemployed persons) to the total population divided into age classes at five-year intervals, the data vividly depict what occurred following the period of rapid growth. The labor force under 19 years of age naturally declined between 1955 and 1990, reflecting higher levels of formal education for both males and females, but another important fact is that the labor force participation rate for women 35 and over shows a striking increase. Since agriculture was still relatively important in 1955, the labor force participation rate for women was relatively stable in the area of about 50 percent, even though it showed something of a decline during the busy child-bearing and nurturing ages of 25 to 34. By 1970, however, when the importance of agriculture had declined and urbanization had progressed, there was a sharp rise in the labor force participation of middle-aged and older women, and although the rate was lower for the 25-to-34 age group in 1970, it had risen even for this group by 1990. This testifies to the fact that this group's employment opportunities had increased and that they had been mobilized into urban industries.

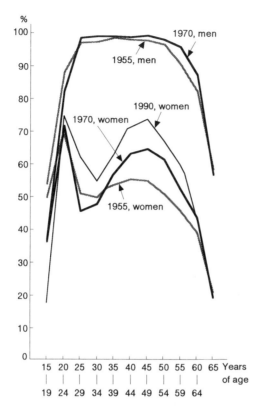

Figure 5.3. Labor force participation rates by sex, 1955, 1970, and (for women) 1990

Source: Statistics Bureau, Office of the Prime Minister, *Nihon no Jinkō* [The Population of Japan].

Let us turn now to conditions on the labor demand side. The labor market in the 1950s was a buyers' market, and labor could be selected and employed in full accord with firms' aims. Herein arose the stratified labor market which was the distinguishing feature of the "dual structure" (see Table 5.5). This was a repetition of the labor pattern of the 1920s, and it displayed the special features of that pattern all the more prominently.

This structure as it existed in the 1950s may be summarized as follows. In the large firms there was a permanent labor force working under the lifetime employment and seniority wage systems. Employees in this group were members of the company labor unions and

Table 5.5. Indexes of the Structure and Level of Wages (Place of Business Aggregates)

	Average wage index for all industries (1975 = 100)		Manufacturing industry wage differentials by size of operation (Places of business employing 500 or more = 100)			
	Nominal	Real	500 employees or more	100–499 employees	30–99 employees	5–25 employees
1950	5.6	24.2	100	83.1	67.3	
55	10.1	32.8	100	74.3	58.9	
60	13.6	41.0	100	70.7	58.9	46.3
65	22.0	49.4	100	80.9	71.0	63.2
70	43.7	75.3	100	81.4	69.9	61.8
75	100.0	100.0	100	82.9	68.7	60.2
80	146.4	106.7	100	80.5	65.3	58.0
85	175.7	112.0	100	79.1	62.9	54.9
90	200.0	123.7	100	79.0	60.3	55.2

received relatively high pay, beginning with wages plus bonuses, retirement allowances, wages in kind such as housing and other items. As a rule selected for employment upon completion of their schooling, such employees generally worked for the same company until a fixed retirement age under the seniority wage system, and were promised comparatively equal advancement. Partly because starting salaries were low, particularly in the early stages of high growth, the seniority wage advancement curve was generally steep, as indicated in Table 5.6. Large firms with 1,000 or more employees showed a trend toward an even more steeply rising slope in their seniority wage curves during the 1950s. Subsequently, as the labor supply grew tighter, wage rates for younger workers increased and seniority-based wages rose more gradually. Some argued that this spelled the demise of the seniority wage system. Yet the seniority wage slope hardly changed after the 1970s and even steepened at the end of the 1980s. It appears the seniority wage system is still alive and well. In addition, as the same table shows, starting salaries for middle-school and high-school graduates in the smaller firms in 1955 were already low compared to those in the large firms. They began to approach large-firm salary levels in the early 1960s.

Moreover, the slope of the seniority curve for the smaller firms has tended to flatten out since the 1950s. Wage rises for the middle-aged

Table 5.6. Indexes of the Structure and Level of Wages

	(A) Starting wages for men (¥ 1000s)	
	Middle-school graduates	High-school graduates
1950	4.0	
55	4.1	6.6
60	5.9	8.2
65	13.2	16.4
70	23.8	28.4
75	58.0	70.4
80	81.1	92.8
85	96.1	112.2
90	117.0	133.0

(B) Wage differentials by age within firms (high-school graduates in manufacturing industry); 20–24 years old = 100
Firms employing 100 or more

Age	18~19	20~24	25~29	30~34	35~39	40~44	45~49	50~54	55~59
1954	71	100	138	172	199	222		226	
61	77	100	139	188	224	261		269	
65	69	100	127	160	190	218		232	
70	70	100	123	143	159	184		195	
75	85	100	122	144	157	168	180	191	172
80	83	100	121	144	163	175	181	191	182
85	85	100	120	144	163	181	189	193	187
89	81	100	126	159	187	208	227	236	223

Firms employing 10–99

	18~19	20~24	25~29	30~34	35~39	40~44	45~49	50~54	55~59
	71	100	136	165	182	194		181	
	75	100	135	167	190	202		190	
	76	100	113	129	138	151		107	
	81	100	126	141	149	156		149	
	81	100	122	142	151	156	156	158	141
	85	100	124	147	164	171	173	173	157
	86	100	121	143	164	180	183	181	168
	83	100	123	142	163	181	196	197	184

Sources: Ministry of Labour, *Sengo Rōdō Keizaishi* [History of the Postwar Labor Economy], data section, and Japan Productivity Center, *Katsuyō Rōdō Tōkei* [Useful Labor Statistics], various years. *indicates the source was *Kojin-betsu Chingin Chōsa* [Survey of Wages by Work Force Characteristics] for 1954 data and *Chingin Kōzō Kihon Chōsa* [Basic Survey of the Wage Structure] for 1958 or later data.

all but cease; in fact wages start to decline. For this reason, too, workers began to accept jobs in smaller firms while at the same time hoping to eventually strike out on their own. Many of the more capable ones seized opportunities to do so and also changed jobs frequently. If we look at the proportion of entering employees and the separation rate by age category, we find that while in large companies both entrance and separation rates are high for the twenty-and-under age bracket and decline after the age of thirty, these rates in small firms are rather high even beyond the age of thirty. In small firms having 99 or fewer employees, it seems that workers could not really count on lifetime employment. From that time until recently, however, wage levels for middle-aged and older workers in firms with 10–99 employees have improved, and a seniority wage system has gradually come into being. This may be the result of efforts by these small companies to hold on to their skilled labor force.

However, the stratified structure of the labor market does not stop here. In both large and small firms there are a considerable number of temporary workers and day laborers with limited periods of employment. Throughout the 1950s, such workers at places of business employing 30 or more persons averaged about 6 percent of the work force for all industries, and about 7 percent in manufacturing. These workers' wages were about half those of permanent employees, and they had to put up with working conditions inferior to those of regular employees in the smaller firms and, needless to say, in the large firms as well.

From the companies' point of view, numbers of temporary and day laborers could be reduced at will in response to business fluctuations since they were hired for limited time periods or on a day-to-day basis. It was also an easy matter to induce them to increase their efficiency in the hope of being promoted to the status of permanent employees. So long as employers were guaranteeing lifetime employment for their permanent employees, a cushion against business fluctuations in terms of employment levels was particularly indispensable. That employment conditions so disadvantageous to workers could exist on such a large scale was a result of the excess labor supply. Even worse labor conditions prevailed in the various household industries. For example, according to a March 1954 survey, the average hourly pay for an hour's work by women engaged in domestic employment was ¥15.75. Even assuming 200 hours of labor per month, this would provide a monthly income of only ¥3,150. This was no more than 50 to 60 percent of the average monthly income of female workers in small manufacturing firms. The most common reason given for taking this kind of work was to supplement the household income, followed by unemployment.

In summary, against the background of a surplus in labor markets in the early postwar period, the conditions of the demand side—employers—were accepted in a lopsided way. The result was a tiered labor market—where there were wide disparities between large and small firms and within firms, between regular workers on the one hand and part-timers, day laborers, and workers at home on the other. Labor suppliers had to accept their disadvantageous position. Eventually Japan's low wages became an issue as the situation deteriorated to a point where the dual structure, described below, became a problem.

However, after the shift to a labor shortage in about 1960, things changed rapidly. The labor shortage first appeared in the form of a shortage of new school graduates, as indicated by increases in the ratio of openings to applicants and by higher starting salaries. The effects of the labor crunch extended in more directions than this, though. Forced to seek labor elsewhere besides among new graduates, firms had to turn to labor flowing out of the farm villages and to yet another source, worker transfers from one firm to another. And as firms began welcoming workers transferring in from other companies in the 1960s, young workers seeking better working conditions became exceedingly mobile. In order to attract such employees, the smaller firms also had to pay wages in line with the going rates. Wage differentials for younger workers on the basis of firm size were swiftly extinguished, and a counter-differential developed as the smaller firms began paying higher than average wages instead, in an attempt to assure themselves of the necessary labor force (see Table 5.6). Similarly, the wages of employees hired away from other firms had until that time been inferior to those of long-time regular employees doing similar work, but this difference gradually began to narrow.

This situation had a great impact on the labor policies of firms. First, the seniority wage system had to change along with the wage increases for younger employees. However, this should not be interpreted as having posed a threat to the seniority wage system. The slope of the seniority wage curve flattened out, but neither labor nor management was well disposed toward doing away with the principles of seniority wages and lifetime employment, because these principles maintained the company union system. The seniority wage system was in fact strengthened when the growth rate declined in the 1980s.

Second, the disadvantageous conditions under which temporary and day laborers were employed gradually became more difficult to sustain. This was because workers would move on in search of more favorable conditions as long as employment opportunities for workers in their prime were increasing. In order to retain these workers, firms were forced to adopt measures such as pay increases and promotions to the status of permanent workers, but the number of temporary workers declined rapidly until they eventually disappeared.

Thereupon, and thirdly, first unmarried women and then the over-35 middle-aged and elderly female work force appeared on the scene to replace the temporary and day laborers in this cushioning role. The rise in the female labor force participation rate shown in Figure 5.3 substantiates this. From the latter half of the 1960s onward the female labor force was mobilized, doing side jobs as family workers, as pieceworkers at home, and as part-time help. The increase in part-time work was particularly notable. The changes in "workers for whom the job is secondary" shown in Table 5.7 illustrate this. Some regular workers are included among those who are conscious that their job is secondary, but the concept refers mainly to those whose principal activity is something other than their job, such as keeping house, attending school, and so on. The rapid increase in this type of worker after 1965, the fact that over 95 percent of these people have consistently been women, and that more and more of them have been becoming employees rather than self-employed workers, all testify to their having been mobilized into the labor force as part-time employees. According to the same survey, the reason most frequently cited by housewives for seeking employment was, "Not because we are having trouble making ends meet, but because we would like to increase household income." The second-ranking reason was a desire for "money to cover school expenses and pocket money." These motives replaced "low income" and "unemployment" as reasons for joining the work force.

This kind of female labor, a "marginal labor force" as Umemura Mataji once called it, enters the labor market if there are employment opportunities, but if not, it returns to the household; it differs in character from the "mainstay work force" of men who remain in the labor market in order to make a living until they retire.[3] Yet in the last ten years, this labor force has become a permanent feature of the labor market; women are working for many years at a stretch and becoming something close to a "mainstay work force" in their own right. At the same time, however, such women often refrain from enrolling in health insurance programs as dependents of the householder, and wish to keep their gross income below one million yen in

Table 5.7. Changes in That Part of the Non-agricultural Labor Force Consisting of Workers for Whom "My Job is Secondary"

(1000s persons)

		Totals	Self-employed	Family workers	Hired employees	Sectoral components total		
						Manufacturing	Wholesale & retail	Services
Total for males and females	1965	1,934	490	718	727	570	742	416
	71	3,997	1,097	1,271	1,627	1,370	1,320	878
	77	5,375	1,177	1,571	2,627	1,688	1,867	1,224
	87	7,987	1,565	1,507	4,916	2,133	2,762	2,123
Females only	1965	1,772	438	690	592	486	689	375
	71	3,699	1,036	1,237	1,428	1,294	1,233	811
	77	5,063	1,120	1,544	2,400	1,629	1,762	1,141
	87	7,325	1,471	1,473	4,378	2,059	2,511	1,913

Source: Statistics Bureau, Office of the Prime Minister, Shūgyō Kōzō Kihon Chōsa [Basic Survey of the Employment Structure], various years.

order to claim dependents' income tax exemptions. Firms, for their part, were seeking in this kind of labor force a cushion against economic fluctuations in place of the former temporary and day laborers. The mobilization of a part-time labor force progressed rapidly from the latter half of the 1960s to the beginning of the 1970s, and thereby sustained growth under labor shortage conditions. After the oil crisis the part-timers were the first to be dismissed, but they increased rapidly again to replace retired workers and others, in the process of employment adjustment. Today there are about 5 million such part-timers, as well as high-school and university students working part time, and perhaps one million foreign workers, who are also used as a relatively low-waged, temporary labor source. During the labor shortage of 1988–90 the unusual phenomenon arose that the wages of these temporary workers actually rose well above those of regular workers. Is it perhaps true that without a cushion against business slowdowns in the form of some kind of labor force that can be readily sacrificed, Japan's employment system is untenable?

3. The Problems of Small Business

(1) Small Business and the "Dual Structure" Theory

In the interwar period, small and medium-sized businesses (the term "small business" as used here includes indigenous industry and petty firms) were engaged in fierce competition and were increasing in number. Operating in the midst of a labor surplus and making use of labor-intensive technology, these firms continued to maintain their vitality. During the war the government forced a reorganization of business, liquidating small businesses in order to absorb their labor force into the munitions industry. Thus, by the final stages of the war most small businesses not directly connected with munitions had disappeared. After the defeat, however, the various kinds of small business rapidly began to increase again. Let us attempt to pinpoint the reasons for this phenomenon.

The changes in the size of small businesses are summarized in Table 5.8. Just how important the small businesses were in the non-primary industries can be seen from the data on changes in the numbers of places of business and persons employed. Moreover, a period-by-period examination reveals the following trends. To begin with the manufacturing industries, the proportion of employees in this sector's smallest firms (1–29 persons) has consistently declined since the war, although their absolute numbers have grown. Both the absolute numbers and the proportion of employees in firms with 30–49 persons have continued to rise. On the other hand, the marked personnel

Table 5.8. Number of Business Establishments and Number of Employees by Size of Business

		Number of establishments (1000)					Number of employees (1000)				
		Total	1–29	30–99	100–299	over 300	Total	1–29	30–99	100–299	over 300
Non-primary industries (excluding govt. employees)											
Total numbers	1954	3,309	3,239	57	10	3	18,788	10,878	2,738	1,598	3,494
	63	4,014	3,863	120	23	7	30,040	15,113	5,876	3,757	5,294
	75	5,524	5,304	178	34	9	43,159	22,567	8,735	5,345	6,511
	86	6,641	6,368	225	40	9	52,343	28,855	10,990	6,767	6,231
	91	6,687	6,375	257	45	10	57,983	31,233	14,534	7,099	7,116
Composition ratio	1954	100	97.9	1.7	0.3	0.1	100	57.9	14.6	8.5	18.6
	63	100	96.3	3.0	0.6	0.1	100	50.3	19.6	12.5	17.6
	75	100	96.0	3.2	0.6	0.2	100	52.3	20.2	12.4	15.1
	86	100	95.9	3.4	0.6	0.1	100	55.1	21.0	12.0	11.9
	91	100	95.3	3.8	0.7	0.2	100	53.9	25.1	12.2	12.3
Manufacturing industries											
Total numbers	1954	528	499	22	5	2	6,196	2,704	1,087	740	1,665
	75	814	747	51	12	4	12,699	4,513	2,521	1,901	3,764
	91	857	777	61	14	5	14,096	5,001	3,074	2,323	3,698
Composition ratio	1954	100	94.5	4.2	0.9	0.4	100	43.6	17.5	12.0	26.9
	75	100	91.8	6.2	1.5	0.5	100	35.5	19.9	14.9	29.6
	91	100	90.7	7.1	1.7	0.5	100	35.5	21.8	16.5	26.2

Table 5.8. (continued)

		Number of establishments (1000)					Number of employees (1000)				
		Non-primary industries (excluding govt. employees)									
		Total	1–29	30–99	100–299	over 300	Total	1–29	30–99	100–299	over 300
Wholesale and retail industries											
Total numbers	1954	1,609	1,601	7	1	0.1	4,963	4,454	304	109	96
	75	2,636	2,594	36	5	0.8	12,368	9,383	1,719	735	533
	91	2,923	2,854	61	6	0.9	16,913	12,448	2,873	985	608
Composition ratio	1954	100	99.5	0.4	0.0	0.0	100	89.7	6.1	2.2	1.9
	75	100	98.4	1.4	0.2	0.0	100	75.9	13.9	5.9	4.3
	91	100	97.6	2.1	0.2	0.0	100	73.6	17.0	5.8	3.6
Service industries											
Total numbers	1954	825	810	12	1	0.2	3,341	2,460	578	173	130
	75	1,232	1,185	40	6	1	8,295	4,590	1,974	999	733
	91	1,715	1,630	69	14	3	14,614	7,474	3,416	2,101	1,624
Composition ratio	1954	100	98.3	1.5	0.1	0.0	100	73.6	17.3	5.2	3.7
	75	100	96.1	3.2	0.5	0.1	100	55.3	23.8	12.1	8.8
	91	100	95.0	4.0	0.8	0.1	100	51.1	23.4	14.4	11.1

Source: General Affairs Agency, Bureau of Statistics, *Jigyōjo Tōkei Chōsa* [Census of Business Establishments].

expansion by large firms employing 300 persons or more was limited to the period of rapid growth from the latter half of the 1950s through the 1960s, while both the absolute number of their employees and their proportion of the work force declined in the 1970s and 1980s.

The overall rate of work force growth in the wholesale and retail industries far surpassed that in the manufacturing industries. Although the proportion employed in petty firms of one to four persons in this sector is declining, their absolute numbers show a large increase. However, the greatest increases occurred in businesses employing 30 to 99 persons during the 1950s and thereafter in firms of larger size. In the field of commerce, then, there has actually been an expansion in the scale of firms from petty businesses to small and medium-sized enterprises. However, employment in petty firms increased somewhat in 1975, as though reflecting an easing of the labor shortage.

As can be seen from these fluctuations, small businesses have absorbed the greatest part of the employed population, even during the period of rapid growth. Therein arose the wage differential problem described in the section on labor markets. With the help of Figure 5.4, this situation may be formally explained as follows. Let us assume that the work force is homogeneous and moreover that the entire work force must be hired (total employment).[4] That is, all workers appearing in the labor market (N_0) must be hired. If there is no wage differential between the large firms and small businesses, the wage in this society will be determined at the level (W_0) equivalent to the marginal productivity of the N workers. Now, however, let us assume that the wage in large firms must actually be determined at a level (W_L) higher than W_0 for institutional reasons such as the pressure of the lifetime employment system, seniority wages, and labor unions. Accordingly, with W_L as the marginal productivity of labor, the number of workers hired by large firms (N_L) must be determined at a level lower than the number hired (N'_L) when W was regarded as the marginal productivity. On the other hand, if we assume total employment, the small firms must absorb all the labor $(N_0 - N_L = N_S)$ other than the N hired by the large firms; it naturally follows that N_S will be larger than N'_S, and marginal productivity W_S will be less than W_0. This is how wage differentials (W_S/W_L) arose. The mechanism operated swiftly during the 1950s, when there was a continuing labor surplus. Small businesses absorbed a large volume of labor, and the differential between their average wages and those of large firms widened. Under these conditions the so-called dual structure theory emerged, and the situation began to be seen as a problem.[5]

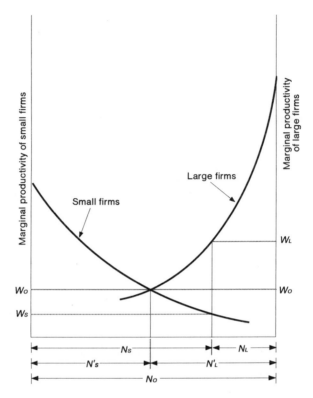

Figure 5.4. Formation of a wage differential under full-employment conditions

Due to the gap in wage levels between workers in small businesses and the employees of large firms, workers in smaller firms naturally had a lower standard of living even if they had the same experience and abilities, and were also exposed to the danger of unemployment should their company go bankrupt or reduce its size. They envied workers in the large firms who were protected by the lifetime employment and seniority wage systems, and many permanent employees in small businesses in fact gave up their positions to become temporary workers in large firms. Tolerating low incomes and unstable employment conditions for a while, they tried to seize every opportunity for promotion to the status of permanent employees of the large firms. At the same time, a large rural labor force seeking urban employment opportunities was waiting in the wings. Thus, the small firms' source of labor supply was not exhausted. The dual structure theory, in recognition of the above, is erected on the view that this kind of stratification is built into the Japanese economy and that it would be extremely difficult to break down. A number of disputes have developed over this, but we will not delve into the controversy here.[6]

The emergency of the wage differential set off a number of further chain reactions. The character of the labor market as a buyers' market for the big firms was reinforced, so that these firms took precedence over others in selecting and hiring new school graduates, while at the same time they forced disadvantageous working conditions on their temporary and day laborers. However, the "subcontractorization" of the small firms by the large was seen as the greatest problem. The subcontracting system itself had been in use since the mid-1920s, but because of the widening wage differential gap, using the low-wage labor of the small firms indirectly via subcontracting was more profitable for the large concerns than producing goods themselves. This was one of the principal reasons that subcontracting came into general use.

Of course there were other reasons besides the advantage of cheap labor for the subcontracting system's spread in the 1950s. Most important among these were capital economies and the spreading of risk, particularly the latter. When business was poor, parent firms would drop their subcontractors and postpone payment on their accounts, while in good times they would increase subcontracting. Citing the need for rationalization among subcontractors, they would beat down prices to low levels. It was not without reason that the subcontracting system called for "ordering externally on unequal terms." The large firms got away with this kind of thing because the small companies were at a great relative disadvantage. For example, in the 1950s banks went ahead and made loans to small businesses during periods of monetary ease when funds were abundant, but when money became tight, they would hurriedly call in these loans.[7] On the other hand, of course, there were some advantages for small businesses in the subcontracting system. They were guaranteed a continuous flow of orders, and there were many examples of small firms being taken care of financially by their parent companies and receiving technological guidance from them. Table 5.9 shows the number of small businesses in the manufacturing industry which were subcontracting firms. According to these figures, the bulk of small and medium manufacturing was carried out via subcontracting relation-

Table 5.9. Subcontracting Circumstances of Small Firms (Year-end, 1966)

(%)

	Doing business exclusively with one (A)	Taking subcontracts from several firms (B)	Doing both subcontracting & non-sub-contracting business (C)	(A) + (B) + (C)
Manufacturing	24.2	18.8	10.6	53.6
Steel	15.7	35.1	15.1	65.9
Metals other than steel	13.0	22.5	15.5	51.0
Machinery manufacturing	26.6	26.9	18.1	71.6
Electrical equipment	28.8	34.3	14.4	77.5
Transportation equipment	27.7	32.0	9.6	69.3
Precision machinery	25.0	27.8	10.1	62.9
Textiles	50.6	22.2	6.8	79.6
Clothing & other textile products	42.0	21.0	6.7	69.7
Chemicals	15.1	13.5	4.1	32.7

Source: Kiyonari Tadao, *Nihon Chūshō Kigyō no Kōzō Hendō* [Structural Changes in Japan's Small Business] (Shin Hyōron, 1970), p. 166.
Original data source is Small Business Agency, *Daisankai Chūshō Kigyō Sōgō Kihon Chōsa Hōkokusho* [Report on the Third Comprehensive Basic Survey of Small Business].

ships, which was the mode of production for approximately 70 percent of small and medium-sized businesses in the textile, electric machinery, machinery, clothing and other textile products, and steel industries.

The subcontracting problem began to attract attention in the early half of the 1950s just after the Korean War, and the Law to Assure Prompt Payment to Subcontractors, which had been pending since the recession of 1954, was passed in 1956. Then, after agitation by the Small and Medium Business Federation (Chūseiren), the Small and Medium Business Enterprise Organizations Law was enacted in 1957. Small businessmen formed associations, organizing trust cooperative associations and enterprise cooperative associations which shared production, selling, and equipment. Their cartelization on a large scale was tolerated as an exception to the Anti-Monopoly Law.

At about the beginning of the 1960s small businesses' low productivity of value added, due to the fact that they were technologically behind the large firms, began to attract attention. Moreover, it was said that the future of small business looked grim because of international competition and the impending labor shortage. For these reasons, the Basic Small Business Law was passed in 1963. The law defined small businesses as firms capitalized at or below ¥50 million and/or employing 300 persons or less (in the commerce and service industries, firms capitalized at or below ¥10 million and/or having 50 or fewer employees). It obligated such firms to make efforts to prevent excessive competition, to rationalize subcontracting transactions, and so on. In return, the government would introduce modern equipment; improve technology; rationalize management and administration; "rationalize the scale of enterprises; provide for cooperation among firms; provide for the aggregation of factories, shops, etc.; convert businesses into modernized establishments; provide for the modernization of the conduct of retail business"; and "correct the adverse terms under which these firms did business." This resulted in the passage of the Small Business Modernization Promotion Law (1963), under which a system was created to provide for funding and guidance. Industry categories were specified, "modernization" plans were drawn up, and the national government was to provide guidance in the formation of cartels, the provision of funds, and so on. These measures are still being implemented, with the addition of the "restructuring" policies which since 1968 have accompanied the move toward joint business arrangements, joint management, and mergers.

The concept of small businesses that guided the drafting of this legislation was that they are weak compared to large firms and deserving of protection. The idea was that in order to improve them, they would have to have the same kinds of plant and equipment, management methods, technology, and so on, as the large firms—in other words, small firms that were miniature replicas of the large ones would have to be created. Let us look at the logic behind this thinking. Certainly, the practices of dropping subcontractors and delaying payments to them during times of recession should not be allowed to go on unchecked. However, freedom to form cartels, or equipment installations comparable to those of large firms, are not indispensable to the survival of small businesses. These companies have their own distinct characteristics. In the section below, we identify these features by comparing large and small firms from two different angles.

(2) Value-added Productivity Differentials
The fatal flaw of small businesses is considered by many economists to have been their low prevailing value-added productivity. However,

is this factor actually that important? Consider the following. If value added is the sum of profits (P) and wages (W), and if N indicates the number employed, then the productivity of value added is given by $(P + W)/N$. Then if K_1 is gross capital employed and K_2 is fixed capital stock, the following identity is established:

$$\frac{P + W}{N} = \frac{P}{N} + \frac{W}{N} = \frac{K_2}{N} \frac{K_1}{K_2} \frac{P}{K_1} + \frac{W}{N}$$

Value-added productivity = capital equipment ratio × gross capital employed/fixed capital stock × gross capital profit ratio + per-capita wage cost.

In other words, the value-added productivity may be broken down into profit per employee and per-capita wage cost (including employee benefits), and the former may be rewritten as the product of the degree of capital concentration, the ratio of gross capital (including land) to fixed capital (referred to below as the fixed capital ratio), and the gross capital profit ratio. The data for this equation were obtained from the Finance Ministry's *Corporate Statistics* (Hōjin Kigyō Tōkei), and values were calculated on the basis of the size of firms' capital stock to obtain Table 5.10. The following facts should be noted. First, the value-added productivity differentials have been extremely large right down to the present. This was attributed to the "weakness" of small businesses. However, it is clear from the regression coefficients and coefficients of determination in the note to Table 5.10 that this is almost entirely explained by the differences in degree of capital concentration from industry to industry. In this way it can be seen that disparities in value-added productivity do not arise as a result of differences in firms within the same industry; the problem is rather one of differences in capital concentration among industries.

On the other hand, in a capitalist economy the profit rates of firms are supposed to equalize, but it can be seen that for all years, the lower the capitalization of the small firm, the higher the profit rate was.[8] Might it not be that the "weakling" companies' high profit rates offer some pluses that compensate for the many negative factors already described? Table 5.11 calculates fixed capital ratios and for small firms this ratio is low, as is the capital equipment ratio. Small businesses are competing with the large firms by raising their capital turnover rates and taking advantage of their maneuverability.

A comparison of the largest and the smallest firms shows that wage-cost differentials by size of firm, which have shrunk from almost four times in 1953, to slightly over double in recent years are still

Table 5.10. Analysis of Corporate Value-added Productivity

(Units: ¥1000s, except $\frac{K_1}{K_2}$ in units of 1, and $\frac{P}{K_1}$ as %)

Totals for manufacturing industries	1953 (¥1,000)					1960 (¥1,000)					1970 (units ¥1,000)					1989 (units ¥1,000)				
	$\frac{P+W}{N}$	$\frac{K_2}{N}$	$\frac{K_1}{K_2}$	$\frac{P}{K_1}$	$\frac{W}{N}$	$\frac{P+W}{N}$	$\frac{K_2}{N}$	$\frac{K_1}{K_2}$	$\frac{P}{K_1}$	$\frac{W}{N}$	$\frac{P+W}{N}$	$\frac{K_2}{N}$	$\frac{K_1}{K_2}$	$\frac{P}{K_1}$	$\frac{W}{N}$	$\frac{P+W}{N}$	$\frac{K_2}{N}$	$\frac{K_1}{K_2}$	$\frac{P}{K_1}$	$\frac{W}{N}$
Averages	265	213	3.30	18.7	134	531	608	2.89	15.5	259	1.67	1.96	3.18	11.9	0.93	5.82	4.75	3.70	5.7	4.39
Capital funds under ¥2 million	130	49	4.30	31.3	63	320	217	3.08	20.6	182	1.09	0.57	3.28	24.5	0.63	3.03	1.27	4.29	4.3	2.79
200–500	238	128	3.95	21.3	130	404	304	3.56	18.7	201	1.16	0.73	3.19	20.7	0.68	3.65	2.06	4.11	5.3	3.20
500–1,000	269	149	4.22	17.7	158	438	407	3.35	15.4	228	1.21	0.86	3.45	17.0	0.71	3.75	1.99	5.77	4.8	3.21
	322	247	3.49	16.9	177	534	551	3.21	15.6	258	1.32	1.21	3.32	14.5	0.78	4.58	2.87	5.34	6.2	3.63
5,000–10,000	348	298	3.39	14.9	198	693	905	2.86	13.4	348	1.50	1.42	3.45	12.0	0.91	5.23	3.93	4.95	6.3	4.01
10,000–100,000*	486	508	3.04	15.9	240	1,035	1,588	2.71	14.0	428	1.72	1.98	3.09	11.2	1.03	6.42	5.22	4.66	6.2	4.91
											2.53	4.08	3.14	9.7	1.29	9.47	9.85	5.49	5.6	6.44

* for 1970 and 1989, 10,000–100,000

Source: Calculated from Ministry of Finance, *Hōjin Kigyō Tōkei Nenpō* [Corporate Statistics Annual].
The table below shows the estimated parameters and their R^2 coefficients of determination for the equation $P+W/N = \alpha + \beta(K_2/N)$, which explains value-added productivity in terms of the degree of capital concentration. (Figures in parentheses are *t*-values.)

	α	β	R^2
1953	133.4	0.5739	0.9614
		(9.98)	
1960	235.3	0.5067	0.9963
		(32.67)	

	α	β	R^2
1970	0.8647	0.4126	0.9958
		(11.54)	
1989	2.2583	0.7474	0.9940
		(3.98)	

Table 5.11. Objectives of Plant and Equipment Investment

(%)

Scale of business	Primarily for labor-saving purposes	Investments for which labor economies were a significant consideration	Investments more for the purpose of expanding productive capacity than economizing on labor	Other	Period in which labor economies became primary goal of investments*			
					1961 or earlier	1962–64	1965–67	1968 and after
Total for manufacturing industries	18.9	29.9	48.4	2.7	5.7	17.1	52.6	24.6
1000 employees or more	19.6	35.6	42.9	1.9	6.5	14.1	55.4	23.9
500–999 employees	15.3	28.1	54.1	2.6	6.7	20.0	60.0	13.3
300–499 employees	12.4	23.4	60.6	3.6	5.9	23.5	52.9	17.6
100–299 employees	22.0	26.4	48.2	3.4	4.5	18.0	47.2	30.3

* For the proportions shown under "period in which labor economies became the primary goal of investments," places of business which "are primarily investing for labor-saving purposes" = 100.

Source: Ministry of Labour, "Rōdō Keizai Dōkō Chōsa" [Survey of Trends in the Labor Economy], as cited in Kiyonari Tadao, Nihon Chūshō Kigyō no Kōzō Hendō [Structural Changes in Japan's Small Business], p. 143.

relatively large. There are probably two major reasons for this. One is the differences in the ages and lengths of employment of the labor forces in large and small firms, as we have already seen. Suppose we call this the labor force factor. Another is the labor market factor arising from the total employment of the surplus labor force, particularly in the 1950s. This second factor may be regarded as having weakened since the period of high economic growth. If so, the labor force factor, based on qualitative differences in the work force, may be considered the major factor in the currently frozen differentials. In the midst of the transition from labor surplus to shortage from the 1950s to 1960, small businesses had no choice but to change. In this sense, the view that small businesses were able to establish themselves initially only on the basis of a low-paid work force needs to be reconsidered.

In response to the growing impossibility of using low-wage male labor in labor-intensive work, small firms too shifted their production technology little by little in the direction of capital intensiveness. Table 5.11 which gives the survey data indicating this situation, clearly indicates that labor-saving plant and equipment investment (the introduction of automated machinery beginning with the automatic lathe, improvement of manufacturing methods and production processes, etc.) progressed in small firms through the mid-1960s. Advances in the machinery industry, and the development of specialist machines to perform a wide range of specific tasks, enable small businesses to purchase equipment at low prices. However, while on the one hand the modernization of plant and equipment has been advancing, a number of firms have been trying to scrape through the labor shortage by using temporary workers, part-time help, and moonlighters, or by using the low-paid local labor force of subcontractor factories in such places as Korea, Taiwan, and later Southeast Asian countries.

(3) The Diversity of Small Firms: Start-ups, Failures, and Changes in Scale

Small businesses have their own *raison d'être*; while they produce average profits surpassing those of large firms, there are reasons for their having been treated as "weaklings." One reason is probably the diversity of small firm management. The term "diversity" here refers to the fact that the profitability of small businesses, including their technology and the managerial capabilities of their executives, is widely distributed. While the same is true to a certain extent of large firms as well, profitability is dispersed over a much narrower band than for small businesses. Figure 5.5 summarizes the situation.[9] Dur-

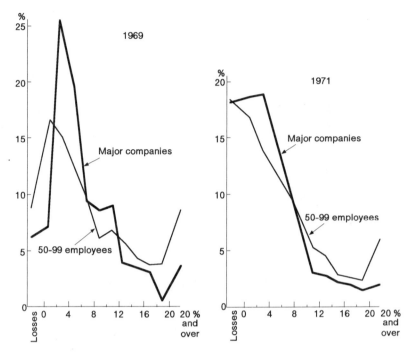

Figure 5.5. Distribution of gross profit rates for large and small firms (component ratios; number of firms = 100), 1969 (left) and 1971 (right)

Sources: Constructed from Bank of Japan, *Chūkigyō Keiei Bunseki* [Analysis of the Operations of Medium-sized Firms], FY 1969 edition, and *Kigyō Kibo-betsu Keiei Bunseki* [Analysis of Firms by Scale of Operations], FY 1971 edition.

ing the prosperous year of 1969, the distribution of profit rates was skewed to the left. Small firms with losses or profit rates of 2 percent or less and those with high profits of 12 percent or more were rather numerous, while there were by comparison few large firms in either of these categories. In the recession year of 1971, both curves indicate that businesses showing losses were the most numerous. As profit rates rise, the number of firms declines, and both distributions slope downward from the left in times of recession. However, there is a clear-cut contrast between the higher proportion of large companies with profit rates of 8 percent or less, and the greater percentage of small businesses with rates above 8 percent.

This attests to the fact that there are great managerial differences among small companies. In the world of small business, severe fluctuations in firms's fortunes are unavoidable because competition

Table 5.12. Fluctuations in Number of Business Establishments Covered by Unemployment Insurance

	Number of business establishments covered (1000s)	Percentage new entrants into program %	Percentage cancellations & withdrawals %
1956	253	13.7	6.4
60	361	14.2	4.7
64	521	14.5	5.4
68	641	10.5	3.7
72	740	8.8	4.0
76	1,045	3.3	0.7
80	1,313	3.0	0.5
84	1,451	5.8	4.2
88	1,612	7.2	3.3
90	1,734	6.1	2.9

Source: Employment Security Bureau, Ministry of Labour, "Shitsugyō Hoken Jigyō Tōkei" [Statistics on Unemployment Insurance Operations] and "Koyō Hoken Jigyō Tōkei" [Statistics on Employment Insurance Operations].

develops among firms with strikingly different general managerial capacities. Indicating start-ups, liquidations, and increases and decreases in firm size, Table 5.12 portrays the situation to a certain extent. While on the one hand firms of all sizes opened for business at a yearly rate of 14 to 15 percent in the 1950s and even at present are entering business at a rate of about 10 percent, 3 to 5 percent of all firms at the same time have either been going out of business or withdrawing from the unemployment insurance program—the majority most likely consisting of those going out of business. Moreover, according to Kiyonari Tadao, 22.6 percent of the places of business in the manufacturing industry employing nine persons or less changed trades or failed between 1964 and 1966.[10] The proportion of such firms was especially high in the chemical and heavy industry sector, reaching 41.4 percent in the general machinery industry. Moreover, the number of small businesses was increasing overall during this period. Small business is characterized by a "high start-up, high failure rate."

Furthermore, as Kiyonari shows in his unequivocal research findings, a total of as many as 63 percent of those opening small businesses have previous experience as employees of small firms. The most common age of those opening their businesses is 30–34 equivalent to 56 percent if all those 34 years of age and under are taken together. These men chose small business as "work in which they could be independent in the future," and the hope of "independence" becomes stronger as the number of years of employment increases. The average amount of funds with which they started up their businesses was somewhat more than ¥2 million (10 thousand U.S. dollars in the 1970s), of which about half was equity capital and the remainder "for the most part consisted of borrowings from relatives, acquaintances, and friends, and business credit."[11] It is easy to understand why there were so many new entrants.

The reality of the high start-up and failure rate naturally means that, even if a small business survives, the expansions and contractions in the course of its existence are violent. Thus, the small business sector is in an overall state of flux, with old firms constantly being replaced by new ones. When considered in the light of these facts, the problems of small business policy as represented by the Small Enterprise Organizations Law and the Modernization Promotion Law become clear. Taking for granted that the currently extant group of "small and medium firms" should continue to exist as is, neither increasing nor decreasing, these laws are based on the idea that a cartel can be formed from the given membership group, and plant and equipment modernization carried out.

However, whereas small business in reality continues to be highly volatile, the problem with these policies is that they protect groups specially designated by region or by type of industry and also run the risk of not producing the hoped-for results due to the activities of new industry entrants who are non-members of such groups. Herein lies the reason that the so-called modernization promotion schemes often did not produce results.

The textile industry is an example of the application of these policies. Because of excess plant and equipment and excessive competition, the industry formed associations that scrapped obsolete equipment and introduced a few modern, up-to-date installations; and from the 1960s onward the national government repeatedly implemented policies to assist in these efforts. But these activities have always been disrupted by new entrants from outside the industry. If the objective were only to temporarily suppress plant and equipment expansion, that would be quite another matter; but the present policy certainly seems to have missed the mark. Rather than concentrating on such things as partial protection and the nurturing of small business, the main line of policy should be in the direction of improving small business finance and redressing the disadvantages of subcontractors, rectifying the competitive handicaps of small businesses, and providing the conditions under which fair competition can take place.

(4) The Conditions for the Existence of Small Business

The character of small business as described above may be more readily grasped through an understanding of the complexity of the functions it performs. Before the war, traditional industry assumed the burden of the production and distribution of non-agricultural consumption goods and took care of exports, absorbing a portion of the population second in size only to agriculture. Did this situation change after the war? If one assumes that there was no major change, small business must have inherited the functions of the traditional industries. Let us attempt to shed some light on this point by means of an input–output analysis.

This author, in cooperation with Sakura Itasu, at one time had occasion to construct, on the basis of the 1955 input-output table, an input–output table by scale of firm which consolidated the sectors in the manufacturing field in which large firms (300 or more employees) or small firms (300 employees or less) were dominant (Table 5.13).[12] The method of classifying the industries as small-firm or large-firm-dominated was essentially "to categorize the industrial groupings (or a combination of several of them) of the Census of Manufactures corresponding to the industrial sectors of the input–output table as large-firm-dominated if the value of shipments from establishments employing 300 persons or more consisted of 50 percent or more of the total value of shipments for that industry, and to classify as small-firm-dominated those sectors in which this amount was 50 percent or less (the value of shipments from establishments employing less than 300 persons was 50 percent or more of the total). After each of the sectors in the input–output table (detailed industrial classification) had been identified as either large- or small-firm-dominated, they were consolidated on this basis into large-firm and small-firm components of each of the sectors in manufacturing—textiles, chemicals, metals and machinery, and other light industry." Let us consider below the facts that may be observed from the input–output table constructed in this manner.

First, let's examine the input–output table's component ratios by type of demand. The sectors with high endogenous inter-industry demand were, in rank order, mining, textiles (large firms), energy, chemicals (large), chemicals (small), and metals and machines (large). The ratios of endogenous to total demand for all of these sectors were

Table 5.13. Input-Output Table for 1955

	Agric., forestry & fisheries (A)	Mining (Min)	Energy industries (E)	Metals & machinery industries (M) Small (S)	Large (L)	Chemicals (C) Small (S)	Large (L)	Textiles (T) Small (S)	Large (L)	Other light industries (L) Small (S)	Large (L)
A	392	1	10	0	1	22	40	47	61	524	83
Min	0	0	0	0	80	14	20	0	0	0	0
E	26	4	207	13	93	32	82	14	14	36	4
M_S	16	1	5	84	54	1	3	3	2	22	1
M_L	9	2	9	251	833	5	2	0	0	5	0
C_S	11	3	6	14	23	98	58	10	15	88	9
C_L	103	0	4	5	13	159	156	19	39	10	1
T_S	14	0	1	2	2	3	3	243	2	13	9
T_L	2	—	—	0	2	0	0	390	54	1	0
L_S	37	1	2	11	20	3	2	6	1	232	1
L_L	15	0	2	4	16	6	13	1	0	23	0
S	173	16	97	79	315	157	147	108	63	302	23
Tu	17	1	25	8	25	25	22	9	4	34	2
Sub-totals	814	30	368	472	1,476	526	549	850	256	1,291	132
Value added & indirect taxes	1,682	84	351	271	386	263	234	183	258	679	212
Totals	2,495	114	719	743	1,862	789	783	1,033	514	1,970	344

Source: Sakura Itaru and Nakamura Takafusa, "Sangyō Renkan no Kigyō Kibo-betsu Bunseki" [Size of Business in Industry Relations] (Keizai Kenkyū, Oct. 1960).

0.7 or higher. On the other hand, the sectors with low ratios, all 0.5 or below, were, in order from the smallest, transportation and communications, textiles (small firms), other light industry (large), other light industry (small), metals and machines (small), and agriculture, forestry, and fisheries. From this it can be seen that the functions of the former traditional industries have clearly been passed on to the textile industry, other light industry, etc.; and consumer goods production, of course, as well as most exporting, has likewise been done by small businesses. Even though in the 1960s the bulk of exporting shifted to large firms, the major share of consumption goods was still produced by small firms.[13] Small business is still maintaining a secure hold on the stable segment of demand—namely, consumption demand.

Next, let us look at the relationships between large and small firms within the manufacturing sectors, as indicated in the boldface figures in the tables. In all three of the manufacturing industries other than

% (¥ billions)

Commerce & services (S)	Transport, communications & construction (Tu)	Sub-totals	Comsumption	Gross capital format-tion	Exports	Total final demand	Com-petitive imports	Gross output	Gross supply
137	18	1,338	1,227	151	28	1,406	−249	2,495	2,744
2	38	156	—	−3	1	−2	−40	114	154
65	114	703	126	−1	14	139	−124	719	842
92	83	368	65	242	103	409	−34	743	777
122	121	1,360	49	328	160	537	−34	1,862	1,897
249	60	642	130	1	31	163	−16	789	805
87	63	659	89	9	38	136	−12	783	795
32	5	328	386	61	262	709	−4	1,033	1,037
27	—	477	19	−3	22	38	−1	514	515
379	179	874	1,059	33	88	1,179	−83	1,970	2,053
46	6	132	206	0	7	214	−2	344	346
1,328	317	3,125	3,221	51	236	3,508	−62	6,571	6,633
263	60	498	343	1,065	154	1,561	−5	2,053	2,059
2,828	1,066	10,658	6,920	1,935	1,143	9,998	−666	19,900	20,656
3,745	988		438	—	1		—	9,772	
6,571	2,053		7,359	1,935	1,144		−666	29,672	

light industry, there are sizable flows of goods from the large firms to the small, while flows in the opposite direction are quite minimal. The prevailing pattern is that large firms are in charge of the raw materials sector while small firms handle the transformation of these materials into manufactured goods. Of course, in assembly industries such as electrical machinery and automobiles, there are many instances in which the parts industry consists of small firms, and here there are flows from the small to the large firms. It is well known that the proportion of such flows has increased in recent years. But the prevailing pattern has given rise to a situation in which final demands on the large-firms sector induce comparatively little demand in the small-firms sector, while final demands on small firms stimulate a great deal of demand among large firms. This can be understood if we look at the power of dispersion coefficients and the sensitivity of dispersion coefficients (Table 5.14) derived from the inverse matrix. Generally, the power of dispersion generated by final demand in the manu-

Table 5.14. Power of Dispersion and Sensitivity of Dispersion Coefficients

	Power of dispersion	Sensitivity of dispersion
A	0.7262	1.2735
Min	0.6526	0.5896
E	0.8611	1.1126
M_S	1.2104	0.6845
M_L	1.3798	1.4440
C_S	1.1235	0.8969
C_L	1.1350	1.0561
T_S	1.3090	0.6813
T_L	0.9227	0.8244
L_S	1.0186	0.8200
L_L	0.7878	0.5478
S	0.8893	2.3271
Tu	0.9919	0.7423

Source: Same as for Table 5.13.

facturing industries is larger than that which it generates in other sectors; and within the manufacturing sector itself, demand directed toward small business has a greater power of dispersion than that directed toward large firms. Furthermore, the sensitivity of dispersion index is, by contrast, by far the largest for the commerce and service industries, and is also quite high for agriculture, forestry, and fisheries. (The high index of the primary industries is probably due to the large figures appearing in this table because competitive imports are included.) However, for all industries within the manufacturing sector, the sensitivity of dispersion index is far higher for large firms than for the small ones. This would naturally follow for small firms engaged in activities close to the final demand stage of production and distribution, but as an economy-wide effect, it gives cause for fresh reflection on the magnitude of the demand directed toward small business (see Table 5.15).

It can be seen from the above analysis that the conditions for the existence of traditional industry in Japan have been passed on into the postwar period and that the reasons for the formation of small businesses have not changed. Neither has there been any change in this situation since the era of rapid growth. The only thing that has changed is that small businesses are shifting to capital intensiveness since, as has been seen, they are no longer able to get along as before with only labor-intensive technology that relies on what had once been cheap labor, now that they are surrounded by a labor shortage and great technological progress. It is not without reason that by

Table 5.15. Composition of Demand for Value Shipped in 1955 (as a proportion of total value supplied)

	Intermediate demand totals	Consumption	Gross capital formation	Exports	Total final demand	Competitive imports
A	.4876	.4544	.0550	.0102	.5127	−.0907
Min	1.013	—	−.0195	.0065	.0123	−.2597
E	.8349	.1496	−.0012	.0166	.1651	−.1473
M$_S$	.4736	.0837	.3115	.1326	.5264	−.0438
M$_L$	.7169	.0258	.1729	.0843	.2831	−.0179
C$_S$	.7975	.1615	.0012	.0385	.2025	−.0199
C$_L$	.8289	.1119	.0113	.0478	.1711	−.0151
T$_S$	.3558	.3722	−.0588	.2527	.6365	−.0039
T$_L$	.9262	.0369	−.0058	.0427	.0738	−.0019
L$_S$	.4257	.5258	.1610	.0429	.5743	−.0404
L$_L$	.3815	.5954	0	.0202	.6185	−.0058
S	.4711	.4856	.0077	.0356	.5283	−.0003
Tu	.2419	.1666	.5172	.0748	.7581	−.0024
Subtotals	.5160	.3350	.0937	.0553	.4840	−.0322

Source: Same as for Table 5.13.

virtue of these changes, and using their own technology and management methods, firms have arisen from among the small businesses which have produced results the large firms cannot rival. Called the "reliable mainstay firms" (*chūken kigyō*) and "venture businesses," these growth firms have appeared in rapid succession.

The *chūken kugyō* are a group of firms which first attracted attention in the 1960s. According to Nakamura Hideichirō, who pioneered research on this subject, the phrase refers to a group of firms under the management of strong individuals who may be "more readily characterized as innovative administrators and organizers ... rather than private individual capitalists"; firms which have "independently selected ... growth products," "succeeded in putting these products on a mass-production basis, improving their quality, and developing mass markets," "achieved economies of scale," and "secured comparative superiority," even relative to the large firms.[14] This does not mean that there were no such firms prior to the war or in the 1950s. Matsushita Electric of prewar days, and Sony and Yoshida Industries postwar, are good early examples. However, the creation of an environment of high growth and technological progress in which firms of this type could easily develop stimulated an increase in their numbers.

While they inherited the characteristics of the "mainstay" firms, the venture businesses which were a special feature of the 1970s carried these qualities yet one step further. Nakamura Hideichirō has characterized them as follows. (1) The inclination to find their *raison d'être* in the demonstration of their special abilities is much stronger. (2) They start out by producing on a commercial basis a new product which is the fruit of independent research (including design development). (3) Concentrating on specialty products, few pursue economies of scale in production. (4) They develop and systematize new markets. (5) As a result of concentrating the firm's efforts on product development, they depend to a large extent on external sources for actual production. (6) They invest heavily in technostructure. (7) There are few of the managerial succession problems that tend to occur in small businesses and the "mainstay" firms, nor do they generate organizational pressures the way large firms do.[15]

4. Changes in Postwar Agriculture

Following the defeat in World War II, agriculture absorbed an employed population in excess of 17 million people, but the farm population declined rapidly after that. It played, so to speak, the role of supplying a labor force for rapid economic growth. However, during the growth process, agriculture also underwent sweeping changes. Let us take a look at these changes as indicated by the data presented in Table 5.16.

Along with the population increase, the number of agricultural households also climbed, to a figure in excess of 6 million. This was because workers returning to the farm established households of their own rather than clustering together on the family homestead. The resulting state of agriculture in the 1950s was such that the land reform had solved the tenant farmer problem, but the growing trend toward intensive farming on tiny plots was viewed with apprehension. During the course of growth following the Korean War, however, labor gradually began to migrate out of the farm villages. We have already noted the great population outflows that occurred from that time onward in the process of rapid growth. What was going on in the farm villages during that time?

First, let us summarize the course of agricultural policy from the land reform onward. Aimed at preventing the revival of a landlord system like that of the prewar era, the Agricultural Land Act was passed in 1952, imposing severe restrictions on land transfers, tenure, tenant rents, etc. However, this law also had the undeniable effect of preserving without modification the much more dispersed, minutely

Table 5.16. Number of Farm Households and Farming Population

| | Number of farm households (1000s) | | | Population employed in agriculture (1000s) | |
	Total	Farming full time	Farming part time Class I	Farming part time Class II	Employed population	Population engaged in Key areas of agriculture
1941	5,499	2,304	2,040	1,155	—	—
47	5,909	3,275	1,684	951	—	—
55	6,043	2,105	2,275	1,663	—	—
65	5,665	1,219	2,081	2,365	11,514	8,941
75	4,953	616	1,295	3,078	7,907	4,889
85	4,229 (3,315)	(498)	(758)	(2,058)	6,363	3,696
90	3,835 (2,971)	(473)	(521)	(1,977)	5,653	3,127

Source: Data are from Census of Agriculture (*Nōgyō Sensasu*) and Survey of Agriculture (*Nōgyō Chōsa*). 1985 and 1990 figures in parentheses are for households marketing their produce. Totals include households engaged in self-sufficient farming as well.

fragmented pattern of landownership. It was the public works projects in the farm villages that really made a difference—water supply improvements, soil improvement, adjustments of cultivated fields (*kōchi seiri*), culvert drainage, the use of intermediate ponds to raise the temperature of paddy irrigation water, farmland irrigation, agricultural land conservation, and so on. The exploitation of water supplies through their joint use for flood control, electric power, industrial water, and city water supply, as in the Aichi Reservoir, also attracted attention. Public works expenditures related to agriculture and forestry were poured into these kinds of "basic improvements."

The main emphasis in the food supply administration system since the war has gradually shifted away from an assured food supply and toward income security for rice farmers. For example, as the postwar food shortages abated, the rice price determination formula was also changed in 1952 from the price parity formula which had been used until that time to an income parity formula. Under the price parity formula, the rice price had been determined in accordance with changes in the prices of goods purchased by farm households, and had maintained farmers' real incomes. The income parity formula, however, attempting to increase farmers' real income, took into consideration changes in the amount of production inputs and the gap between the rates of increase in consumption levels in urban versus rural household budgets as well as changes in the prices of goods purchased by farm households. The formula was changed yet again in 1960 to the production-cost income compensation formula, which calculated the rice price by evaluating at the average industrial wage rate the self-employment wages the marginal rice producer paid himself. The result was that rice prices slid upward in tandem with urban wages, which were soaring under labor shortage conditions.

At about the beginning of the 1960s, however, there was growing recognition that this type of agricultural policy was out of step with changes in the economy. In 1961 the Basic Agricultural Law was passed, attempting to set out the broad lines for subsequent agricultural policy. First, the preamble asserts that since it is placed on adverse terms naturally, economically, and socially relative to other industries, agriculture has reached a turning point under economic growth; in order to compensate for such conditions, the law seeks the modernization and rationalization of agriculture in such a way that farmers can carry on lives that are more in balance with those of the other classes of the population. The main text of the law sets forth as three policy goals the redress of such differentials, improved productivity, and income equilibrium between farmers and those employed in other industries. This law tried to extend the concept of economic rationality to agriculture, introducing the idea of using the price mechanism to expand a profitable field of activity and to raise productivity. At the same time, it displayed a directly protective stance, stating that it sought the "stabilization" of agricultural commodity prices as a matter of policy in order to rectify the income differentials between agricultural and non-agricultural industries. This combination united those who were trying to change the direction of farm policy with their opponents who were attempting to preserve that policy and hand it on. This position has become the basis of agricultural policy and has continued unchanged from that time to the present. For example, in the midst of the foreign trade liberalization drive, Japan supported import restrictions on agricultural commodities and comparatively high tariff rates. These policies conformed to the principle of domestic price "stabilization," as can be seen from the way in which the pending liberalization of such items as beef, oranges, and grapefruit between Japan and the United States became a political problem at home and more recently the liberalization of the rice market and tariffication met with fierce resistance from farming interests. Undeniably, however, the result was a tendency toward an excessive exaltation of "stability," at the cost of making Japan's agricultural commodity prices conspicuously high by international standards, as exemplified by the fact that the domestic price of rice in the 1990s is some eight times the international price.

Against the background of a policy which, so to speak, attempted to maintain agriculture and the rural villages close to the national status quo, the farming industry and villages themselves have responded sensitively to modification in their economic environment and changed rapidly. The population employed in agriculture decreased dramatically, but agricultural production continued to increase. On the whole there were striking increases until 1960, and thereafter the tempo of growth was precipitous, mainly centered on livestock raising. One reason is that, as farmers' incomes rose due to the land reform in areas such as Tōhoku and Hokuriku, where the tenant farmer system had been most deep-rooted, the level of their technology also advanced and with it productivity rose. For example, the rice crop per hectare in these areas achieved large increases, from 327 kilograms in 1950 to 431 kilograms in 1955, far exceeding the national average. The other major factor in this connection was the progress in agricultural technology realized in this period. The sequence of advances was as follows: (1) the appearance of cold-resistant, early-ripening plant varieties and the spread of such technology as heated nurseries for rice crossbreeding; (2) the development of new urea and chemical fertilizers, then compound fertilizers, and advances in fertilization technology; (3) the advent of public works projects such as land improvement; (4) the spread of insecticides and germicides like BHC or organic mercury preparations (whose manufacture was later discontinued since they were shown to be harmful) and herbicides like PCP; (5) the spread of agricultural machinery (Table 5.17). These improvements primarily expanded the

Table 5.17. Holdings of Agricultural Machinery

(1000s of items)

	Rice planting machines	Power reapers for rice & other grains	Reaping & hulling combines	Power cultivators and farm
1970	32	263	45	3,452
80	1,746	884	1,524	4,233
90	1,983	1,215	1,282	4,328

Source: Kayō Nobufumi, ed., Kaitei Nihon Nōgyō Kiso Tōkei [Revised Basic Statistics on Japanese Agriculture] (Nōgyō Tōkei Kyōkai, 1977), pp. 168–69.

rice crop, but their effects gradually extended to other crops and into the area of livestock breeding as well.

Let us trace the diffusion of this technology in, for example, rice growing. Basic technology in plant varieties and in fertilization advanced in the first half of the 1950s. Agricultural chemicals also emerged at this time. Small tractors were produced domestically and began to be used on a large scale from the latter part of the 1950s, and the data indicate that by 1965 farmers owned over two million of them. Ownership of power dusters and sprayers followed suit, and power reapers and reaping and hulling combines came into general use from the latter part of the 1960s. At the beginning of the 1970s, the rice-planting machine, which had until that time been thought to pose formidable technical difficulties, came into practical use, and the mechanization of rice growing was completed. As plant strains were improved, their ability to withstand changes in the natural environment increased, while at the same time the use of chemical germicides, pesticides, and herbicides reduced the risks of disease and insect damage and saved weeding time. On the other hand, labor economies became possible through mechanization, which, as it extended to rice planting and harvesting where its development had been late, further reduced the need for large quantities of seasonal labor inputs. Herein lies the reason for still further declines in the agricultural population in the 1970s, in spite of the slackening economic growth rate.

Mechanization and labor savings also proceeded rapidly in other areas of agriculture, as the agricultural productivity increases shown in Table 5.18 testify. A major feature of livestock breeding was the greater efficiency achieved by raising larger herds. In 1962 the number of breeders raising fattened hog herds of one hundred head or more amounted to less than one percent of all hog breeders, but this figure exceeded 2 percent in 1970, and reached 11 percent in 1975. Less than one percent of all dairy cattle raisers had herds of ten head or more in 1960, but their numbers increased to 14 percent in 1970 and 35 percent in 1975. One hardly need add to the list egg-laying hens and broilers with their heated "chicken apartments." In these ways, livestock raising gradually began to assume a form close to that of an industrial production process.

Agriculture's increased ability to get along without massive seasonal inputs of labor as a result of technological progress made possible still further outflows of labor from the farm villages. This in turn heightened the possibility that the agricultural industry would resolve itself into two groups, a small number of full-time farmers who could

Table 5.18. Increases in Agricultural Productivity
(A = yield per unit land area; B = labor time per unit land area; C = labor time per unit of yield)

Units	Rice			Potatoes			Mandarin oranges			Fattened hogs	Milk
	A	B	C	A	B	C	A	B	C	Labor per head of swine	Annual labor per dairy cow
	kg/10a	hours/10a	hours/kg	kg/10a	hours/10a	hours/10a	kg/10a	hours/10a	hours/kg	hours	hours
1950	359	204.5	0.57	1,496	95.1	0.063	2,741	519.7	0.190	—	872.9*
60	443	170.9	0.39	2,249	58.3	0.026	3,239	428.7	0.132	75.3	633.2
70	484	117.9	0.27	3,416	24.6	0.007	2,882	249.3	0.087	1.6	294.6
80	489	68.6	0.12	4,152	18.2	0.004	3,058	189.2	0.062	4.2	—
90	533	57.8	0.08	4,347	15.3	0.003	3,402	209.2	0.061	2.8	—

* 1951 data.
Source: Kayō (see Table 5.17), pp. 429, 435, 471, 479, 483.

secure incomes at or above the level of urban workers by means of
large-scale labor-saving operations, and part-time farmers who primarily relied on income from by-employment while farming on the
side just to keep from giving up their land. As was shown in Table
5.16, part-time farmers in the second category (those for whom half
or more of their income is non-agricultural in origin), constituted
barely 20 percent of the total in 1950, but exceeded 30 percent of all
farm households in 1960, were 50 percent in 1970, rose beyond 60
percent in 1975, and reached 67 percent of marketing farmers in 1992.
Due to technological progress in rice paddy cultivation and the
mechanization of rice harvesting, there was a particularly large
increase in the number of part-time farmers who partially relied on
those engaged in agriculture full-time for the cultivation of their lands
(job contracting) and in the number of those who contracted out the
cultivation of all their land (subcontract farming). According to the
Ministry of Agriculture and Forestry's Agriculture Survey, farmers
who job-contracted part of their agricultural operations for performance by others have amounted to about 40 percent of the total since
1965. The Ministry's figure for those subcontracting all operations is 5
percent. Even though these families live in farm villages, own farm
land, and have agricultural income, they cannot be referred to as
actually engaged in agriculture any longer.

At the opposite extreme is a group of farmers who pursue agriculture full-time, specialize in it, expand their operations using high-
level technology, and attain earnings which compare favorably with
those of the top-performing small businesses, not to mention those of
urban workers. In this group one can find, for example, hog-raising
operations with annual incomes exceeding ¥100 million. The number
of so-called independent farm operators (producing per-capita farm
income equivalent to or exceeding the household member per-capita
income of town- and village-dwelling worker families) is about 12
percent of all farm households, and it is only these that are maintaining stable operations primarily in agriculture. As can be seen
from Table 5.19, the proportion of gross total agricultural output, full-
time farmers, and fixed capital stock supplied by these farmers is
gradually rising. At the same time, the proportion of what had once
been single-crop rice-growing operations or multiple-crop combined
operations has begun to decline, while single-crop vegetable growing,
fruit orchard and cash-crop farming, hog-raising, dairy farming, and
so on has begun to increase. There has been a remarkable shift to
large-scale operations in rice cultivation which has promoted mechanization, has expanded the scale of operations through the renting or

Table 5.19. Indexes on Independent Farm Operators

	Minimum agricultural income per household (¥10,000s)	As a proportion of all farm households (%)				
		No. of households	Value of gross of agricultural industry	Cultivated land area	Full-time farmers	Value of fixed capital in agriculture
1960	48	8.6	23	24	16	19
70	150	6.6	25	18	19	19
80	408	5.2	30	19	21	21
90	496	6.3	39	26	28	28

Sources: Kayō (see Table 5.17), pp. 117, 119. Ministry of Agriculture and Forestry, *Nōrin Suisan Tōkei* [Agriculture Forestry and Fisheries Statistics].

subcontracting of farm land, and has also involved some job contracting. Vegetable raising is achieving successes with intensive cultivation using vinyl-covered structures and greenhouses. In hog raising and dairy farming, too, large-scale operations which have equipped themselves with a number of labor-saving devices have been outstanding. "Selective expansion" in this field is at last producing results. By contrast, fruit growers have produced some surpluses, such as the over-supply of mandarin oranges, as a result of which producers suffer from declining prices. In any event, however, most of these large-scale farmers are increasing productivity, sensitively responding to market trends, and transforming their operations into undertakings worthy of being called business enterprises.

Should we then regard as having missed the bus (in terms of commercial profitability) those farm households which have not become independent businesses but have instead, for all practical purposes, virtually left agriculture? Not necessarily. It would be more accurate to say instead that, after comparing their scale of operations and profitability with non-agricultural employment and income opportunities, many farmers chose to leave agriculture, judging this to be the most advantageous course; they provide rice for their own consumption as well as a little cash income while at the same time preserving the family property. Table 5.20 shows farm households' total income, the proportion of that total obtained from agricultural income, agricultural family budget expenses, and the proportion of farm household budget expenses covered by agricultural income for the years 1950 to 1975. From these data we may observe the following. In 1950, farm households having one hectare or less of arable

Table 5.20. Changes in Farm Household Economics
A = Farm household income (¥ 1000s); B = Family budget expenses
(¥ 1000s)
C = Agricultural income as a proportion of total farm household income
(%)

| | Less than 0.5 ha | | | 0.5–1 ha | | | 1–1.5 ha | | |
	A	B	C	A	B	C	A	B	C
1950	138.5	130.5	40.5	170.7	153.5	66.9	220.4	186.0	78.5
60	372.2	338.4	21.4	368.8	348.2	52.0	436.4	390.4	72.0
70	1,362.8	1,182.5	9.3	1,328.8	1,182.4	29.0	1,409.8	1,251.5	51.6
80	4,605	3,897	3.2	4,512	3,885	13.4	4,380	3,812	29.4
89	6,337	5,289	1.6	6,561	5,301	8.6	6,639	5,173	19.6

| | 1.5–2 ha | | | 2 ha or more | | |
	A	B	C	A	B	C
1950	275.2	219.0	85.6	341.7	256.6	89.0
60	526.6	449.2	79.4	695.5	555.6	87.3
70	1,448.8	1,296.5	65.8	1,665.5	1,416.8	77.4
80	4,381	4,063	42.1	4,634	4,186	61.1
90	6,650	5,216	29.6	7,449	5,430	54.2

Source: Kayō (see Table 5.17), pp. 503, 505, 507, 509, 511;
Ministry of Agriculture statistics.

land were already unable to cover their expenses out of their agricultural income alone; those having 0.5 hectare or less could not meet even half their expenses with such income. The tiny farm households inevitably had no choice but to take on side employment. Thus, in many cases those who were early in seeking such work succeeded in finding positions as steady employees or laborers, whereas those who delayed could find nothing but unstable employment. However, by 1960 farmers with more than one hectare of land but less than two were also finding it difficult to make ends meet on their agricultural income. Accordingly, in this group, too, side jobs become common, and agricultural income constituted less than half of total household income for this group from 1970 on. After the beginning of the 1970s, those who could support a family on agricultural income alone were the farmers owning two hectares or more, who did not even amount to 7 percent of all farm households.

As has been seen, however, such calculations are based on a

compartmentalized perception that views these people exclusively as farmers. This myopia arises from the gap between the rather inflexible categorizations of policymakers and the practical situation of the farmers themselves—a gap similar to that which we have previously noted with respect to the modernization promotion policies for small and medium businesses. That is, agricultural policymakers considered farmers only within the context of agriculture and classified them exclusively as either farmers who stayed in the rural villages or those who left farming; and on the basis of this view they attempted to achieve rationalization and increasingly large-scale operations by accumulating in the hands of those who stayed on the farms land left behind by those who departed for work in the cities. Meanwhile, the farmers themselves, while continuing to live in their farm villages all the while, were engaged in a process of comparing agricultural and non-agricultural opportunities and trying to choose the most advantageous.

These demographic changes were also tied in with the dual structure phenomenon: farmers either leaving agriculture or taking by-employment up through the 1950s were a major factor adding to supply pressure in labor markets. The urban–rural income differential turned farmers toward the cities, creating severe labor surpluses and wage differentials. The outmigrations of labor from the farm villages underlay the wage differentials between small and large businesses. Then, when the labor shortage arrived, urban entrepreneurs had to raise starting salaries and increase wages for workers hired in mid-career in order to attract even farm labor. There were good employment opportunities for the outmigrating farmers, and for those who were left in the farm villages the situation also presented an opportunity to raise agricultural commodity prices, especially that of rice. Thus, the shift to a labor shortage in the midst of rapid growth was, for the farmers as well, a golden opportunity to increase their income levels. This was another aspect of the changes whose cumulative impact steered the dual structure toward disintegration under the altered labor market conditions.

In the sense described above, present-day agriculture is being conducted as economically rational behavior. Of course, it is the continuation of the government's liberal protective policies that makes such rationality possible, and the present form of agriculture will survive as long as those policies do not change. Yet there are numerous and growing problems in the existing situation. Examples are the continued dependence on imports for animal feed, and the continued expansion of livestock production. Another is rice growing, which relies on purchases of the crop by the national government and tends to produce surpluses. The result, agricultural commodity prices in Japan which are on the whole higher than international levels, is also a major problem. Agricultural administration authorities counter by insisting that these policies are necessary both for the sake of the "security" of the food supply and in order to maintain a certain level of agricultural production and prop up the food self-sufficiency ratio, which continues to decline at present (68 percent in 1965, 77 percent in 1975, 74 percent in 1985, and 67 percent in 1990). But should consumers also have to endure (as a cost of preparedness against unforeseen disasters) food prices which are conspicuously high by international standards? Isn't it about time to reconsider the fiction which sees as a homogeneous "agricultural industry" what is really a compound of a professional agricultural industry made up of business firms, and an admixture of part-time farmers primarily engaged in non-agricultural industries? The time is at hand not to preserve all presently existing "farmers," but to separate the question of how efficiently they produce agricultural commodities from the question of commercial returns to farmers otherwise employed. The first step will be for the government to bestir itself to classify marketing farmers separately from self-sufficient farmers and direct its agricultural policy primarily at the former. Such are the new problems facing today's agriculture and the agricultural administration as they move forward in the aftermath of the breakdown of the dual structure.

Notes

1. The effective ratio of openings to applicants is the number of employees sought by firms as registered with the Employment Security Bureau, divided by the number of job-seekers registered. If the value of this ratio is greater than one, the number of positions for which employees are sought exceeds the number of those seeking work, and a manpower shortage is indicated. If the ratio is less than one, it indicates that the number of persons seeking work exceeds the number of employees sought, and there is a manpower surplus.

2. Minami Ryōshin, in *The Turning Point in Japanese Economic Development: Japan's Experience* (Kinokuniya Bookstore Co., Tokyo, 1973) [a translation of *Nihon Keizai no Tenkanten* (Sōbun-sha, 1970)], using an econometric model, gives a detailed analysis of the Japanese economy's transition to a labor shortage.

3. See Umemura Mataji, *Rōdōryoku no Kōzō to Koyō Mondai* [Labor Force Structure and Employment Problems] (Iwanami Shoten, 1971) and Nakamura Takafusa, "Rōdōryoku Kōzō no Henbō" [Changes in the Labor Force Structure], Chapter 7 of *Nihon Keizai no Shinrō* [The Path of the Japanese Economy] (University of Tokyo Press, 1975).

4. Japan's explicit unemployment was quite low even immediately after the war: only 2% in 1946, as we saw in Chapter 2. This phenomenon can be explained as follows. If a man cannot survive without a job, he cannot choose his conditions of employment. He has to work at something; to put the matter another way, he has no freedom to be jobless. Tohata Seiichi called this phenomenon "total employment." Since about 1960 the phenomenon ceased to be applicable to Japan; however, there are many examples of total employment today in other parts of Asia.

5. Arisawa Hiromi's "Nihon ni okeru Koyō Mondai no Kihonteki Kangaekata" [A Basic Conception of the Employment Problem in Japan] (in Japan Productivity Center, ed., *Nihon no Keizai Kōzō to Koyō Mondai* [Japan's Economic Structure and Employment Problems], 1957) was the first work to take up the question of the "dual structure." It was then discussed in the Economic White Paper published in 1957.

6. For a useful contemporary summary of the debate, see Kawaguchi Hiroshi, Shinohara Miyohei, Nagasu Kazuji, Miyazawa Ken'ichi, and Itō Mitsuharu, *Nihon Keizai no Kiso Kōzō* [The Basic Structure of the Japanese Economy] ("Nihon Keizai no Genjō to Kadai" [The State of the Japanese Economy and Issues], Shunjūsha, 1962).

7. Kawaguchi Hiroshi presents a detailed analysis of this point in "Chūshō Kigyō e no Kinyūteki 'Shiwayose' Kikō" [The Mechanism of financial "Burden-shifting" to Small Businesses], in Tachi Ryūichiro and Watanabe Tsunehiko, eds., *Nihon Keizai to Zaisei Kinyū* [The Japanese Economy and Fiscal and Monetary Policy] (Iwanami Shoten, 1965).

8. This question was first taken up by Komiya Ryūtarō, "Dokusen Shihon to Shotoku Saibunpai Seisaku" [Monopoly Capital and Income Redistribution Policy] (*Sekai*, March, 1961).

9. For details on this point, refer to Nakamura Takafusa, *Keizai Seichō no Teichaku* [Economic Growth Takes Root] (University of Tokyo Press, 1970), Chapter 5. Since the period from 1957 to 1965 has already been analyzed in this book, the data shown above are for subsequent years. However, there has been no change in the general trend.

10. Kiyonari Tadao, *Nihon Chūshō Kigyō no Kōzō Hendō* [Structural Changes in Japan's Small Business] (Shin Hyōron, 1970), p. 245 ff.

11. Kiyonari, *ibid.*, p. 259.

12. Sakura Itasu and Nakamura Takafusa, "Sangyō Renkan no Kigyō Kibo-betsu Bunseki" [Analysis of Inter-Industry Relations by Size of Firm] (*Keizai Kenkyū*, October 1960).

13. See for example Kasuya Shinji, "Chūshō Kigyō" [Small Business], in Ouchi Tsutomu, ed., *Gendai Nihon Keizai Ron* [On the Contemporary Japanese Economy] (University of Tokyo Press, 1971), Table 111.

14. Nakamura Hideichirō, *Chūken Kigyō Ron* [A Discussion of the Reliable Mainstay Firms] (Tōyō Keizai Shimpōsha, 1968). The above quotations are from Kiyonari Takao, Nakamura Shūichirō, and Hirao Kōji, *Benchū Bijinesu* [Venture Businesses] (Nihon Keizai Shimbunsha, 1971), pp. 137–38.

15. Kiyonari, Nakamura, and Hirao, *Venture Business*, pp. 138–39.

Part III

Stable Growth and Internationalization

6

The End of Rapid Growth

Japan's position in the global economy changed as a result of increased production and exports during the 1960s. In 1968, Japan's GNP in U.S.-dollar terms ranked third in the world after the United States and the Soviet Union, and had jumped to the number two position if the socialist bloc countries were excluded. Thus, Japan emerged as a GNP "superpower." Around this time the composition of Japan's exports changed to one based on the heavy and chemical industries, with spectacular increases in steel production and ship-building, whose share in the world economy rose dramatically. Symbolic of this was the fact that the short-term deficit of 1967 was Japan's last balance-of-payments deficit, after which the balance of payments showed a stable surplus. From 1965 onward it was no longer necessary for Japan to liquidate international payments deficits by adopting tight-money policies that suppressed domestic demand and dampened business prosperity. The monetary stringency imposed in 1967 was relaxed before it caused an economic slowdown.

This testifies to Japan's growing international competitiveness and to the continued low valuation of the yen at the 360-yen rate set in 1949 (see Table 6.1), which enabled Japan to build up its gold and foreign currency reserves and transform itself from a debtor to a creditor nation from 1967 onward. Japan's position in the international economy underwent a complete change in the latter half of the 1960s, as can be clearly seen from the external assets and liabilities balance sheet shown in Table 6.2.

This transformation naturally stimulated Japan's foreign investments, the gross value of which had been less than $1 billion until 1965. During the five years from 1965 to 1970 their value reached $3.6 billion, and it grew even more explosively through the early 1970s. Forty percent of this investment was in resources, primarily the mining industry; 22 percent was in markets and labor—with a view to

197

Table 6.1. Worldwide (A) and Japanese (B) Production, Trade, and Gold and Foreign Currency Reserves

		Production volumes of key goods						Gold & foreign currency reserves (US$ millions)	Foreign trade (US$ billions)	
		Crude steel (millions of tons)	Nitrogen fertilizer (millions of tons)	Cement (millions of tons)	Ship tonnage (thousands of tons)	Passenger cars (millions)	Electric power (billions of kWh)		Exports	Imports
1938	A	109.7	2.6	85	2,976	3.05	459	27,700	21,100	23,700
	B	6.5	0.256	5.9	442	0.002	32.7	289	1,109	1,070
	B/A	5.9%	9.9	6.9	14.9	0.06	7.1	1.04	5.26	4.51
1955	A	269.3	6.7	217	5,317	11.01	1,545	52,400	84,300	89,200
	B	9.41	0.633	10.6	829	0.020	65.2	768	2,011	2,471
	B/A	3.5	9.5	4.9	15.6	0.18	4.2	1.47	2.39	2.77
1960	A	346.6	9.9	317	8,356	12.81	2,304	56,900	113,000	119,400
	B	22.14	0.922	22.5	1,732	0.165	115.5	1,824	4,055	4,491
	B/A	6.4	9.3	7.1	20.7	1.29	5.0	3.21	3.59	3.76
1965	A	459	19.2	433	12,230	19.1	3,379	70,520	165,830	175,970
	B	41.17	1.615	32.5	5,363	0.696	188.4	2,107	8,452	8,169
	B/A	9.0	8.4	7.5	43.9	3.6	5.6	2.99	5.10	4.64
1970	A	581	30.2	569	21,690	22.7	4,923	92,806	282,180	296,600
	B	91.9	2.13	57.2	10,476	3.18	359.5	4,399	19,318	18,881
	B/A	15.8	7.1	10.05	48.3	14.00	7.30	4.74	6.85	6.36
1975	A	643	43.9	690	35,668	25.2	6,439	227,579	795,703	815,741
	B	102.3	1.56	65.5	17,740	4.57	475.8	12,815	55,753	57,863
	B/A	15.9	3.5	9.5	49.7	18.1	7.4	5.63	7.01	7.09

			Semi-conductors ($ millions)	Televisions (millions)					($ billions)	($ billions)
1980	A	712.0	10,857	65.1	13,572	31.4	7,999.0	445,348	1,642.8	1,689.1
	B	111.7	3,674	13.6	7,308	6.2	589.6	25,232	129.8	140.5
	B/A	15.7	33.8	20.8	53.8	19.7	7.4	5.7	7.9	8.3
1990	A	676.0	50,854	120.2	14,680	35.3	10,879	820,210	3,019.4	3,152.0
	B	107.9	25,942	13.3	6,531	9.1	799.8	85,072	274.6	186.5
	B/A	16.0	51.0	11.1	44.5	25.7	7.4	10.4	9.1	5.9

Source: Bank of Japan, *Nihon o Chūshin to suru Kokusai Hikaku Tōkei* [International Comparative Statistics Focusing on Japan], 1971, 1977.

Table 6.2. External Asset and Liability Balance
(A) 1962–70 (Long-term assets)   ($ millions)

	1962	1963	1964	1965	1966	1967	1968	1969	1970
Long-term assets	1,478	1,760	2,041	2,503	3,209	4,082	5,181	6,689	8,745
Long-term liabilities	2,428	3,243	3,898	3,932	3,825	3,880	4,538	5,891	6,326
New assets	−950	−1,483	−1,857	−1,429	−616	202	643	798	2,419

(B) 1971–75 (Gold assets)

	1971	1972	1973	1974	1975
Assets	32,753	43,595	47,551	55,942	58,334
Liabilities	22,980	29,728	34,535	46,999	51,316
New assets	9,773	13,867	13,016	8,943	7,018

Source: Figures from 1971 on are Ministry of Finance estimates. Prior data are estimates by a private institu-
tion (Nihon Keizai Shimbun).

making inroads into local labor forces and markets in such fields as
textiles, electrical equipment and metals; and 38 percent was in commerce and finance (data for 1970).[1] By region, 25 percent of investment was in North America, 22 percent in Southeast Asia, 18 percent
in Europe, 16 percent in Central and South America, and 9 percent in
the Middle East. Investment in Southeast Asia, where Japanese
advances aroused severe criticism, represented little more than a fifth
of Japan's total overseas investments. However, the direct investments of all the developed nations (through the Development Assistance Committee) in the developing countries of Asia came to more
than $1.23 billion between 1956 and 1970, of which Japan accounted
for 63 percent, or $780 million. And this level of investment did pro-
voke anti-Japanese sentiment, particularly when coupled with the
behavioral style of Japanese corporations, which tended to stimulate
nationalism by ignoring local customs and lifestyles. "Modern Japanese Imperialism" became a theme in foreign journalism, while the
Japanese persisted in their unconcern.[2]

Misunderstandings between Japan and the rest of the world over
Japan's international position and its economic power began to arise
during the latter half of the 1960s. U.S.–Japan relations started to
cool first as a result of entanglements over the U.S.–Japan textile
negotiations and the negotiations for the return of Okinawa in 1969,
then due to Nixon's New Economic Program of August 1971 and the
problems that arose over the revaluation of the yen. In the eyes of

Europe and America, Japan was already a highly competitive industrial nation; without a yen revaluation, the United States would be
hard-pressed to meet its balance of payments obligations, while many
European industries (for example shipbuilding and automobiles) felt
their markets would be stolen away. There was a gradually widening
gap between the Japanese perception of the Japanese economy as
backward and underdeveloped and the much more positive way it
was viewed by the international community.

Japanese economists were by no means oblivious to this kind of
criticism, but they also took pride in the fact that it was through the
efforts of the Japanese people themselves that the nation had risen
from the ashes of defeat, rebuilt a modern industrial base, developed
products that were internationally competitive, and opened up sales
channels to world markets. They felt it was natural that Japan should
come out on top of other nations that had not tried so hard, and that
there were no grounds for complaint over the outcome of what was
only fair competition. The Japanese also felt they were at a competitive disadvantage not only in farm products like rice, livestock
products, sugar and fruit, but also in fields like airplanes and computers. The official view in government and business circles was that
Japan had only just managed to catch up and overtake the West in
mass-consumption industrial products and must now redouble its
efforts to develop the high-technology industries where it still lagged
far behind. It was thought that the 360-yen exchange rate was a
standard that had to be maintained if Japanese industry was to go on
expanding and to catch up in the fields that remained. This view was
all well and good so long as Japan was catching up and overtaking,
but the international community would no longer accept its validity
once Japan had risen to the status of a "great power."

1. Monetary Restraint and the "Plan for Rebuilding the Japanese Archipelago"

The generation that brought about Japan's rapid growth was born
during the period from the 1910s to the early 1930s. Economic growth
was a shared goal for this generation, which held in common the
experience of the war and had seared in their memories the wartime
and postwar privations. It was the cumulative efforts of the "intense
salarymen" of this time, who threw all their energy into their work
and had neither hobbies nor amusements, that made Japan an
economic superpower. As members of labor unions they may have
demanded wage increases and shorter working hours, and many
voted for reformist parties in general elections. Yet it is self-evident

that the unions were company unions whose fates were intertwined with those of their firms, and the advent of progressive administrations did not breach union-company solidarity.

However, as this generation was displaced, little by little the national consciousness began to change. One reason is that a generation with no memory of the years during and right after the war began taking an active part in society. The storms which raged on university campuses in Tokyo as they did in Paris and New York at the end of the 1960s were the postwar generation's expression of opposition against their wartime and war-era elders. In contrast to the previous generation, which strove for growth because of its poverty, the new generation had grown up amidst growth and never known poverty. Sick and tired of a society whose only goal was economic growth, they rebelled in search of a change in values. It was only natural that growth would no longer be the supreme value for those who were already enjoying its fruits. They perceived the re-humanization of an affluent society and escape from an over-organized, oppressive way of life as more appealing goals.

The changes in the lifetime employment and seniority wage systems that accompanied the labor shortage under rapid growth gave added impetus to these trends. Through the end of the 1950s, changing one's place of employment almost always meant accepting a drop in wages and other working conditions. With the labor shortage of the 1960s, however, young workers in their twenties began changing jobs in search of better working conditions and more personally satisfying employment. The slope of the seniority wage system's salary increase curve began to gradually flatten because of the high rates of wage increases for younger workers. Not surprisingly, the charms of the lifetime employment system also gradually faded, at least for the younger generation.

The industrial pollution generated during rapid growth at length attained the status of a major social problem in the 1960s. It was only after rapid economic growth had afforded people some security in their lives, however, that serious attention began to be focused on its attendant ills. At the beginning of the 1960s many local governments attempted to entice firms into their areas by granting them special privileges including tax exemptions and land for industrial development. But in the latter half of the decade they began to direct their efforts toward preserving nature and the living environment, rather than industrializing. Industrial complexes such as those at Sakai, Mizushima, and Fukuyama had been completed in rapid succession along the Pacific coast, the last of such installations being at Kashima,

Ibaraki Prefecture. But subsequent plans for complexes at Mutsu-Ogawara, Tomakomai, and Shibushi Bay were never brought to completion.

The nationwide spread of a negative reaction to economic growth which continued into the 1970s might have suggested that the end of rapid growth was approaching. However, the industries and individual firms which directly sustained growth continued as before to make large-scale expansion investments, for the double purpose of increasing production capacity and economizing on the use of labor. Their equity capital alone was inadequate to supply the funds for these investments, so they borrowed still more money, which continued to further decrease the equity capital proportion of their gross capital employed. The overwhelming majority of firms during this period were dominated by the bullish attitude that, even with the burden of interest payments and depreciation, profits could be produced just as anticipated if plant and equipment were expanded by reliance on borrowed funds and if the completed facilities were operated at full capacity. These expectations had always been fulfilled throughout the 1960s. Even when businesses were confronted with pollution problems and difficulties in securing industrial sites, there was no shift away from this fundamental optimism.

For the outlying regions, left behind in the rush for growth, rapid economic growth had charms that were difficult to gainsay. It was not due merely to chance or political payoffs (though these did play a role) that Tanaka Kakuei was chosen as Prime Minister in 1972 on the basis of his slogan "Rebuilding the Japanese Archipelago," which might be called a second edition of Ikeda Hayato's Income-doubling Plan. Assuming that a 10-percent annual rate of growth could be continued through the year 1985, Tanaka's plan envisaged the elimination of regional inequities by relocating industry, concentrated in the Pacific coast belt, to the interior and the Japan Sea side of the country, and linking together the entire nation by constructing 9,000 kilometers of Shinkansen (bullet train) rail lines, 10,000 kilometers of superhighway, and 7,500 kilometers of oil pipeline. At that time no more than 700 kilometers of Shinkansen and superhighways combined had been opened to traffic, and this scheme was the blueprint for Tanaka's dream of distributing the benefits of growth throughout the country. The idea of building modern cities with populations of 250,000 across the nation, thus decentralizing the functions of the major conurbations, also swelled the hopes of people in provincial areas. In the event, the ensuing Rebuild-the-Archipelago boom only served to raise land prices nationwide, and soon evaporated under the onslaught of strict price stabilization policies and the oil crisis that struck the following year. Nevertheless, the episode illustrates the continued strength of people's aspirations for economic growth.

The maintenance of the 360-yen to the dollar exchange rate was seen as a prerequisite for continued economic growth. People's attitudes at the time were not sufficiently detached to enable them to listen to criticism from abroad. There was a gap between the Japanese perception of the economy and the way it was viewed overseas, and this gap was growing wider all the time. But it was the monetary restraint of September 1969 which was directly responsible for making the Japanese posture a policy issue and giving rise to a major international problem. In September 1969 the Bank of Japan raised the official discount rate from an annual 5.84 percent to 6.25 percent. In conjunction with this, it raised the reserve deposit ratio and, moreover, by means of window guidance, directly limited the supply of funds in the market. The problem, however, lies in the reasons why a tight-money policy was considered necessary at this point in time.

In the summer of 1969 Japan's exports were continuing to improve and the balance of payments was sustaining a large surplus. Since output of mining and manufacturing increased by 3–4 percent in quarterly data, it was maintaining growth at an annual rate of over 10 percent. What was responsible for the idea that a tight-money policy had become necessary was anxiety over wholesale prices, which had shown signs of a rapid increase from the beginning of that year. Underlying this phenomenon was a large-scale increase in import prices, an effect of the worldwide inflation that occurred during the Vietnam War. Wholesale prices rose steadily at an annual rate of 4 percent in the U.S. and England, and at 9 percent in France during this period, but price rises in international commodities markets began to be more pronounced. The monetary authorities judged that domestic demand had to be restrained and international price increases prevented from impacting on the domestic economy in order to head off inflation.

From the latter half of 1969 through the beginning of 1970 international prices rose inexorably, and import prices climbed in step. Prolonged far beyond what had been anticipated, the tight-money policy was finally lifted in the summer of 1970, by which time international prices had stabilized and domestic demand had been more or less completely curbed by funds shortages. By that time, however, domestic business conditions had already slumped, and it was no easy matter to turn around plant and equipment investment in the direction of a recovery. The mining and manufacturing production growth rate wound up registering negative values from April to June of 1971.

In the past, tight-money policies had been implemented with the intention of restraining domestic demand when it grew too vigorous, leading to expanded import demand and balance of payments deficits. This time, however, conditions were different. Despite the fact there was a balance of payments surplus, the authorities tightened credit and undertook to restrain domestic demand with the aim of preventing domestic wholesale price increases, mainly generated by soaring international prices, from causing a general inflation. But all monetary restraint can hope to achieve in cases such as this, when import prices are rising, is to blunt the impact of import price rises on domestic prices in general. And it can be expected to have the side-effect of contracting domestic demand and cooling the economy. If the growth in domestic demand stalls, pressure to export increases while imports stagnate, and the international payments surplus grows even larger. The correct and effective policy that should have been adopted at that time was the revaluation of the yen exchange rate by about 5–8 percent, but discussion of a change in the 360-yen rate was then taboo in Japan's government offices and economic circles.

In fact, Japanese wholesale prices at last began to stabilize after international prices slipped in the second quarter of 1970. Meanwhile domestic demand was quiet, exports increased a notch from the latter half of 1970 while imports were nearly flat, and the balance of payments surplus further expanded. Moreover, domestic demand fell autonomously after tight money controls were relaxed. Such results suggest that the tight-money policies were not very effective in attaining their original goals, and that their achievements were outweighed by the side-effects they produced.

2. The End of Rapid Growth

U.S. President Richard Nixon's announcement of the New Economic Program in August 1971 was aimed at restraining inflation, which was gradually becoming more serious, and, additionally, at checking the sudden increase in the U.S. balance of payments deficits, which had begun growing at an alarming rate at the beginning of that year. Along with measures such as ending the dollar's convertibility to gold, freezing wages and prices, and reducing taxes to induce demand, an import surcharge was also announced at that time, with the clearly expressed object of checking exports from Japan. These moves signified a call for the other major trading nations to adjust their exchange rates. The Western European nations all responded by shifting to the floating exchange rate system. But since Japan continued to maintain the ¥360 exchange rate for about 10 days thereafter, a glut of dollar sales occurred in anticipation of a rise in the yen rate, and Japan's foreign exchange reserves increased by $4.6 billion to reach a total of $12.5 billion in the space of the single month of August. In the face of these conditions, the government and the Bank of Japan gave up their efforts to maintain the ¥360 rate and switched to the floating exchange rate system. Afterwards, the yen continued to rise until a new ¥308/U.S.$1 rate was established under the Smithsonian agreement in December of that year. In taking this step, Japan bade farewell to the ¥360 rate which had been maintained for 22 years, since April 1949.

During that time, Japan's international competitiveness had strengthened dramatically. As Table 6.3 indicates, export prices had dropped continuously from 1951 to 1965; by contrast, West European prices for this period had been fairly steady, and in America they had tended to rise. During all this time, the ¥360 rate had been left undisturbed. Japan's unit export prices rose in the latter half of the 1960s, but for the two decades of the 1950s and 1960s taken as a whole, its export price competitiveness improved remarkably. At the beginning of the 1970s, unit prices in other countries showed large-

Table 6.3. International Comparison of Unit Value of Exports

(1963-100)

	Japan	U.S.A.	Western Europe	Advanced industrial countries	Developing countries	Free world
1951	134	93	101	100	128	108
55	103	95	95	96	111	100
60	107	99	97	98	103	100
65	98	104	104	103	103	103
67	100	110	105	105	103	105
70	111	114	112	114	109	112
71	110	121	130	130	126	128
75	165	201	223	219	233	240
77	162	218	243	237	404	260

Unit values for Japan converted to U.S. dollars become 129 for 1972, 201 for 1975, and 219 for 1977, giving an 85-point increase since 1951.

Source: Calculated from Bank of Japan, *Nihon Keizai o Chūshin to Suru Kokusai Hikaku Tōkei* [International Comparative Statistics Focusing on Japan], 1969, 1975, and 1979.

scale increases while in Japan alone they declined very slightly. The monetary restraint of 1969–70 caused exports to expand still more. Hence ¥308/U.S.$1 can be seen as the appropriate exchange rate, corresponding to Japan's effective international competitiveness. However, most people in Japan at the time took the pessimistic view that, since exports had only been enabled to expand by virtue of the ¥360 rate, they would be crippled by the ¥308 rate. Hence the Japanese economy was assailed by the panic dubbed the "Nixon shocks."

The domestic economy was at the bottom of a recession at that time, and the government was already expanding fiscal expenditures while the Bank of Japan was boldly increasing the money supply in order to restore prosperity. Policy authorities reasoned that if there were no hope of achieving a recovery through exports, they would have to make up for it by stimulating domestic demand. As illustrated by Fig. 6.1, from the latter half of 1970 to the first half of 1971, moves were made to stem the recession by rapidly easing monetary conditions (lowering interest rates and increasing the money supply) and increasing the level of public investment through fiscal spending. Fearing that the economy would take a further turn for the worse, the government adopted even stronger business stimulation measures and made efforts to promote domestic demand. But the panic was partly psychological. There was no particular decline in contract closings for exports either before or after the exchange rate was fixed at ¥308 in December of 1971. Rather, there was even a flurry of efforts to move up contract dates in the fall of 1971 before the yen increased in value.

However, the revaluation did not altogether fail to influence exports. The rates of increase over the previous year in customs-cleared exports valued in dollars for 1970, 1971, and 1972 hovered around 20 percent, but valued in yen the rate of increased plunged to 4.3 percent in 1972, reflecting the influence of the higher exchange rate. Despite the increased value of the yen, the yen-based export price index actually fell to a level of −2.9 percent in 1972. The effect of the revaluation was not as destructive as had been anticipated, though it did give rise to a shortfall in export earnings. However, the expansive monetary and fiscal policies aimed at counteracting its influence were carried to excess, and set the stage for inflation.

The reasons for this may be found first of all in business firms' remarkably high liquidity, which enabled them to buy up land in anticipation of higher prices, and to pile up intentional inventories. As Fig. 6.2 shows, corporate liquidity (ratio of cash and deposits on

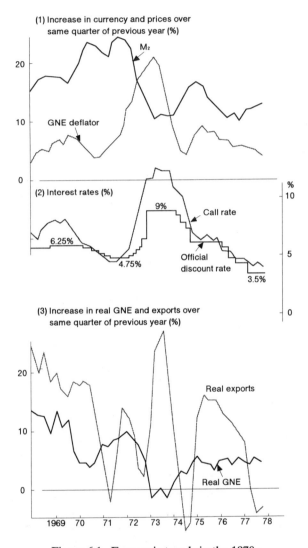

Figure 6.1. Economic trends in the 1970s

hand to turnover) started to increase at the beginning of 1971, and continued to rise at an extraordinary rate after the "Nixon shocks," maintaining a level of 12 percent from 1972 to the beginning of 1973. These idle funds were used primarily to purchase land for specula-

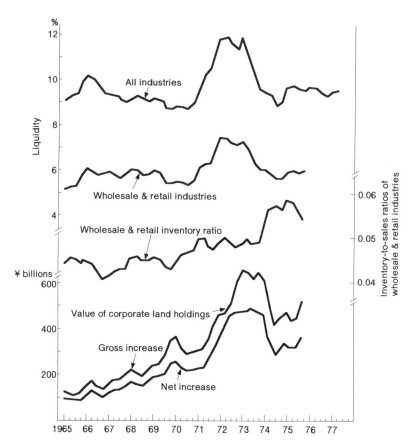

Figure 6.2. Corporate liquidity, inventories, and land holdings
Source: Calculated from Ministry of Finance, *Hōjin Kigyo Chōsa* [Survey of Corporations]. Values shown are three-period moving averages.

tion, but also to build up inventories. Land was being bought up not only in areas within commuting distance of the big cities, but throughout the country. This trend, stimulated by the Tanaka "Plan for Rebuilding the Archipelago," continued throughout 1973, and land prices rose steeply. The nationwide land price index for urban property (surveyed annually in March; March 1955 = 100) sky-rocketed by more than 50 percent in the period from 1972 to 1974 (see also Table 3.12 in Chapter 3). As we will see, this kind of land speculation was repeated on an even greater scale during the late 1980s.

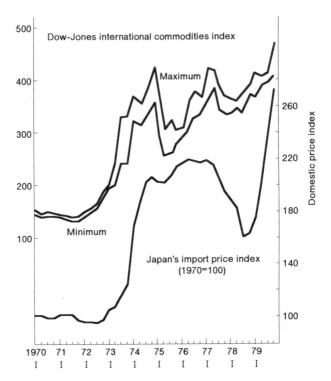

Figure 6.3. Domestic and international prices, 1970s
Source: Bank of Japan data.

The rise in land prices was followed in swift succession by rises in general commodity prices. The process was spurred by the sudden jump in international prices which began in 1972, as shown in Fig. 6.3. This reflected the fact that, due to worldwide growth, the supply and demand balance of primary products, which had been in excess supply throughout the 1960s, had switched to a condition of excess demand. OPEC (the Organization of Petroleum Exporting Countries) had concluded a contract with the major international oil companies in 1970 providing for crude oil price increases of about 50 percent in stages over a five-year period. Moreover, under the terms of the Riyadh Agreement, OPEC had acquired capital participation rights in the major oil producing firms and direct selling rights to oil they themselves produced. The background to these events was that crude oil had been in excess supply through the 1960s and had only just regained supply–demand equilibrium. Then, occasioned by the

Soviet Union's massive grain purchases on the American market due to the 1972 grain crop failure in the socialist bloc, international price increases for primary commodities rapidly became manifest. The situation prompted Japanese trading companies and wholesalers, who had spare funds on hand, to increase inventory ratios in hopes of higher prices.

Until halfway through 1972, Japan's export prices followed a downward trend, showing the effects of the upward yen revaluation. After that time, though, price increases for imported goods became apparent, and wholesale prices also began to rise. In February 1973 the United States prohibited soybean exports to Japan because of soaring domestic grain prices. This led to fears of bean curd (*tofu*), miso paste, and soy sauce shortages, and the price of *tofu* in particular shot up. In the same month, Japan shifted once more to a floating exchange rate system, and the yen was revalued upward by more than 10 percent, but the rise in domestic prices could not be restrained. Due to apprehension over price increases and shortages of raw materials, supplies of hides, lumber, textiles, metals, and petroleum products were hastily bought up, and Japan's balance of payments surplus turned into a large deficit. With growing alarm over rising prices, there was a striking trend toward panic buying in 1973, extending right down to the general consumer. The wholesale price index for September 1973 was up 18 percent over the same quarter of the previous year, the worst figure since the 1950s. A vicious cycle began where the increase in real demand spurred anticipatory demand, which invited price rises, leading to still more panic buying.

The policy-making authorities did not simply stand by while all this was going on. Tight-money measures were imposed from March 1973, and fiscal expenditures postponed from May onward. As shown by Fig. 6.1 and Table 6.4, the fiscal and monetary authorities began adopting measures to restrain inflation in early 1973, and started really coming to grips with the problem in April of that year. The fiscal 1973 budget which the Tanaka Cabinet first drew up was larger by 24.6 percent than the budget for the previous fiscal year, with a 32.2 percent increase in public investments. Hence there was some foot-dragging over the adoption of an all-out tight-money policy until the budget actually passed the Diet at the beginning of April 1973, and the opportunity to curb inflation was lost.

The more austere subsequent monetary restraint was stringent. Window guidance in particular was substantially tightened, and in July strict regulations were imposed not only on the city banks but also on regional banks, long-term credit banks, mutual savings and

Table 6.4. The Restrictive Monetary and Fiscal Policies of 1973

	Fiscal policies	Discount rate	Deposit reserves ratio	Window guidance
1973 Jan.–Mar.		4.5%	Raised twice, on Jan. 16 and March 16.	Lending restricted to increases of 12.7% over same period previous year. Further restricted thereafter.
Apr.–Jun.	Decision to defer execution of public works projects (April 12). Policy further extended June 29.	5.25% (April 5) 5.75% (June 2)	Raised for third time May 30.	Lending to be reduced by 16% relative to same period previous year.
Jul.–Sept.	8% of public works spending & public investment finance deferred to the following fiscal year (over ¥ 1 trillion including local government finance). (August 31)	6.25% (July 5) 7.25% (Sept. 1)	Raised for fourth time August 28.	Lending to be reduced by 24% relative to same period previous year; later revised to 40%.
Oct.–Dec.				Lending to be reduced by 41% relative to same period previous year.
Jan.–Mar.		9.25% (Jan. 4)	Raised for fifth time Jan. 4.	Lending restricted to 34.6% of level in same period previous year.

Source: Fiscal policies, discount rates, and reserve ratios from Economic White Paper, 1974. Data on window guidance compiled from *Nihon Keizai Shimbun* [Japan Economic Journal].

loan companies, and even foreign banks. Until September 1973, however, despite the tightening of financial conditions, firms still had large surpluses, and the severe effects of international inflation made themselves felt in Japan as well.

3. The Oil Crisis

The decisive factor which pushed the high rate of international inflation to a critical stage was the oil crisis accompanying the Middle East
War of October 1973. When the long-standing Arab–Israeli dispute
broke into open conflict for the fourth time, the Arab oil-producing
states set in motion their oil strategy. First they suspended shipments
to countries that did not support their position, and then they
announced an almost fourfold increase in the price of crude oil. This
step obviously had a tremendous impact on Japan, which was
dependent on crude oil for three quarters of its primary energy supply and lacked domestic energy resources. At a time when domestic
inflation was running rampant, the massive hike in the crude oil price
led to price increases on a range of other goods, not only petroleum
and oil-based products but many other commodities as well. With
supply and demand conditions for many goods already tight, the
shock of the oil crisis sparked panic buying and opportunistic price
hikes. For example, in October 1973 a rumor to the effect that it was
no longer possible to buy toilet paper began circulating in the Osaka
area and was carried by a newspaper at the end of that month. This
triggered a wave of panic buying, and one person was seriously
injured in a supermarket stampede. The government took emergency
measures and ordered an urgent release of inventories, but there
were large subsequent increases in the price of toilet paper, and consumers went on trying to obtain the commodity regardless of price.
Suppliers, meanwhile, mindful of cost increases for raw materials and
labor, withheld goods from the market in anticipation of higher
prices. Hence the supply–demand gap grew wider and wider, and
prices climbed steeply, out of all proportion to production costs.[3]
Such seems to have been the case for many other items, not only for
consumer goods but for producer goods as well. This was Japan's
bout with the "crazed prices" (*kyōran bukka*) inflation.

The government was forced to switch policies and channel all its
efforts into restraining inflation. Existing tight-money policies were
strengthened further. At the behest of Fukuda Takeo the newly
appointed Finance Minister, the Tanaka Cabinet temporarily—and,
in the event, permanently—abandoned its plan for "rebuilding the
archipelago" and devoted all its energy to bringing inflation under
control.

Table 6.5 shows the severity of the monetary restraint at this time,
which centered on lending by private financial institutions. Lending
by the city banks, which was the principal target of window guidance,
had already stopped increasing by the second quarter of 1973, and in

Table 6.5. Fluctuations in the Supply of Industrial Funds

(¥ millions)

	Total supply of industrial capital	Total lending by private financial institutions	Lending by city banks
1972			
Jan.–Mar. QI	31,234	25,824	11,702
Apr.–June QII	33,635	29,111	11,683
Jul.–Sep. QIII	57,932	50,494	19,831
Oct.–Dec. QIV	77,752	68,562	23,144
1973			
Jan.–Mar. QI	45,250	35,379	14,865
Apr.–June QII	48,422	38,800	11,759
Jul.–Sep. QIII	60,458	51,996	13,759
Oct.–Dec. QIV	63,519	54,137	13,677
1974			
Jan.–Mar. QI	33,056	25,891	8,855
Apr.–June QII	34,464	26,606	8,061
Jul.–Sep. QIII	42,608	34,978	9,582
Oct.–Dec. QIV	56,460	45,984	13,546

Source: Bank of Japan, *Keizai Tōkei Nenpō* [Economic Statistics Annual] The "supply of industrial funds" here refers to financial institutions' end-of-period loans and other debt issues outstanding, and the increases or decrease in each period.

the third quarter of that year lending actually declined over the same quarter of the previous year. The table shows how, from October to December 1973, when window guidance was extended to other financial institutions as well, the entire supply of industrial funds was tightly restricted. Figure 6.1 also illustrates the abnormal situation that obtained between the end of 1973 and early 1975, when the growth rate of M_2 was substantially lower than that of the GNE deflator. Thus, in terms of both its severity and its duration, this period of monetary restraint far surpassed anything that had been seen previously. Former periods of restraint did not cause any decline in lending by financial institutions over the same period of the previous year, but at most blunted the growth in lending, and they had never been sustained for more than a year. The credit restraint of 1973 lasted a full two years, and it was far more stringent. This was due to the strong determination of the government and the Bank of Japan, which were willing to make any sacrifice for the sake of containing the abnormal inflation. It is clear from the international comparison

Table 6.6. International Comparison of Price Increases Relative to Previous Year

(%)

	Japan		U.S.A		England		West Germany		France	
	W	C	W	C	W	C	W	C	W	C
1970	3.7	7.7	3.6	5.9	7.1	6.4	4.9	3.4	7.3	5.9
71	0.8	6.1	3.2	4.3	8.9	9.4	4.3	5.3	3.7	5.3
72	0.8	4.5	4.6	3.3	5.3	7.1	2.6	5.5	5.9	6.1
73	15.8	11.7	13.1	6.2	33.1	9.1	6.6	6.9	12.7	7.3
74	31.4	24.5	18.9	11.0	22.6	16.0	13.4	7.0	23.7	13.7
75	3.0	11.8	9.4	9.0	23.0	24.0	4.6	5.9	-5.7	11.8
76	5.0	9.3	4.6	5.8	16.2	16.6	3.6	4.4	5.8	9.7
77	1.9	8.1	6.2	6.5	18.2	15.8	2.8	3.6	7.0	9.3
78	-2.6	3.8	7.7	7.6	9.9	8.3	1.1	2.7	4.3	9.1
79	7.3	3.6	12.5	11.2	10.9	13.5	4.7	4.2	13.4	10.8
80	17.8	8.0	14.2	13.5	14.0	17.9	7.6	5.4	14.8	13.5
81	1.4	4.9	9.1	10.4	9.5	11.9	7.8	6.3	11.7	13.4
82	1.8	2.7	2.0	6.1	7.8	8.6	5.8	5.3	11.4	11.8
83	-2.2	1.9	1.3	3.2	5.4	4.6	1.5	3.3	8.8	9.6
84	-0.31	2.2	2.4	4.3	6.2	5.0	2.9	2.4	8.9	7.4
85	-1.14	2.1	-0.5	3.5	5.5	6.1	2.2	2.2	4.5	5.8

W: Wholesale Price Index.
C: Consumer Price Index.
Source: Statistics Department, Bank of Japan, Nihon Keizai o Chūshin to Suru Koku-sai Hikaku Tōkei [International Comparative Statistics Focusing on Japan].

of price increases shown in Table 6.6 that these policies succeeded in achieving their intended goal of curbing inflation. Although from 1973 to 1974 Japan's inflation was second only to that of England in severity, it rapidly subsided thereafter. It contrasts conspicuously with the inflation that persisted through the 1970s in countries like America and France. Here, inflation became a fact of economic life and developed into so-called stagflation, which led to stalled production and rising unemployment. The same was true of the period following the second "oil shock" at the beginning of the 1980s. Japan's success in curbing inflation cannot, of course, be wholly ascribed to monetary and fiscal policy. As will be discussed below, significant contributions were also made by the unions' self-imposed restraint on wage increases and firms' efforts to rationalize.

However, the unsparing anti-inflationary policies were of course accompanied by great sacrifices. The business indexes from 1971–79

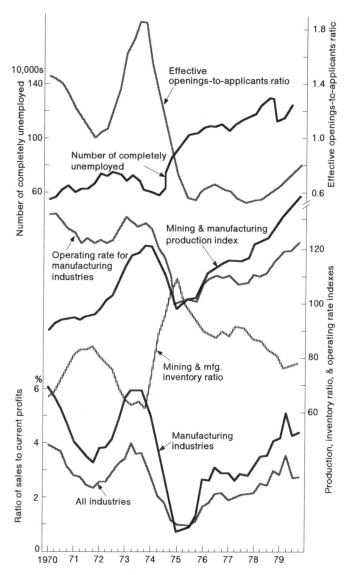

Figure 6.4. Trends in the domestic economy, 1970–79 (quarterly data, seasonally adjusted)

Sources: Unemployment figures from Statistics Bureau, Office of the Prime Minister, *Rōdōryoku Chōsa* [Labor Force Survey]. Effective openings-to-applicants ratios from Ministry of Labour, *Shokugyō Antei Tōkei* [Employment Security Statistics]. Mining and manufacturing output, inventory ratios, and manufacturing industries operating rate indexes from Ministry of International Trade and Industry (1975 = 100). Sales to current profit ratios from Ministry of Finance, *Hōjin Kigyō Tōkei Nenpō* [Corporate Statistics Annual].

shown in Fig. 6.4 clearly point up this fact. First, during the severe inflation of 1973–74, firms' operating profits fell drastically. The reasons for this were declining demand and rising costs. The tight fiscal and monetary policies combined with a decline in real demand (consumption volume) due to inflation to produce a sudden drop in demand growth.

Moreover, as costs rose due to large wage increases and soaring raw materials and fuel prices, businesses were no longer able to cover their outlays by increasing the prices of their products, so margins declined. In addition, they were heavily burdened with interest repayments on funds borrowed during the period of growth, and with the costs of depreciation on plant and equipment. Furthermore, mining and manufacturing production declined by 19 percent from the last quarter of 1973 through the first quarter of 1975. This was the most severe production decline in postwar Japan. The most acute production declines occurred in chemical and heavy industries such as metal products, cement, and non-ferrous metals, and in the lumber and pulp and paper industries.

Since exports were comparatively buoyant for the shipbuilding and steel industries, the trough for these industries was relatively shallow, although they suffered a tremendous blow during the later slump. In the textile industry, there was a frenzied boom until the middle of 1973 due to soaring prices and consumer efforts to buy up available goods on the market. But as 1974 began, prices quickly dropped as reaction set in, demand declined, and the industry fell into a pronounced recession.

Only a few of the strongly export-competitive industries, like the automobile industry, and those producing everyday necessities, like the food industry, escaped major declines in production. The index of firms' finished goods inventory ratios—the index of the ratio of finished goods in stock to goods shipped—shows an extraordinary increase, reflecting sudden unintended additions to inventories. For this reason as well, businesses' plant and equipment operating ratios fell by about 25 percent in 1975 as compared with the beginning of 1973. If we assume that roughly 90 percent of the actual capacity of plant and equipment was in operation at the beginning of 1973, this means that about one third of productive plant and equipment was standing idle in 1975. This was a major factor depressing business profits, and at the same time it ultimately stifled firms' desire to invest in plant and equipment.

An unemployment problem rapidly surfaced along with the recession. Figure 6.4 shows that in 1974 there was a steep rise in the number of completely unemployed and, most importantly, a sudden drop in the ratio of effective job offers to effective job openings[4] at public labor exchanges. Part-time workers, principally housewives, also found themselves instantly without jobs, in far greater numbers than suggested by the increase in the number of totally employed as shown in the figure. Most of these people did not remain in the labor market to be counted as "completely unemployed" but stayed at home and dropped out of the labor force altogether.

In addition, since nearly all Japanese firms in principle abide by the lifetime employment system, they cannot simply launch into personnel reductions when the economy is in recession. Instead, there is a tacit understanding between firms and the labor unions that in times of recession the firm will not specify individual employees to be fired. This is the reason labor–management relations have always been good in Japan. And therefore, as explained below, employment restructuring became an increasingly serious issue in the late 1970s and early 1980s.

The policies to curb inflation that were begun in 1973 had serious effects on the Japanese economy. They signalled a complete end to the rapid growth that had continued for over twenty years, since the 1950s. As we have seen, the rapid growth of the economy had previously been supported from the inside by the bullish management attitudes of firms anticipating growth. Large-scale plant and equipment investments stimulated the domestic economy, providing the capacity for growth, which in turn raised productive capacity, strengthening international competitiveness and creating the possibility for still further growth. But domestic demand declined extensively. Business firms which, more than anything else, were bulging with idle plant and equipment, had already abandoned their former bullishness and lost their appetites for plant and equipment investment. For reasons of public finance which will be taken up below, policies to stimulate the economy became difficult to implement. With some difficulty consumption and exports became the mainstays of growth. Thus, in the short run the Japanese economy suffered a recession, but for the medium term these events ushered in a new era in which the economy broke out of the high-growth mold.

4. Disengaging from Growth

The United States was hit by a second currency crisis in February 1973, which led Washington to demand that all nations abandon the fixed exchange rate system and shift together to a managed float. Japan acceded to the demands from America and Europe, moved to a floating exchange rate system, and had to accept an upward revaluation of the yen by some 17–20 percent against the U.S. dollar. The float was expected to be a relatively long-term measure rather than a temporary palliative, and it has in fact continued unchanged ever since. The postwar IMF regime, conceived as an attempt to preserve as far as possible the features of the prewar gold standard system, was deprived of its essential role by President Nixon's new economic policies in 1971, but the floating exchange rate fundamentally altered its character.

Theoretically, the floating exchange rate system was expected to function as follows. When a country's international competitiveness improved (weakened) and the balance of payments went into surplus (deficit), an increase (decrease) in the exchange rate would suppress (expand) exports and expand (restrain) imports. Thus, so the theory goes, exchange rates under the float should arbitrate international payments imbalances and restore equilibrium. In the long run these expectations would probably be fulfilled. In the short run, however, due to such factors as the *J*-curve effect (discussed below), international capital movements, and policy interventions by the currency authorities, exchange rates have not always responded Immediately to balance-of-payments fluctuations, and have had a strong impact on the domestic economy as well.

Figure 6.5 shows trends in Japan's and the world's foreign trade and exchange rates from the 1970s to the first half of the 1980s. By the end of the 1970s world import prices had reached 3.5 times their 1970 level, but trade volume increased by little more than half this amount, reflecting international inflation and a worldwide slowdown in economic activity. The advanced industrialized nations and the non-oil-producing developing nations sustained large trade deficits from the mid-1970s through the early 1980s. The oil-exporting nations naturally maintained trade surpluses throughout this period. Oil money from Saudi Arabia and the other oil producers greatly influenced the movements of the international money markets. Only West Germany and Japan were able to adapt to these changes with any rapidity.

The yen, having risen against the dollar from ¥308 to ¥265 in 1973, began to decline again following the oil crisis, and hovered at just above the ¥300 level from 1974 to 1976. From 1975, however, Japan's exports began to climb steeply again. This increase was led by machinery and appliances such as automobiles and color television sets, and was an early demonstration of the success of rationalization measures implemented after the recession of 1974, about which more will be said later. In ten years Japan's exports increased 3.2 times,

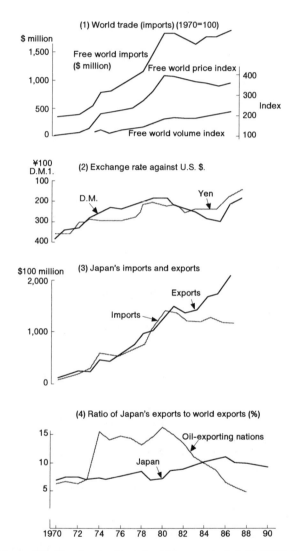

Figure 6.5. Foreign trade and exchange rate trends, 1970–90

from $55.7 billion in 1975 to $175.6 billion in 1985. World trade increased by approximately the same factor during this period, but the increase was due mostly to the expansion of crude oil and raw materials exports, and the ratio of Japan's exports to the exports of the industrialized nations as a whole increased dramatically.

Japan was able to eliminate the trade deficit that had accompanied the oil crisis by 1976, and both Japan and Germany then proceeded to gradually expand their trade surpluses. This led to increasing criticism of the two nations, and the economist Lawrence Klein proposed that Japan and West Germany raise their domestic economic growth rates and increase the level of their imports so as to join America as loco-motives of world economic growth in providing the stimulus for a world economic recovery. America demanded the revaluation of the Deutschmark against the dollar, and Treasury Secretary Michael Blumenthal announced that an upward revaluation of the yen would also be desirable.

Here it is worth looking more closely at the reasons why dollar-based exports declined so little even under an appreciated yen. First, we can point to the fact that the rate of increase in Japanese and German dollar-based export prices was actually lower than that of America, Britain, and France since, during this period, prices in these countries had continued to rise under stagflation (see Table 6.6). Second, we have to take into account the so-called J-curve effect. When the exchange rate increases, exports denominated in foreign currency increase for some time thereafter, since ex-ports are subject to pre-existing contracts and ongoing trends, so there is a certain time-lag before contracts are closed under the new exchange rate and exports actually decrease. In the same way, when the exchange rate decreases, exports denominated in foreign cur-rency decline for a time and only begin to expand after a delay.

Since exports do not suddenly decline once the exchange rate begins to rise, but continue to increase for a time, the exchange rate rises beyond the desirable equilibrium level (assuming that such a level can be determined) and later subsides again. In the reverse sit-uation, when the exchange rate begins to fall, exports do not expand rapidly and only show a clear increase once the exchange rate has dropped below the equilibrium level and then recovered. According to the 1979 White Paper on the Economy, after any single increase in the yen exchange rate the J-curve effect acts to increase the dollar-based value of exports for a period of six to seven months, after which the value of exports declines. However, when the exchange rate rises continuously, as it did in Japan from 1976 to 1978, exports just go on increasing and the decline may not appear for more than twelve months, as successive exchange rate increases spur additional increases in exports, which blot out the decreases due to earlier increases in the exchange rate.

5. "Operation Scale-Down"

During the period of rapid growth from the 1950s through the 1960s business firms consistently pursued bullish management policies. In many fields of industry, competition for market share was extremely fierce; in order to keep up with the competition, firms invested in plant and equipment and expanded production without hesitating to go further into debt. They made increasingly bold investments in equipment, operated it at full stretch, and forged ahead in the conviction that the increased turnover would enable them to cover interest repayments and depreciation without sacrificing profits. As firms continued to use borrowed funds to purchase plant and equipment, their levels of indebtedness inevitably increased while their self-owned capital ratios declined. During the period of rapid economic growth these aggressive policies rarely worked against them, and management attitudes became increasingly bullish.

As a result, the health of Japanese firms deteriorated throughout the era of rapid growth. This can be seen from Table 6.7. As the data in the table show, the self-owned capital ratio fell to 14 percent in the 1970s. The ratio had also been tending to decline in other countries, but a 1976 comparison of major firms shows that, in contrast to ratios of 52 percent in the United States, 42 percent in England, and 29 percent in West Germany, the proportion was 21 percent in Japan.[5] Since this phenomenon was primarily a result of increased plant and equipment investment on borrowed funds, the fixed assets ratio of course increased, as did the rate of depreciation. For these reasons, finance costs (interest payments, discount charges) and depreciation costs as a proportion of sales inevitably rose. Thus, once the economy went into recession, since fixed costs like interest payments and depreciation stayed the same while business profits declined, the rate of recurring profits—the rate of business profits minus fixed costs—plunged even further. It was in 1974–75 that these conditions manifested and that, as we have seen, the rate of recurring profits reached its nadir.

Following the oil crisis, firms set about improving their financial health with "operation scale-down" (*genryō keiei*). Broadly speaking, they scaled down in three different ways. First, they curtailed numbers of employees and reduced labor costs. Second, they cut their financial costs by paring down the interest burden. And third, they made efforts to rationalize by cutting down on all other costs.

Let us first consider personnel cuts and the reduction in labor costs. From the fall of 1973, when the oil crisis reduced energy supplies and industry was forced to scale down or stop production, until 1974,

Table 6.7. Firms' Financial Ratios

(%)

	1970	1973	1976	1979	1982	1985	1988	1990
All industry								
Self-owned capital ratio	16.1	14.4	13.7	14.3	16.0	18.3	18.3	19.1
Fixed assets ratio	226.9	234.4	258.7	241.7	234.2	223.8	218.0	216.6
Ratio of interest								
expenses to sales	2.5	2.5	2.8	2.1	2.3	2.2	1.9	2.4
Ratio of interest								
expenses to added								
value	15.2	14.3	16.9	12.5	14.4	13.1	10.8	14.0
Ratio of interest on								
borrowings		8.3	9.1	7.2	8.0	7.0	5.2	6.6
Ratio of operating								
profits to sales	4.7	5.2	3.2	3.6	2.8	2.8	3.4	3.5
Ratio of current profits								
to sales	4.8	4.1	2.8	5.9	4.6	4.3	4.7	3.5
Manufacturing industry								
Self-owned capital ratio	19.9	21.1	17.0	19.3	22.6	25.7	29.1	30.6
Fixed assets ratio	195.3	199.8	214.4	180.0	159.5	146.5	132.4	131.9
Ratio of interest								
expenses to sales	1.7	3.1	3.7	2.5	2.7	2.2	1.7	2.1
Ratio of interest								
expenses to added								
value		12.7	16.8	11.3	12.3	10.5	7.3	9.4
Ratio of interest on								
borrowings		8.4	9.4	7.7	8.4	7.2	5.1	6.7
Ratio of operating								
profits to sales	7.3	8.0	4.5	5.7	4.2	3.9	4.9	4.8
Ratio of current profits								
to sale	5.9	7.1	3.2	8.1	5.6	5.4	6.2	5.2

Source: Ministry of Finance, *Hōjin Kigyō Tōkei Nenpō* [Corporate Statistics Annual].

firms first of all dismissed their temporary female workers and their part-time workers, who were mainly housewives. However, any further personnel reductions after this first round were difficult to implement without coming into conflict with the principle of lifetime employment. To maintain their traditionally good labor-management relations, firms had to avoid large, sweeping cutbacks in their work forces. They rarely went so far as to designate specific workers for dismissal, which has been particularly taboo in Japan. Every imaginable device to reduce employment within the constraints of these values was used, from leaving the positions of retiring employees unfilled to personnel reshuffles, transfers to other companies, and calls for voluntary resignation. But it took several years to achieve personnel reduction targets by these methods alone. Table 6.8 shows changes in numbers of employees by industry and size of firm.

The number of employees at large firms employing more than 500 people in industry as a whole shrank by more than 330,000 between 1973 and 1979, but the number employed by manufacturing firms of more than 500 employees fell by over 800,000 during the same period. Of this number, 440,000 were men and 360,000 women. The total number employed in industries other than manufacturing, especially commerce and the service sector, increased during this period, and there was no decline in the number employed by the largest non-manufacturing firms. It was first and foremost the large-scale manufacturing firms that were compelled to downsize.

Cutting back requires firms to economize as much as possible on labor-related expenses. Thus, firms switched from male to female employees and took on more low-wage part-time workers such as housewives. According to the Ministry of Labor's Survey of Labor Trends, the number of part-time workers in the labor force has risen dramatically: from 700,000 in 1975 to 1.46 million in 1980, 2.3 million in 1985 and 4.67 million in 1991. Whereas part-timers comprised 2.9 percent of the labor force in 1975, this rose to 5.8 percent in 1980, 8.6 percent in 1985, and 12.6 percent in 1991. In manufacturing, part-timers accounted for 2.7 percent of the work force in 1975, 5.3 percent in 1980, 8.5 percent in 1985, and 10.4 percent in 1991, while in the trade sector the figures were still higher at 5.6 percent, 11.3 percent, 14.6 percent, and 25.5 percent, respectively. One indication of firms' success in cutting labor-related costs was the fact that they gained the cooperation of the company labor unions and managed to hold down annual wage increases to a level only slightly in excess of the rate of increase in the consumer price index. Spring offensive wage hikes dropped from 33 percent in 1974 to 13 percent in 1975, and thence to 8.8 percent for the following two years. By the end of the 1970s the level of wage increases was down to around 6 percent, and after rising to 7 percent in 1980 due to the second oil crisis, it settled at around 4 percent in the mid-1980s when the growth in labor-related costs stabilized. It can be said that industrial firms had succeeded in their effort to scale down employment and trim their total wage costs.

Second, let us turn to the problem of economizing on finance costs. The burden of such costs is of course determined both by the scale of borrowing (including corporate bonds, etc.) and by interest rate lev-

Table 6.8 Numbers of Employees in Non-Primary Industries by Size of Firm (Female employees in parentheses)

(10,000 persons)

		Total employed	1–29	30–99	100–199	over 500	civi
All industry	1973	3,562 (1,172)	1,164 (437)	536 (183)	506 (165)	921 (256)	426 (127)
	76	3,682 (1,195)	1,237 (457)	572 (198)	513 (162)	902 (239)	451 (137)
	79	3,846 (1,300)	1,329 (509)	596 (213)	545 (183)	888 (236)	483 (157)
	82	4,068 (1,408)	1,390 (552)	628 (232)	589 (201)	961 (262)	492 (159)
	85	4,285 (1,539)	1,426 (590)	673 (257)	654 (233)	1,017 (288)	503 (168)
	88	4,507 (1,660)	1,508 (623)	715 (281)	708 (261)	1,065 (323)	499 (167)
	91	4,972 (1,907)	1,635 (703)	793 (317)	815 (312)	1,200 (391)	514 (179)
Manufacturing industries	1973	1,200 (403)	324 (127)	211 (82)	234 (84)	430 (109)	1 (0)
	76	1,133 (370)	316 (126)	216 (86)	216 (73)	383 (85)	1 (0)
	79	1,107 (373)	325 (134)	215 (89)	215 (76)	350 (73)	2 (0)
	82	1,151 (392)	324 (136)	220 (94)	226 (83)	378 (78)	1 (1)
	85	1,235 (435)	335 (147)	238 (103)	253 (96)	407 (88)	1 (0)
	88	1,245 (440)	337 (148)	244 (108)	259 (99)	403 (85)	1 (0)
	91	1,357 (489)	355 (160)	251 (116)	288 (110)	451 (103)	1 (0)
Commerce, finance, insurance, real estate and service industries	1973	1,434 (640)	583 (279)	201 (82)	183 (70)	264 (119)	199 (88)
	76	1,595 (695)	635 (297)	229 (94)	208 (79)	291 (125)	229 (100)
	79	1,729 (789)	687 (334)	255 (107)	239 (96)	312 (136)	233 (115)
	82	1,906 (875)	746 (371)	277 (119)	268 (105)	367 (155)	246 (119)
	85	2,051 (962)	778 (400)	304 (135)	305 (126)	403 (174)	257 (127)
	88	2,240 (1,071)	828 (425)	335 (154)	349 (139)	464 (213)	257 (128)
	91	2,518 (1,235)	905 (479)	381 (178)	415 (185)	55 (259)	262 (133)

Source: Statistics Bureau, Prime Minister's office, *Rōdōryoku Chōsa Hōkoku* [Survey of the Labor Force].

els. As was shown in Table 6.7, firms' financial ratios underwent a major change beginning in the second half of the 1970s. There are unmistakable trends toward an improvement of the self-owned capital ratio, a decline in the asset ratio, a fall in the interest ratio after monetary restraint policies were implemented at the time of the second oil crisis, and a decline in the ratio of interest rates to sales and value added. Firms with a heavy burden of interest repayments cut back on equipment investment, clamped down tightly on increases in new borrowing, redeemed old bonds, and then succeeded in reducing the interest burden by taking advantage of lower interest rates to refinance their borrowing. They had managed to shrug off old patterns of financial behavior appropriate to a period of rapid growth, and learn new ones that were better adapted to a time of slow growth. As we will see below, this was to bring about a change in the mechanisms of Japanese finance, which had always been centered on corporate finance.

Third, let us consider some examples of various other cutback strategies. Inventory reductions are a case in point. As a result of their bitter experience with abnormal inventory increases in 1975, firms had taken great pains to resist increasing their inventories even when good business conditions were anticipated. As was shown in Fig. 3.2, the ratio of private inventory increases to GNP dropped markedly from the late 1970s to remain at a level below 1 percent. Developments in inventory management techniques made such economies possible. Signs of similar efforts can also be seen in the suppression of plant and equipment investment. Due to production cuts in 1975, firms were suffering from a decline in operating rates. Thereafter, with the exception of unavoidable items such as pollution prevention and improvements in efficiency, they curtailed plant and equipment investment as much as possible and, rather than expanding production capacity, went on trying to increase their operating ratios.[6] Construction of major industrial complexes came to a halt after the first oil crisis, and petrochemical and shipbuilding plant and equipment started to be dismantled instead. As we will see below, this reflects a change in the industrial structure towards the more specialized electronics and machinery industries and towards the tertiary sector.

In every field, firms contrived ways to reduce costs and economize on raw materials. For example, the adoption of such technologies as the NSP kiln in the cement industry and the continuous casting method in the steel industry sharply increased fuel efficiency. In one old tire factory that used piped-in steam power, fuel costs were cut nearly in half by mobilizing idle workers to wrap insulation material around the pipes. In television set production, substantial reductions in numbers of assembly workers were achieved through the use of integrated circuits, while large gains in the efficiency of machine parts production were achieved through the adoption of the NC lathe and of robots for engineering.

The combination of the government response and the various efforts of firms such as those outlined above achieved some measure of success for Operation Scale-Down. An indication of this is the fact that profit rates made a clear-cut recovery from the end of 1978 and into 1979. In this respect, Operation Scale-Down, over a period of five years or so, may be said to have borne fruit. Nevertheless, the measures adopted had a great impact on every aspect of society. Let us now summarize the effects of those measures.

6. Worsening Employment Conditions, Improved Productivity, and Energy-Saving

The most important consequence of Operation Scale-Down was the deterioration in employment conditions that it produced. Table 6.8 shows there was a contraction in the number of employees in the manufacturing industries, particularly in large firms, and a marked levelling off in the number of male employees. Looking at the number employed in all non-primary industries including manufacturing, we see that here, too, the rate of increase in the number of male employees was 6.5 percent as against 10.9 percent for females, during the six years from 1973 to 1979. And although high rates of increase are indicated at establishments employing 1–29 employees, with 12.8 percent for males and 16.5 percent for female workers, establishments with 30 or more employees show a growth rate of a mere 3.8 percent for male employees and 7.6 percent for females. Since wages and other working conditions at small places of business are inferior to those at larger establishments, the concentration of the employment increase in small establishments in itself attests to a deterioration in employees' working conditions. During this period the number of employees in the wholesale and retail trades increased at practically the same rate for both men and women, while in the service industries the growth rate was higher for women. Overall there is a conspicuous increase in the number of low-wage female part-timers and students in the work force, reflecting a thorough rationalization of the employment side of operations.

As shown by Fig. 6.6, the unemployment rate, which is the denominator of the number of people employed, rose continuously from

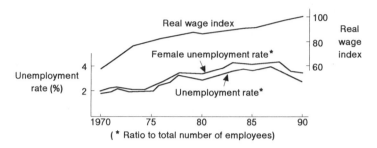

Figure 6.6. Real wage index and unemployment rate

1975 to the second half of the 1980s. Although it is not shown in the figure, the effective ratio of job openings to applicants, which indicates the supply and demand balance of labor at employment security offices, indicates that labor was in a state of continuous over-supply from 1975 through 1987. The biggest problem in this area was the increase in the number of older people unemployed. From the 1960s the government had encouraged people to retire later. This meant that, while mandatory retirement at age 55 was adopted by close to 60 percent of all firms in 1970, the figure had dropped to 27 percent by 1985, and more than 50 percent of firms had extended their retirement age to 60. But although they qualified for retirement pensions, a large number of old people still sought employment, and in the 1980s, when the ratio of job openings to applicants as a whole was quite favorable, it was as low as 0.1 to 0.2 for the over-55 age-group. Older people tend to expect high salaries and so are highly selective about applying for jobs; nevertheless firms are still very reluctant to employ them. The situation is likely to prove increasingly problematic as the Japanese population continues to age.

Next, we should consider rationalization—the result of productivity increases—as a positive aspect of Operation Scale-Down. During the rapid growth period, Japan's rate of increase in labor productivity was extremely high, particularly between 1955 and 1970, when the overall rate for manufacturing industries recorded an annual 10.1 percent, and 1970–73 when it averaged 11.7 percent (Japan Productivity Center, labor productivity statistics). Principally responsible for these gains were the technological innovations which were a concomitant of the vigorous plant and equipment investment up to this time. We can say that increased productivity was the end result of enlarging plants to achieve economies of scale, installing the latest

Table 6.9   Average Annual Growth Rate of Labor Productivity Index by
            Industry

	1955–70	70–75	75–80	80–85	85–91
All industry	10.1	5.4	8.3	4.4	6.4
Public works	11.4	5.5	4.8	5.1	5.1
Manufacturing	10.1	5.5	8.6	4.0	5.3
Steel	12.4	6.5	7.7	2.7	5.9
Non-steel metals	10.9	5.4	9.5	1.5	5.5
Metal products	10.3	4.0	7.9	1.2	3.9
Machinery	14.2	6.6	11.2	7.6	7.1
Ceramics	8.3	4.0	8.6	2.5	7.1
Chemicals	11.8	4.8	9.6	5.3	7.1
Pulp, paper, paper products	9.4	5.9	9.0	4.8	6.8
Fibers	7.8	4.9	5.8	2.9	2.0
Lumber & wood products	3.1	−0.4	3.4	0.1	0.9
Foodstuffs, cigarettes	2.2	5.0	1.0	−0.5	0.9

Source: Japan Productivity Center, *Rōdōseisansei Shisū* [Labor Productivity Statistics].

technology, and automating. Table 6.9, which summarizes these trends, indicates that productivity increased at a particularly high rate in the machinery and chemical industries, on which industrial expansion centered in the late 1970s and early 1980s.

7. Changes in the Industrial Structure

The oil crisis came as a tremendous shock to the Japanese economy, which had developed primarily on the basis of the chemical and heavy industries. The expansion of industry had centered mainly on the steel and petrochemical industries, which consumed enormous amounts of energy, and the principal source of that energy was imported crude oil. The low price of crude oil during the 1960s was the foundation on which the heavy and chemical industries were built, and it made possible the growth of the high-volume energy-consumption industrial materials industries like steel, aluminum refining, and petrochemicals. Most of these plants were located on the seacoast, where they had their own harbor facilities for the off-loading of raw materials and the on-loading of finished products.

After the oil crisis, however, the prices of both crude oil and the other primary commodities rose, and while this did not completely destroy the chemical and heavy industries, it greatly impaired their profitability. This can be seen plainly from Table 6.10, which shows the extraordinary relative increases in the prices of raw materials and fuel during this period.

Table 6.10. Import Price Index (Special classification)

(1973 = 100)

	Overall average	Foodstuffs and animal feed	Row materials and fuel	Light industrial products	Heavy industrial products
1968	81.7	64.3	82.6	69.7	98.4
76	189.9	150.0	230.6	112.0	132.8
78	150.1	112.9	178.3	109.6	112.6
82	303.7	138.0	430.9	130.8	164.0
85	265.3	122.6	363.6	124.7	157.7

Source: Bank of Japan, *Oroshiuri Bukka Tōkei* [Wholesale Price Statistics].

A closer look at Table 6.10 shows that import price indexes rise steeply after the first oil crisis, fall back slightly due to the appreciation of the yen in 1978, and then rise sharply again to peak at the time of the second oil crisis in 1982. Furthermore, the two principal sources of demand for these industries, plant and equipment investment and construction investment, stagnated. Under the cumulative impact of these conditions, economic growth stressing the chemical and heavy industries had to turn a corner. The machines industry and tertiary industries, primarily wholesaling-retailing and the services, played an important role in this process. Table 6.11 shows changes in the GDP by industry from 1970 to 1990, with 1973 as the base year, while Table 6.12, also based on 1973, shows changes in manufacturing output indexes. The tables show clearly that growth in output in the secondary industries was slow up to 1985, with a particularly sharp decline in 1975, and many industries had difficulty recovering thereafter.

After the oil crisis those sectors of the manufacturing industry that had previously registered growth in output went into decline due to the leap in imported raw materials prices and the effects of the worldwide recession. Not only the textile industry, which was already stagnating in the period of rapid growth, but prestigious sectors like steel, non-ferrous metals, and shipbuilding, which had been the flagships of industry during the period of growth, now went into a long-term depression. This led the Trade and Industry, Transport, and Labor Ministries in May 1978 to draw up countermeasures for "structurally depressed industries" (*kōzō fukyō gyōshu*), directed at the hardest-hit industries and regions. Basically the government designated structurally depressed industries by passing the Emergency

Table 6.11. Indexes of Real Gross Domestic Product (Factor price indicators)

(1973 = 100)

	1970	1975	1980	1985	1990
Gross domestic product	81.1	100.8	127.9	154.6	197.3
Agriculture, forestry & fisheries	86.8	97.5	87.6	97.9	100.5
Mining	87.0	81.9	111.4	90.4	90.3
Manufacturing	76.4	95.5	130.5	172.8	228.5
Light industry	81.1	98.9	116.7	132.6	149.9
Industrial materials	71.4	93.9	119.3	146.3	170.9
Machinery	74.7	92.4	159.1	250.6	386.1
Construction	81.9	102.9	108.7	104.8	145.3
Electricity, gas & water	85.5	110.4	132.2	166.6	214.3
Wholesale & retail	74.7	102.2	157.0	176.7	228.1
Finance & insurance	58.7	100.6	139.2	198.2	295.7
Real estate	75.5	106.2	139.6	136.9	202.9
Transportation & communication	89.3	107.6	115.8	143.7	175.5
Services	90.8	102.5	127.1	163.1	195.1
Public Sector	88.8	110.9	134.9	149.7	153.3
Primary industries	86.8	97.5	87.6	97.9	100.5
Secondary industries	78.1	97.3	123.6	151.3	201.5
Tertiary industries	80.9	104.7	135.5	165.2	205.4

Light industry includes food products, textiles, pulp and paper, and others. Industrial materials industries include steel, non-ferrous metals, chemicals, and petroleum and coal products. Machinery industries consist of general machinery, electrical equipment, transportation equipment, precision instruments, and metal products.

Source: Calculated from Economic Planning agency, *Kokumin Keizai Keisan Tōkei Nenpō, Heisei 4-nen Ban* [National Accounts Statistical Annual], 1992, and *Chōki Sokyū Shuyō Keiretsu Kokumin Keizai Keisan Hōkoku* [Long-term Retroactive National Accounts for Major Business Groupings], 1955–1989.

Measures to Stabilize Designated Depressed Industries Act, which made provisions for the cooperative scrapping of excess plant and equipment, government cooperation in drafting plans for the disposal of equipment, and the establishment of a joint fund for the purpose. The government then enacted an Emergency Measures for the Unemployed in Designated Depressed Industries Act, an Emergency Measures for the Unemployed in Designated Depressed Regions Act, and an Emergency Countermeasures for Small Businesses in Designated Depressed Regions Act. The Emergency Measures to Stabilize Designated Depressed Industries Act designated thirteen "structurally depressed industries": open-hearth and electric furnaces, aluminium refining, long nylon fibers, short acrylic fibers, long and short polyester fibers, urea and ammonia, phosphoric acid, cotton

Table 6.12. Movements in Manufacturing Output Indexes

(1973–100)

	1970	1975	1980	1985	1990
Total	78.6	85.4	118.2	140.1	168.9
Steel	79.3	84.2	105.3	106.3	113.5
Non-ferrous metals	73.0	77.8	109.4	110.1	136.2
Metal products	72.7	75.0	102.1	99.3	115.7
Machinery, average	74.7	85.1	141.6	207.0	268.3
General machinery	81.7	77.8	122.8	151.1	186.3
Electrical machinery	71.4	82.0	166.3	340.1	485.4
Transport machinery	70.9	96.7	125.7	136.8	160.3
Transport except shipping and railways	72.9	96.8	163.5	180.5	218.2
Precision machinery	81.8	101.9	278.3	387.6	471.3
Ceramics	79.8	79.1	104.7	100.6	115.5
Chemicals	78.8	90.7	129.4	157.2	202.4
Petroleum & coal products	74.9	93.8	95.0	80.1	83.0
Plastic products	70.1	73.9	102.7	118.6	140.7
Pulp, paper, paper products	82.3	83.8	112.4	125.5	161.5
Textiles	88.8	84.4	91.5	89.3	83.0
Food products & tobacco	90.8	100.9	114.4	116.4	120.6
Other manufacturing	76.0	81.1	110.2	109.2	152.6

Source: Calculated from Ministry of International Trade and Industry, *Kōkōgyō Seisan Shisū Nenpō* [Yearbook of Mining and Manufacturing Output Indexes].

spinning, wool spinning, ferrosilicon, cardboard, and shipbuilding. These industries formed cartels to dispose of plant and equipment cooperatively. By 1981 the four synthetic fiber industries had disposed of production plant capacity corresponding to 18 percent of annual production, the urea and ammonia industry 34 percent, and the shipbuilding industry 37 percent (3.58 million tons). More than 100,000 workers were laid off as these industries scaled down production. Measures were introduced to extend the period those laid off could claim unemployment benefit, allowances were made available while they retrained in new skills, and a placement scheme lined up new positions for them in public corporations. Small businesses in structurally depressed regions were afforded low-interest loans and certain tax advantages. In April 1983, after the second oil crisis, the Emergency Measures to Stabilize Designated Depressed Industries Act was converted into the Emergency Measures for the Restructuring of Designated Industries Act, which provided for business tie-ups and investment in modernization as well as the disposal of plant and equipment. Fiscal investment and loan programs were expanded and depressed industries were given subsidies and preferential tax treatment.

One exception to the general stagnation of manufacturing was the machinery sector, which experienced impressive growth during this period. Since the industry had a high rate of value added and a low level of dependency on raw material imports, there was still considerable scope for technical improvement, and despite the fact that it contained depressed industries like shipbuilding within it, it made rapid progress. Output of the so-called mechatronics products in particular—which combined machine tools and electronics products such as micro computers—grew dramatically as their domestic diffusion rate increased and exports boomed. Computerized engineering machinery, VCRs, Japanese-language word-processors, low-priced, high-performance personal computers and the new microelectronics products like semiconductors that served as their components, were all initially developed with the export market in mind. A look at labor productivity growth rates in manufacturing bears out the performance of the machinery industry: average productivity for manufacturing as a whole increased 4.7 percent annually between 1973 and 1980, and 5.6 percent from 1980 to 1990, but electrical machinery registered 9.5 and 9.6 percent while labor productivity in precision machinery grew at 15.2 and 9.0 percent.

The tertiary industries, in the meantime, were seizing new opportunities for growth as the domestic lifestyle underwent rapid changes, and the field of services to businesses expanded. Lifestyle changes have been linked to the inter-regional equalization of incomes which is one of the prominent features of the post-oil-crisis Japanese economy (see Table 6.13).

Despite the depression of the secondary industries, rural incomes continued their stable growth, as guaranteed by government policy. Patterns of consumption became homogeneous throughout the country, so much so that the diffusion rate for automobiles came to be higher in rural areas than in the cities. Western styles of living centered on beds and sofas gained general acceptance in the rural districts, and new markets were created for the retail and service industries. The range of new services to businesses expanded to include computer software development, industrial waste disposal, and guarding and cleaning city buildings. And as the custom of dining out became more prevalent in both urban and rural areas, attention focused on the chain-store restaurants, which spawned a whole new "dining-out industry" (*gaishoku sangyō*). In the distribution sector, large supermarket chains sprang up rapidly from the latter half of the

STABLE GROWTH AND INTERNATIONALIZATION

Table 6.13. Equalization of Per-capita Income among Prefectures

	Average per-capita income (χ) ¥1000s	Standard deviation (σ) ¥1000s	Coefficient of variation (χ/σ) (%)
1965	230.7	41.2	17.86
70	482.7	77.5	16.40
75	1016.1	144.6	14.23
80	1545.8	227.5	14.72
85	1981.0	296.9	14.99
90	2478.9	407.2	16.43

Source: Calculated from Economic Planning Agency, *Kenmin Shotoku Tōkei* [Statistics on Citizens' Incomes].

1960s. In this way the tertiary industries enjoyed both an overall expansion and, additionally, growth in areas where there had been little activity before. The basis for these changes was the fact that Japanese styles of living and doing business were moving rapidly toward the Western pattern, particularly that of the United States.

Notes

1. Sekiguchi Sueo and Matsuba Koshi, *Nihon no Chokusetsu Toshi* [Japan's Overseas Direct Investments] (Nihon Keizai Shimbunsha, 1974), Appendix.

2. Jon Halliday and Gavin McCormack, *Japanese Imperialism Today: Co-Prosperity in Greater East Asia* (Monthly Review Press, New York, 1973).

3. Tsujimura Kotaro, "Shijo Kyoso Riron no Saiko—Jukyu Baransu to Kyoso Atsuryoku" (A Reconsideration of Market Competition—The Supply-and-Demand Balance and the Pressure of Competition), and Tsuzuki Sachiko, "Sutagufureshon-ki ni okeru Toiretto Pepa Shijo no Bunseki" (An Analysis of the Toilet Paper Market under Stagflation), in Keio University, *Keio Economic Observer*, No. 1 (1975).

4. The ratio of effective job offers to effective job openings is calculated by dividing the number of job openings registered by firms at public labor exchanges by the number of registered job-seekers. Thus values higher than 1 indicate that there are more job offers than job seekers, i.e., a labor shortage, whereas values lower than 1 indicate the reverse, i.e., a labor excess.

5. Ministry of International Trade and Industry, "Sekai no Kigyo no Keiei Bunseki" (Business Analysis of World Business Firms). Since the group of firms surveyed in this study differs from that from which the figures in Table 6.7 were drawn, the data are not consistent.)

6. However, the equipment investment function which was valid during the period of rapid growth did not entirely cease to apply. The model intro-

duced in Chapter 3 is valid for this period as well. (Data are for 1985 prices, and figures in parentheses are for values of t.)

$$1970-90 \qquad I_p = -5957.4 + \frac{0.12558}{(19.4)} K_p + \frac{3531.9}{(3.35)} \pi_c \qquad R^2 = 0.97432$$

The fact that the K_p coefficient in particular, although reduced, indicates a true value probably means that the pattern of equipment investment behavior continued unchanged even though the level of investment declined.

7

In the New International Environment

The Japanese economy was visited by a second oil crisis in 1979, as the yen sharply appreciated in value and an economic policy promoting domestic demand was just beginning to take effect. Since the autumn of 1973 there had been a mounting ferment of revolt in Iran against the rule of the Shah, whose moves to modernize the nation were thought to go against the teachings of the Koran, and the Shiite Islamic regime of the Ayatollah Khomeini was established in 1979. The years of political upheaval severely reduced Iran's output of crude oil, and the revolution was followed by the outbreak of the Iran-Iraq War in 1980.

1. The Second Oil Crisis

From January 1974, when it became clear that Iranian oil production had collapsed, OPEC had embarked on a new round of crude oil price-hikes. The initial plan was to raise prices by a total of 14.5 percent during 1979, but the outbreak of war and other factors led to even larger increases. By October 1981 the crude oil price had in fact rise by almost 300 percent, from $12.70 a barrel to $34 a barrel, in a little less than three years. At the time of the first oil crisis, although prices increased more than fourfold in a single year, the total increase was only $9.10, from $2.60 to $11.70 a barrel. This time, however, they rose by $20 over a period of 20 months and $22.70 over a period of 34 months.

At this time, growth in Japan's plant and equipment investment had slowed due to the post-rapid growth policies of monetary restraint. To survive in this new business environment, as we have seen, firms had to make efforts to scale down their operations, and at the same time there was a shift in the industrial structure as new products were developed and automobiles and electric and precision machinery became the new core industries. Meanwhile exports had

Table 7.1. Growth Rates and Contribution Ratios of Different Elements of GNE

		GNE	Domestic Private Demand	Domestic Government Demand	Exports	Imports	Exports-Imports
5-year growth	1970–75	24.3	21.2	34.4	59.7	39.7	—
rate (%)	75–80	25.2	21.8	22.2	59.5	25.8	—
	80–85	20.6	17.7	4.0	47.5	6.9	—
	85–90	25.5	34.1	14.3	39.5	84.8	—
Contribution	1970–76	24.3	18.3	6.2	4.8	Δ5.0	Δ0.2
ratio (%)	75–81	25.2	18.4	4.3	6.2	Δ3.6	2.6
	80–86	20.6	14.5	0.8	6.3	Δ1.0	5.3
	85–90	25.8	27.3	2.4	6.4	Δ10.6	Δ4.2

If real GNE is y, and the different elements are B, C, D and E, and the composition ratios for the first year of each period are expressed as

$$b = \frac{B}{y}, c = \frac{C}{y}, d = \frac{D}{y}, e = \frac{E}{y},$$

then making Δ the amount of increase over the period, the contribution ratio can be defined as follows:

$$\frac{\Delta y}{y} = b\frac{\Delta B}{B} + c\frac{\Delta C}{C} + d\frac{\Delta D}{D} + e\frac{\Delta E}{E}$$

Calculated from: Economic Planning Agency, *Kokumin Keizai Keisan Nenpō* [National Economic Accounts Yearbook], 1992

begun to make a larger contribution to economic growth. Table 7.1 shows the growth rates and contribution ratios of each of the elements of real GNE for the four five-year periods from 1970 to 1990. The table shows that from 1970–75 the contribution ratios of domestic private demand and government demand were 18.3 percent and 6.2 percent, practically equivalent to the 24.3 percent GNE growth rate, while imports and exports, with absolute values of around 5 percent, cancelled each other out, indicating that growth was achieved solely through the expansion of domestic demand. In the late 1970s and particularly in the early 1980s, however, a wide gap opened up between exports and imports, and exports began to make a larger contribution to growth, compensating for the falloff in the contribution made by government demand. Following the Plaza Agreement in the mid-1980s, when imports increased and the trade balance went into deficit, growth could continue because the deficit was set off by the increase in private domestic demand.

However, the period from the second half of the 1970s through the early 1980s was a time of worldwide inflation, slowed production, and rising unemployment. At a time when many other nations were sustaining trade deficits due to the rising cost of oil imports, the growth in Japanese exports became a target for international criticism. From 1977 onward there was growing pressure, particularly from the United States, for a further hike in the yen exchange rate, and the yen, which had hovered around the US$/¥290 mark since 1973, started a relentless climb until it briefly reach the ¥170 mark in October 1978. Despite the appreciation of the currency, however, the yen-based export growth rate declined (see Fig. 7.1), due to the difficulty of raising dollar-based export prices, the net yen income of the export industries decreased, business profits also declined, and from 1977–78 the high-yen recession grew more severe. At this time, as we will see in some detail below, the budget deficit was expanding due to faltering growth in government finances and tax revenue, but an attempt was made, in the fiscal 1978 budget, to float the economy by issuing deficit-covering bonds. The effects of the new policy were just beginning to be felt when the economy was hit by the second oil crisis, whereupon the government quickly changed tack and adopted a policy of monetary restraint.

On this occasion the fiscal and monetary authorities, having learned from the bitter experience of the first oil crisis, reacted to the situation with great alacrity. Figure 7.1 summarizes the movements of the economy before and after the second oil crisis. The official discount rate, which had been lowered to 3.5 percent, was successively raised to reach 9 percent at the beginning of 1980; the money supply was tightened, and the annual rate of increase in $M_2 + CD$ fell from nearly 13 percent to just over 6 percent. Prices rose temporarily due to the higher prices of imported crude oil and oil-related products; even the GNE deflator rose 9.2 percent between the second quarter of 1979 and the last quarter of 1980; the wholesale price index increased by 21.5 percent, and the consumer price index registered an increase of 10.4 percent. Nevertheless these measures had the effect of preventing further steep price rises occurring after the end of 1980. There was no opportunistic price-raising, and the government's response to the crisis must be judged a success. Internationally, however, the second oil crisis dealt the economy every bit as hard a blow as the first. In this environment, Japan's exports declined in 1982–83 but made a striking recovery in 1984. This can largely be ascribed to Japan's good fortune in the fact that its exports were specializing in products such as microelectronics for which there was a growing

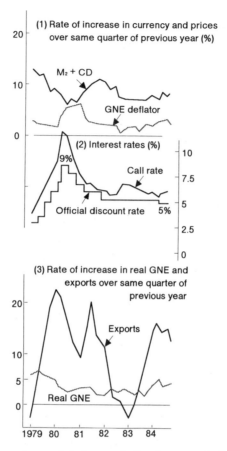

Figure 7.1. Economic trends before and after the second oil crisis

Sources: $M_2 + CD$ is derived from Bank of Japan data, export data from Ministry of Finance surveys, and GNE and the deflator from Economic planning Agency, *Kokumin Keizai Keisan Nenpo* [National Economic Accounts Yearbook]. The data are linked to those in Figure 6.1.

world market at the time. As we have seen, the current account surplus reached 3–4 percent of GNP in the mid-1980s. This eventually led to the change of direction represented by the revaluation of the yen at the Plaza Agreement.

Here let us touch briefly on the question of energy-saving during the period spanned by the two successive oil crises. Centering on this period, Fig. 7.2 illustrates trends in the level of energy consumption, the customs-cleared price of crude oil, and real GNP. The figure

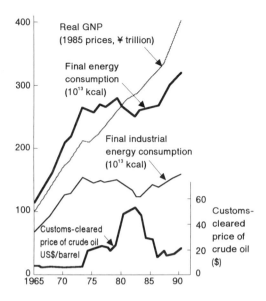

Figure 7.2. Energy consumption, real GNP, and customs-cleared crude oil prices, 1965–90

Sources: Real GNP from Economic Planning Agency data. Energy consumption from Nihon Energii Sangyō Kenkyūjo (Japan Energy Industry Research Institute) data. Crude oil prices from Ministry of Finance data.

enables us to sum up the relationship between Japan's productive activity and energy consumption. First of all, real GNP sustained an annual growth rate of 9.5 percent between 1965 and 1973, and continued to grow at the rate of 4.0 percent from 1973 to 1990. Yet final energy consumption, while it increased at about the same rate as GNP up to 1973, showed an overall levelling off from 1973 to 1986, and dipped sharply during the years 1973–75 and 1984–86, which corresponded to the two oil crises. Industrial energy consumption fell by almost 25 percent between 1973 and 1983. The reason for the slump in demand for energy is that the customs-cleared price of crude oil rose tenfold, from just under $5 to over $50 a barrel, during this same period.

The main factor behind these trends in energy consumption was, as we have seen, Japan's rapid shift from a high-consumption to a low-consumption industrial structure. Even the manufacturing industry came to be dominated by industries with high levels of processing and value-added such as machinery. But a secondary factor was that

Table 7.2. Index of Energy Consumption per Production Index Unit, 1973–
82

(1973 = 100)

	Pulp and paper	Chemicals	Ceramics	Steel	Non-metals
Energy Consumption Index					
(A)	69.3	70.2	76.9	71.6	60.4
Production Index (B)	107.8	131.7	94.6	92.5	99.0
Energy Consumption per unit of production index					
(C)	64.3	53.3	81.3	77.4	61.0

Calculated from: *Nihon Enerugii Keizai Kenkyūjo* [Japan Energy Economics Research
Inst.] *Enerugii Tōkei Shiryō* [Energy Statistics], domestic edition.
(C) = (A) ÷ (B) × 100.

industries made strong efforts to cut their energy consumption. As
Table 7.2 shows, even in high energy-consumption industries the
energy consumption per unit of production fell by 20–40 percent
during the period spanned by the two oil crises. One has to conclude
that the price mechanism played a major role in this reduction.

2. Fiscal Reconstruction

From the second half of the 1970s and into the 1980s the deficit in
government finances came to be a major problem. Table 7.3 gives
three-year average figures for fiscal revenue and expenditure from
1971 to 1991. The table shows that the proportion of government
revenue derived from taxes fell sharply from 1974, and the shortfall
was made up by bond issues and government borrowing. The decline
in tax revenue was most noticeable for corporation tax, reflecting a
decline in corporate profits due to the recession, followed by self-
assessed income tax. Meanwhile government expenditure had to be
increased. Not only had administration and personnel costs swelled
due to the dramatic rise in general prices, but with the revamping of
the social security system in 1973, a number of landmark reforms
were instituted, such as index-linked old-age pensions and free medical care for the elderly, all of which increased fiscal expenditure. In
addition, during the so-called high-yen recession (*endaka fukyō*) of
1977–78, Japan came under pressure from the United States to
expand domestic demand, and public works expenditure doubled in
the four years 1975–79, from ¥3.3 trillion to ¥6.6 trillion. This inevitably led to an expansion of the budget deficit.

Table 7.3. Trends in Government Revenue and Expenditure (1950–91, 3-year averages)

(¥ billions)

	Revenue					Expenditure				
	Total	Tax & revenue stamp income	Receipts from gov't monopolies	Bond issues and gov't borrowing	Balance carried forward	Total	Defense related	Bond expenditure	Social security	Land preservation and development
1950–52	8,970	5,896	1,227	0	961	7,523	1,158	365	740	945
53–55	11,768	7,924	1,332	0	1,836	10,253	1,493	431	1,332	1,183
56–58	13,620	10,106	1,212	0	1,568	11,961	1,462	465	1,490	1,656
59–61	20,247	16,164	1,459	0	1,473	17,671	1,677	401	2,432	3,042
62–64	32,085	25,586	1,651	0	3,431	29,706	2,479	755	4,467	5,395
65–67	45,418	35,164	1,659	5,240	929	44,317	3,463	535	7,396	8,440
68–70	72,093	60,812	2,614	4,072	1,664	70,141	5,092	2,517	11,197	12,028
71–73	13,176	10,354	329	1,634	514	12,091	823	487	1,953	2,219
74–76	22,310	14,815	448	4,880	1,292	21,476	1,387	1,264	4,527	3,146
77–79	34,707	20,994	633	11,236	598	33,982	1,892	3,307	7,452	5,054
80–82	46,495	28,777	790	13,705	716	45,857	2,444	6,351	9,869	6,078
83–85	52,610	35,155	687	12,859	825	51,707	2,987	9,194	10,868	5,994
86–88	60,828	46,500	11	9,275	250	57,614	3,502	12,031	11,951	5,948
89–91	69,082	58,608	9	6,431	1,262	68,619	4,195	14,192	12,641	5,787

Data calculated from Ministry of Finance, *Zaisei Tōkei* [Government Finance Statistics].

Table 7.4. Increase in the Tax Burden Ratio

(¥ trillion, %)

		Tax burden			Tax burden ratio		
	National income	National taxes	Local taxes	Total	National taxes	Local taxes	Total
1970	61.0	7.8	3.8	11.5	12.7	6.1	19.9
75	124.0	14.5	8.2	22.7	11.7	6.6	18.3
80	199.6	28.4	15.9	44.3	14.2	8.0	22.2
85	259.6	39.2	23.3	62.5	15.1	9.0	24.1
90	338.1	61.8	33.7	95.5	18.3	9.9	28.2

Source: Ministry of Finance, *Zaisei Kinyū Tōkei Geppō* [Monthly Fiscal and Monetary Statistics].

The government of course tried every expedient to raise extra revenue. One example of these efforts was the abandonment of the long-standing practise of pegging income-tax revenue to a certain percentage of GNP and lowering the tax rate as nominal income levels increased due to the rise in the cost of living (see Table 7.4). Some revenue was also raised by increasing indirect taxes like those on sakè and beer, but in the end the government had no option but to increase the issue of deficit-covering bonds. This immediately led to increased bond expenditure due to repayments of principal and interest, putting further pressure on the treasury. In the mid-1980s government bond expenditure accounted for as much as 20 percent of total fiscal expenditure, the same level as social security (see Table 7.3).

Faced with these problems, the government tackled the problem of fiscal reconstruction in 1981 by setting up a Provisional Commission for Administrative Reform (Rinji Gyōsei Chōsakai), chaired by Dokō Toshiwo of the Federation of Economic Organizations and charged with reorganizing the administration and government finances. The Commission's bywords were "small government" and "fiscal reconstruction without raising taxes." Industry had already rescued itself from dire straits by scaling down operations in the late 1970s, and now had the confidence to demand an equal level of commitment from the government. The method chosen to reconstruct public finance was first to keep expenditure on new projects below the level of the previous year. At the same time the income and corporation tax burden was to be reduced and a new consumption tax of 3 percent was to be levied on the value-added element of all wholesale and retail transactions. The consumption tax proposal had a rough ride in the Diet due to strong resistance from the opposition parties. After much political infighting it was finally implemented ten years later, in 1989. Beginning that year it was no longer necessary to issue deficit-covering bonds, and fiscal reconstruction was completed, but the principal reason for the eventual success of the reform was the increased tax revenue from the boom economy of the late 1980s. Another factor was the privatization and reorganization in 1987 of the national railways, which had been the source of huge budget deficits.

3. Financial Decontrol and Internationalization

The Japanese economy has become increasingly deregulated and internationalized since the 1970s. It is difficult to treat the two processes separately since they have progressed hand in hand. Deregulation was essential to internationalizing the economy, and it has become further internationalized as more controls have been lifted. Nowhere has this been more apparent than in the finance and securities field. The industry was always strictly controlled by the Ministry of Finance, and banks had to be licensed before they could start operating, establish new branches, or redeploy. The securities industry had been subject to exactly the same kind of controls since 1968. In terms of the business they were allowed to conduct, the banks were restricted to extending short-term credit for up to two years, while trust business was delegated to the trust banks and long-term credit business was confined to the long-term credit banks. The ceiling for interest on deposits was set by the Emergency Interest Rate Adjustment Law. These regulations governing the finance industry came to be known as a "convoy system," where administrative guidance was used to guard against individual bank failures. While this was done under the auspices of protecting depositors, it probably did more to protect the interests of the financial industry.

The situation began to change in the late 1970s, principally because trade friction between Japan and the United States intensified. Japanese exports of products like steel and automobiles were restricted, and there were calls for Japanese markets to be opened to imports of farm products like beef and oranges. America also criticized Japan sharply for failing to open its financial and securities markets, and Japan was forced little by little to accede to American demands. The second reason for the relaxation of controls was that the government came under increasing pressure to adopt an alternative debt management strategy due to rapid increases in bond issues. In order to guard against any fall in government bond prices, the bulk of government bond issues until that time had been underwritten by a syndicate of mainly city and regional banks and then reabsorbed a year later in a buying operation by the Bank of Japan. But with the very large government bond issues of the time it was no longer possible to implement such controls, and government bonds started to circulate on the bond markets. Bond price formation was deregulated, and soon government bond yields were set at the level of long-term interest rates. This eventually created the conditions for the marketing of new financial products like medium-term government bond funds and bond investment trusts.

Meanwhile the internationalization of the yen was pushed in 1984 by the Japan-U.S. Yen-Dollar Commission and a Ministry of Finance report, "Current Situation and Outlook for the Deregulation of Finance and the Internationalization of the Yen," which accepted the Commission's recommendations. Internationalization was given a further boost when the Foreign Exchange Council submitted its report "On the Internationalization of the Yen" the following year. With the publication of these reports, the walls between Japan and the outside world started to come down and deregulation to move ahead.

Financial deregulation falls basically into the following three categories. First, new financial products such as certificates of deposit (CD), maturity-designated deposits and money-market certificates (MMC), medium-term government bond funds, and lump-sum endowment insurance plans were developed. MMCs, which were initially available only for large deposits, have recently been extended to small deposits as well. Second, the money and capital markets were liberalized. During the first half of the 1980s foreign currency deposits and impact loans were deregulated, a yen-based BA market and a Euro-yen lending market were established, investment in overseas securities was deregulated, and foreign-currency-denominated and Euro-yen bonds authorized. The third area of deregulation concerned the financial business that institutions were allowed to conduct. We have seen how the different sectors of the industry encroached on each other's business: banks were permitted to engage in government bond dealings and over-the-counter sales while securities companies were authorized to handle CDs and make bond-secured loans. In addition, foreign banks were allowed to move into the trust business and foreign securities companies permitted to obtain membership on the Tokyo Stock Exchange.

It is clear from this brief summary that the deregulation of the financial and securities industries was closely linked to their internationalization. This obviously meant that investment and fund procurement, which had previously been confined to Japan, could be extended overseas. Table 7.5 shows trends in the internationalization

Table 7.5. Three Indicators of Yen Internationalization

	Fund procurement by firm's head office (bonds convertible bonds, warrant bonds, paid-in capital increase) (¥ billions)		Position of the Euro-yen in the Euro-currency markets (¥ billions)		Commercial Banks' external credit and debt balance (¥ billions)	
	Domestic	Overseas	All currency total	Yen	Credit	Debt
1977	2,113	436				
78	2,623	576	673.4	6.2	33.7	39.0
79	2,326	771	873.8	10.3	45.5	50.5
80	2,251	807	1,056.6	11.2	65.7	80.2
81	3,609	1,410	1,222.5	16.1	84.6	100.4
82	2,528	1,441	1,253.8	16.9	90.9	100.0
83	2,411	2,013	1,614.9	21.7	109.1	106.6
84	3,147	2,824	1,679.2	21.7	126.9	127.0
85	3,235	3,274	1,979.1	49.2	194.6	179.3
86	5,187	4,365	2,521.1	83.8	345.3	346.0
87	8,055	5,348	3,233.8	137.2	576.8	592.0
88	12,295	6,916	3,511.9	141.2	733.7	772.4
89	16,844	11,465	4,196.9	158.7	842.1	879.7
90	4,038	5,037	4,956.1	179.8	950.6	958.5
91			4,889.7	171.7	942.4	845.7

of Japanese finance in terms of three indexes. The first gives the figures for domestic and external fund procurement by Japanese firms. Overseas fund procurement started in the late 1970s, increased in volume through the 1980s, and reached higher levels than domestic fund procurement in 1985 and 1990. Firms started to keep a close eye on interest rate movements in deciding whether to procure funds at home or overseas. The second index—the share of the yen in Euro-currency market trading—shows the gradual rise in the position of the yen on overseas currency markets. Euro-yen dealings took off when financial institutions were authorized to make Euro-yen loans. The third index shows the rapid expansion in overseas dealings by the commercial banks from the beginning of the 1980s. Financial operations, which had been somewhat restricted—though perhaps safer—up to the 1970s, due to extensive controls, now moved out onto the international stage, reflecting Japan's increasing prominence as an economic power. These changes symbolized the internationalization of the Japanese economy.

4. Reaganomics and Japan

In the 1980s the United States engaged in a military buildup to confront the Soviet Union, under the banner of a "strong America," while in its economic policy the Reagan administration espoused monetarism and supply-side economics. The economic policies of the Reagan administration were taken up with much fanfare. But they clearly had negative as well as positive results. On the plus side, high interest rate policies curbed inflation and stopped in its tracks the stagflation that had gripped the American economy since the 1970s. These policies, together with those of British Prime Minister Margaret Thatcher, brought under control the chaos the American and European economies had inherited from the 1970s and signalled a brighter economic outlook for the 1980s. But it must be noted that Reaganomics brought problems as well, in the shape of the "twin deficits," the trade deficit and the budget deficit. The reasons for this can be summarized by the following equation which expresses the relationship [savings = investment] in terms of the personal, corporate, government, and overseas sectors of the economy:

$$\text{personal savings} + \text{corporate savings} + \text{budget surplus} = \\ \text{private investment} + \text{net exports} \tag{1}$$

"Net exports" here is the difference between imports and exports, including services. This indicates that under an export surplus investment flows overseas while under an import surplus investment flows into the country. As Table 7.6 shows, America has had continuous trade and budget deficits since the 1970s, but they both grew much larger during the 1980s. Equation (1) indicates that, assuming a fixed level of private savings (the left-hand side of the equation), when a budget deficit occurs, total savings decline accordingly, and so, assuming a fixed level of private investment (the right-hand side), the net export deficit should increase by the same amount as the decrease in total savings.[1]

However one explains the creation of the twin deficits, an absorption phenomenon occurred in the American economy, whereby the total domestic demand (D) exceeded the GDP, inviting a permanent deficit on the current account, and equilibrium was maintained by drawing in funds from overseas. From the Japanese perspective, high American interest rates created the conditions for excess domestic savings to flow into the United States. As we saw in Chapter 3, with the exception of two short-lasting deficits corresponding to the two oil crises, Japan had maintained a continuous surplus on its current account since the 1970s, and it was this surplus that flowed into the United States to alleviate the U.S. fund shortage.

Table 7.6. The U.S. "Twin Deficits"

(U.S. $100 million)

	1970–74 Nixon	1975–77 Ford	1978–81 Carter	1982–85 Reagan (1)	1986–89 Reagan (2)	1990–91 Bush
GNE	11,872	17,054	26,356	36,174	41,446	55,932
Trade						
Exports	609	1,146	1,951	2,110	2,919	4,076
Imports	618	1,216	2,347	3,069	4,215	4,916
Balance	−9	−70	−396	−959	−1,296	−840
Federal Budget						
Expenditure	2,162	3,120	4,948	6,547	8,807	10,428
Revenue	2,303	3,721	5,578	8,381	10,506	11,874
Balance	−141	−601	−630	−1,834	−1,699	−1,446

Source: Calculated from Bank of Japan, *Nihon Keizai o Chūshin to suru Kokusai Hikaku Tōkei*, [Comparative International Statistics centering on the Japanese Economy].

Broadly speaking, during the period of rapid economic growth the investment–savings balance in the Japanese economy showed a large surplus in the household sector and a deficit in the corporate sector, while the government and overseas sectors remained more or less in equilibrium. Hence the central question for economists was how household savings could be recycled in the form of funds for corporate investment. Here the financial institutions played an intermediary role by taking in household savings and relending them to business, by the method known as indirect finance. From the 1970s to the 1980s, however, in the process of transition to stable growth, the situation changed considerably, as is summarized in Table 7.7. There was no change in the excess of savings in the personal (household) sector, but three significant changes in the savings-investment balance occurred in the second half of the 1970s. First, there was a striking reduction in the corporate savings shortage as firms began to cut back on equipment investment and streamline their operations. Then there was a sudden increase in the general government savings shortage due to the shortfall in central and local government revenues, and there was an expansion of the deficit in the overseas sector, particularly in the mid-1980s when the general government savings shortage started to decline. The funds from the personal sector that flowed into the corporate sector were directed towards alleviating the government deficit and the twin U.S. deficits.

As Table 7.8 indicates, Japan's external asset–liability balance shows a virtually consistent increase from the mid-1970s onwards, with par-

Table 7.7. Japan's Savings–Investment Balance by Sector

(ratio to GNP, %)

	1970–72	1973–75	1976–78	1979–81	1982–84	1985–87	1988–90
Non-finance corporations	-8.7	-11.3	-4.9	-5.7	-4.1	-4.3	-7.5
Financial institutions	0.8	0.8	0.2	0.2	-0.1	-1.0	-1.6
General government	0.8	-0.8	-4.0	-4.1	-2.7	-0.1	2.8
Private non-profit organizations	0.2	0.3	0.2	0.2	0.2	0.1	0.2
Household sector	8.8	10.8	9.6	13.3	8.6	8.9	8.5
Overseas sector	-1.9	0.4	-1.3	0.5	-2.0	-3.8	-1.8
Statistical error	-0.1	-0.2	0.2	0.1	0.1	-0.1	-0.6

Notes: (1) Figures represent the difference between savings and investment in each sector, divided by GNP.
(2) Since data for the overseas sector represent the position as seen from overseas, the register plus values when the Japanese current account is in deficit and minus values when it is in surplus.

Source: Economic Planning Agency, *Kokumin Keizai Keisan Nenpō* [National Economic Accounts Annual Report].

Table 7.8. Japan's External Asset–Liability Balance

(U.S. $ billions)

	Long-term assets			Short-term assets		Total assets	Long-term liabilities			Short-term liabilities		Total liabilities	Net assets
	Total	Direct investments	Securities investments	Total	Financial accounts		Total	Direct investments	Securities investments	Total	Financial accounts		
1976	36.9	10.3	4.2	31.1	30.9	68.0	18.4	2.2	11.2	40.0	29.3	58.4	9.5
77	42.1	12.0	5.6	38.0	37.7	80.1	19.6	2.2	11.9	38.5	28.4	58.1	22.0
78	63.3	14.3	12.2	55.4	54.8	118.7	29.3	2.8	18.0	53.2	40.5	82.5	36.2
79	83.7	17.2	19.0	51.7	50.6	135.4	36.4	3.4	22.6	70.2	54.1	106.6	28.8
80	87.9	19.6	21.4	71.7	70.8	159.6	47.8	3.3	30.2	100.3	81.8	148.0	11.5
81	117.1	24.5	31.5	92.2	90.3	209.3	74.2	3.9	47.9	124.1	104.5	198.3	10.9
82	139.5	29.0	40.1	88.2	85.4	227.7	77.6	4.0	47.1	125.4	105.0	203.0	24.7
83	170.9	32.2	56.1	101.1	97.6	272.0	102.8	4.4	69.9	131.9	111.1	234.7	37.3
84	229.2	37.9	87.6	112.0	104.8	341.2	113.2	4.5	77.1	153.6	133.7	266.9	74.4
85	301.3	44.0	145.7	136.4	127.4	437.7	122.3	4.7	84.8	185.6	165.5	307.9	129.8
86	476.1	58.1	257.9	251.2	238.0	727.3	192.3	6.5	143.6	354.6	329.3	547.0	180.4
87	646.2	77.0	339.7	425.5	402.3	1,071.6	236.2	9.0	166.2	594.7	534.0	830.9	240.7
88	832.7	110.8	427.2	636.7	600.1	1,469.3	311.6	10.4	254.9	866.0	770.3	1,177.6	291.7
89	1,019.2	154.4	533.8	751.8	712.9	1,771.0	447.5	9.2	374.0	1,030.3	911.7	1,477.8	293.2
90	1,096.1	201.4	563.8	761.8	724.2	1,857.9	454.0	9.9	334.5	1,065.8	927.7	1,529.8	328.1
91	1,247.8	231.8	632.1	758.7	714.1	2,006.5	647.4	12.3	443.8	976.0	846.4	1,623.4	383.1

Data for assets, liabilities and the net asset balance are a continuation of Table 6.2.
Source: Ministry of Finance.

ticularly rapid increases in 1978–79 and between 1986–88. Among Japan's long-term assets, securities investment has shown a particularly strong increase. The movements of the differential between U.S. and Japanese interest rates (Fig. 7.3) clearly show that the bulk of this investment was in the United States. Japanese investment in U.S. securities such as treasury notes and bonds was particularly active in 1978–79, due mainly to the surge in U.S. interest rates, and in the mid-1980s, due to the decline in Japanese interest rates. As we saw in Fig. 7.1, these investments were made on the basis of careful interest-rate arbitrage, at a time when the growth in domestic demand for funds was slackening off. From 1990, higher Japanese interest rates dampened investment in overseas securities.

As we have seen, the influx of Japanese funds played a major role in dealing with the twin American deficits of the 1980s, but they were driven primarily by financial deregulation at home and by the difference between U.S. and Japanese interest rates. The Japanese monetary authorities lowered interest rates as a strategy to combat the recession brought on by the high yen, and since prices remained stable thereafter, they stuck to a low-interest-rate policy for the remainder of the 1980s. However, one result of this policy was to swell the domestic money supply, which, as we will see, gave rise to the "bubble economy."

5. The Plaza Agreement

The yen-dollar exchange rate, which had been pegged at around ¥260 at the time of Japan's switch to the floating exchange-rate system in February 1973, fell to almost ¥300 after the oil crisis but, helped by increasing Japanese exports, rose rapidly from 1977–78 (Fig. 7.4). This caused the Japanese economy to suffer a minor recession, and the Fukuda Cabinet was forced to compile a large-scale budget and implement anticyclical measures. Of course the recession was followed by the outbreak of the second oil crisis, and the long-awaited recovery of 1979 was not to last long. For more than five years, from after the second oil crisis until the summer of 1985, the yen-dollar exchange rate showed a general tendency to decline, though it oscillated considerably, with two peaks and three troughs during this period. The Deutschmark fell even more steeply against the dollar, from $US1/DM1.82 in 1980 to $US1/DM2.94 in 1985—a decline of more than 50 percent. One reason for this was that, despite the outflow of dollars to pay for the increased American imports, there was still an excess of demand for dollars because yen and Deutschmarks were being converted into dollars to take advantage of high U.S. interest

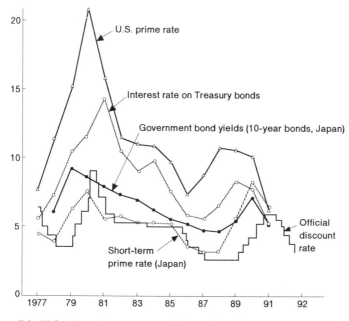

Figure 7.3. U.S.–Japan interest rate differentials, 1977–92

Sources: Compiled from Bank of Japan, *Nihon Keizai o Chushin to Suru Kokusai Hikaku Tōkei* [Comparative International Statistics Based on the Japanese Economy] and *Keizai Tōkei Nenpo* [Annual Economic Statistics].

rates. Under the Reagan administration, even though the "twin deficits" continued to expand, U.S. government monetarists believed that distortions in the exchange rate arose because the market was incomplete and not functioning normally. Based on this theory, they distanced themselves from the market and took the attitude that intervention was justified only when extremely chaotic conditions prevailed. At a time when the yen remained weak despite Japan's enormous trade surplus, they concluded that the underlying cause lay in the barriers and distortions in Japan's financial markets.

By 1985, however, there was growing concern within the U.S. government over the effect of this natural appreciation of the dollar on international competitiveness. The problem was taken up at the Baker–Takeshita Finance Ministers' Conference and, after a few rounds of preparatory negotiations, the so-called Plaza Agreement was signed on September 22 at the G5 meeting of the Finance Ministers and Central Bank Presidents of the major industrialized nations, held at New York's Plaza Hotel. The main thrust of the official statement was that a further orderly rise in the value of major currencies against the U.S. dollar was desirable, and that the G5 nations were prepared to cooperate to see this happen. It was made clear that the yen and the Deutschmark should be allowed to appreciate against the U.S. currency. According to a memorandum circulated unofficially at the meeting, a downward revision of 10–12 percent in the value of the dollar was intended.

6. From High-yen Recession to Boom Economy

On September 23, 1985, all the G5 nations made a concerted move to sell dollars, starting off the transition towards a stronger yen and Deutschmark and a weaker dollar. But events then took control, and the dollar did not stop depreciating when it had declined by the informally agreed level of 10–12 percent. Instead it continued to appreciate until the beginning of 1988, when it reached ¥120. The Louvre Agreement to stabilize exchange rates had been signed by the G7 nations (the G5 plus Italy and Canada) at a summit meeting in Paris in February 1987, but this only halted the rise of the yen temporarily. Furthermore, as the yen appreciated Japan's dollar-based exports started increasing at a much faster rate than before, and its trade surplus steadily expanded.

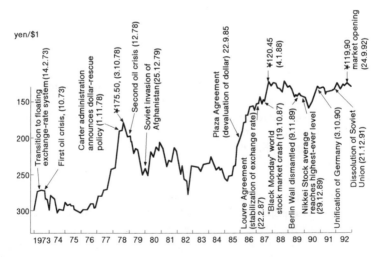

Figure 7.4. The yen–dollar exchange rate, 1973–92 (Tokyo market end-of-month closing rates)

Source: Nihon Keizai Shimbun, Sept. 25, 1992.

The increase in dollar-based exports can be ascribed to the effects of the *J*-curve, which had a much more substantial impact from 1986–88 than it had had in 1977–78. A single upward revaluation of the yen should eventually result in a decline in dollar-based exports, but since the yen was continuously appreciating, new *J*-curve effects were being generated all the time and successively acted to push up the value of exports. Another reason was that industry made strenuous efforts to rationalize and managed to avoid raising export prices due to the stronger yen. As we can see from Fig. 7.5, even looking at the contracted currency-based value of exports (whether yen or foreign currency), and despite the fact that the yen had almost doubled in value, the rise in export prices for the period 1985–91 was held down to less than 20 percent, while yen-based prices were cut on average by 20 percent, and by close to 40 percent for electrical machinery and chemical products. Yet industry was still able to rationalize sufficiently to remain profitable. In fact, the labor productivity index (based on 1985 = 100, data from Japan Productivity Office) shows massive improvements, with precision machinery registering 176, electrical machinery 159, and the chemical industry 146. In bringing down export prices, industry was of course helped considerably by the fall in the yen-based prices of imported raw materials, and by the overseas production of parts, as we will see below, but Japan's export industries deserve credit for meeting a serious challenge and surviving.

Nevertheless they were dealt a severe blow by the appreciation of the yen in its early stages. The yen-based value of exports (see Fig. 7.6), which had risen above ¥40 trillion in the first half of the 1980s, plunged to below ¥35 trillion in 1986–87. Since the volume of exports remained practically static from 1985–87, the resultant fall in income made a sharp dent in corporate profits. Industry was forced to implement serious rationalization measures. Fiscal 1986–87 was the year of the "high-yen recession," reflecting the depressed state of the export industries. Figure 7.7 outlines the features of that recession. Not only did the high yen cause a precipitous plunge in the prices of export goods; the wholesale prices of industrial goods also fell sharply, by an average of 10 percent during 1986. During this period international inflation was already under control, and the appreciation of the yen was mostly absorbed through reductions in yen-based prices. Although firms were quick to take steps and rationalize their operations, there was an immediate collapse in business profits. The ratio of business profits to sales actually fell from 5.0 percent to 3.5 percent in the space of a single year. The already stagnant employment situation grew even worse, and the ratio of effective job offers to open-

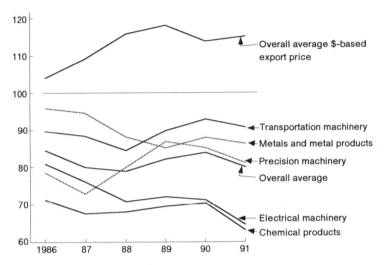

Figure 7.5. Changes in the export price index, 1986–91 (1985 = 100)
Source: Bank of Japan, *Oroshiuri Bukka Shisū* [Wholesale Price Index].

ings, which had just been starting to improve, now turned down again. Since the government was sticking firmly to its hardline fiscal policy, it attempted to revive the economy by successively reducing the official discount rate, from 5 percent to 4.5 percent in January 1986 to a record low of 2.5 percent in February 1987. It was slow to implement government spending increases, and only in May 1987 was a ¥6 trillion (the general account was growing by an annual ¥2.1 trillion) package of countercyclical measures finally agreed on.

In speaking of a "high-yen recession," however, we should note that from the beginning it only affected the export industries; non-export industries actually enjoyed something of a boom during this period. Taken overall, the profit rate of manufacturing industry decreased on average, but this was due almost entirely to the poor performance of exports, whereas corporate profits for the non-export industries actually rose from 1986 (see Fig. 7.8). While the high yen dealt a blow to exporters of highly processed manufactured goods due to lower export prices, the higher exchange rate also worked to sharply reduce the yen-based prices of imports, and the non-export industries, which depended on imported raw materials to manufacture for the domestic market, gained considerable benefit from the improvement in the terms of trade. There are of course many inter-

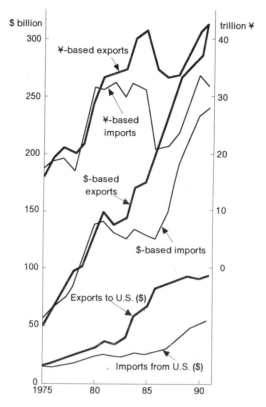

Figure 7.6. Japanese trade ($-based and ¥-based), 1975–90
Source: Ministry of Finance, *Tsūkan Tōkei* [Customs Clearance Statistics].

mediary industries like the steel and petrochemical industries, which use imported raw materials and are also heavily dependent on exports. For these industries, the benefits and drawbacks of the high yen to some extent cancelled each other out, but on balance they were slightly better off, since quite a high proportion of their production was directed to the domestic market. Of course the loud complaints of the export industries throughout 1986 led the business world to believe that the recession was affecting the whole of industry in equal measure, and it was not until the beginning of 1987 that the true situation became apparent.

The principal factor that led the economy to begin an autonomous recovery was the wide permeation of the effects of lower import

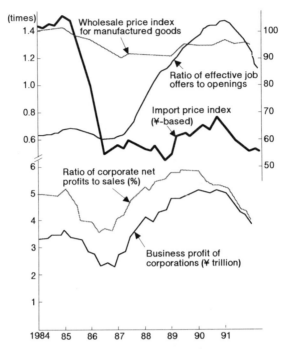

Figure 7.7. Economic indicators, 1984–91 (quarterly data)

Sources: Ratio of effective job offers to openings: Ministry of Labor. Price indices: Bank of Japan. Corporate net profit ratios and business profit data: Ministry of Finance. Figures for corporate profitability are three-term moving averages.

prices, but it was also probably due to the fact that the decline in export prices reached a plateau by the end of 1986 and even the export industries by this time were able to sustain profits at much lower price levels, due to their efforts to rationalize. Figure 7.9 shows that, in the wholesale sector, following the sharp reductions in the prices of imported goods, the prices of domestic products also fell by close to 10 percent. However, the unmistakable gap between domestic and import prices remained, and corporate earnings picked up. As Table 7.9 shows, the input price index, for raw materials and other inputs, is lower in every sector of manufacturing industry than the output price index, plainly indicating an improvement in the terms of trade for industry. The distribution sector also took advantage of lower purchasing prices to increase profit margins. Probably owing to the increase in corporate sector margins and because it includes agri-

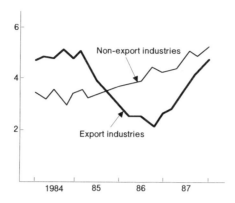

Figure 7.8. Rate of operating profitability in manufacturing, 1983–87
Source: Economic White Paper for fiscal 1988.

Table 7.9. Investment (I) and Output (O) of Manufacturing Industry Price Index (1980 = 100)

	1985		1988		1991	
	I	O	I	O	I	O
Foodstuffs	105	111	95	107	93	103
Textile products	95	100	81	94	90	101
Petrochemicals	86	89	53	67	81	77
Petroleum products	105	107	38	61	49	76
Iron and Steel	98	99	79	90	89	96
Non-ferrous metals	80	66	69	61	95	97
General machinery	101	102	95	98	99	102
Electrical machinery	92	93	83	83	83	79
Automobiles	100	103	92	93	94	93

Source: Bank of Japan.

cultural products and services, the consumer price index continued to rise through the second half of the 1980s. But if we look at the wholesale and consumer price indexes together, we can see that the appreciation of the yen in fact enabled the prices of products and services to remain completely steady through the period 1985–89.

The boom that occurred under stable prices owed much to the renewed vigor of the construction industry, which had remained depressed since the time of the first oil crisis. There was also a long-awaited boom in corporate equipment investment. As Fig. 7.10 shows, it was the first such boom since the end of the 1960s. The

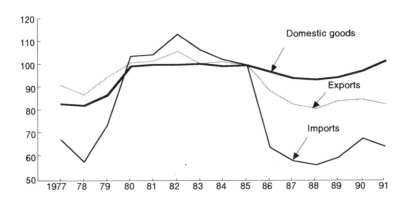

(a) Wholesale price index

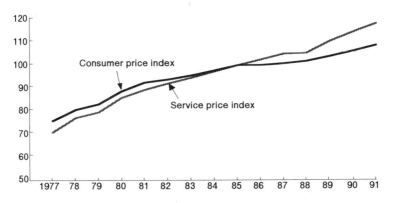

(b) Consumer price index

Figure 7.9. Price trends in the 1980s (1985 = 100)
Sources: (a) Bank of Japan survey. (b) Statistics Bureau, Prime Minister's Office.

reason for the increase in equipment investment is to be found in the principle of stock control, whereby firms sought to expand their existing capital stock in anticipation of future increases in demand. In growth industries like automobiles and electronics there was a rush to install new equipment.

At the same time, in view of the shortage of labor, firms were installing new equipment with the object of labor-saving and automation. They rushed to introduce industrial robots and office automation equipment. Another reason for the increase in equipment investment may have been that equipment installed at the end of the 1960s was coming to the end of its lifespan and was due for replacement. But in any case the mid-1980s brought to a close the long period of adjustment, characterized by a search for stability, that had continued since the oil crisis, and ushered in an entirely new period. In addition, when it was clear that the high-valued yen had become a permanent feature of the economy, many industries transferred their parts-production bases to Southeast Asian countries like Thailand and Malaysia where labor costs were lower. Table 7.10 shows the dramatic increase in overseas direct investments by manufacturing industry beginning in 1986. In value terms the largest portion of this investment was directed at North America, followed by Europe; but for manufacturing North America was followed by Asia. Although the figures are not shown in the table, $11.1 billion worth of manufacturing investments in Asia were made from 1986 onwards.

Another feature of the late 1980s was the increase in the ratio of manufactured imports to imports as a whole, from 31 percent in 1985 to 44 percent in 1987 and 50 percent in 1989. This reflects the rapid switch by manufacturing firms from domestically produced to imported parts.

Firms had to rely once again on overseas capital to procure the funds for direct investment. As we saw in Table 7.7, the investment surplus for non-finance corporations was expanding and household savings were being recycled to the corporate sector. The low interest rates from 1986–87 onward made the period ideally suited to this type of fund procurement. From this time on, the economy was characterized by abnormal monetary relaxation and a swelling of the money supply.

7. The Consequences of a Swollen Money Supply

The government continued its low interest rate policy, begun under the "high-yen recession," from 1986 until 1989. Once rates had been lowered, and no opportunity presented itself to raise them again, the record low discount rate of 2.5 percent ended up being maintained for over two years. The monetary authorities could not very well justify an interest rate hike in a situation where the economy was booming and prices were almost completely stable. The worldwide stock market crash that began on Wall Street in October 1987 also probably made it more difficult to contemplate higher interest rates. Market interest rates followed suit and stayed very low, which caused equipment investment to peak but also gave rise to a number of problems.

Table 7.10. Overseas Direct Investment

(million $)

	Period				Region (total value)		
	1969–75	1976–80	1981–85	1986–90	N. America	Asia	Europe
Agriculture	179	394	172	578	448	330	16
Fisheries	118	171	141	296	186	195	19
Mining	3,526	3,207	4,683	4,783	2,089	7,357	1,559
Construction	86	284	401	1,592	1,176	740	117
Manufacturing	4,478	7,536	11,826	57,213	40,322	18,659	12,540
–lumber, pulp	382	249	362	1,847	2,061	525	20
–chemicals	754	1,852	1,356	6,958	4,824	2,641	1,415
–steel and nonferrous metals	692	1,839	2,544	5,119	4,183	2,804	599
–machinery	355	495	1,077	5,963	3,973	1,649	1,794
–electrical machinery	494	1,057	2,166	16,613	11,099	4,175	4,322
–transport machines	282	619	2,395	7,507	5,030	1,699	1,899
Trade	1,930	3,202	7,269	18,640	16,983	3,792	6,702
Finance & insurance	1,114	1,127	7,713	54,459	19,393	4,231	25,129
Service industries	240	920	3,333	29,981	20,741	5,703	3,264
Real estate	317*	344*	2,533	43,316	31,034	3,028	6,635
Others	1,945	3,370	8,399	16,313	3,811	3,483	3,284
Total	13,934	20,554	47,152	227,157	136,185	47,519	59,265

* indicates real estate acquisition.

Sources: Ministry of Finance Study. International Business Section, Industrial Policy Bureau, Ministry of International Trade and Industry, *Dai Nijūikkai Wagakuni Kigyō no Kaigai Jigyō Katsudō* [Overseas Business Activities of Japanese Firms, no. 21].

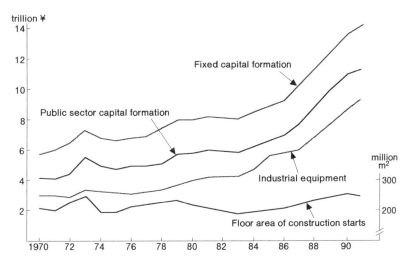

Figure 7.10. Fixed capital formation and construction starts (in floor area), 1970–90

In Japan today, a commonly used indicator of the money supply is $M_2 + CD$. CDs are negotiable certificates of deposit, used to mobilize idle corporate funds. In 1985, the term-end balance of $M_2 + CD$ stood at ¥315 trillion, but by the end of 1990 it had increased 60 percent to ¥505 trillion. It is only since the 1970s that $M_2 + CD$ has come to be seen by financial policymakers as the leading indicator of the money supply, and the rationale for this is a very simple one. Since, omitting CD from the equation, $M_2 = k_2 Y$ (where Y is nominal GNP), ΔM_2 must equal $k_2 \Delta Y$, and therefore, if k_2 is fixed, $\Delta M_2 / M_2 = \Delta Y / Y$. In fact, since the value of k_2 increases by approximately 2 percent a year, an appropriate value for the growth rate of M_2 is seen as a figure 2 percent higher than the growth rate of nominal GNP (which equals the growth rate of real GNP + the growth rate of the GNP deflator). Growth rates for the 1980s are given in Fig. 7.11, which also shows growth rates for nominal GNP. In the second half of the 1980s, and particularly for the three years 1987, 1988, and 1989, the growth rate of $M_2 + CD$ was significantly higher than the growth rate of GNP. The actual figures are 10.8 percent as against 4.9 percent for 1987, 10.2 percent as against 6.0 percent for 1988, and 12.0 percent as against 6.0 percent for 1989. There can be no denying that this discrepancy is what sowed the seeds of excess liquidity. Alongside real economic growth, a large volume of funds was invested in stocks and other financial assets, and in real estate.

Table 7.11 presents the data for the banks' outstanding loans and discounts by industry, as one means of indicating how these funds were supplied. It is clear from the table that there was hardly any growth in the level of borrowing by manufacturing industry, which had previously been the main target of bank lending. From 1985 onwards, the principal growth areas for bank lending were finance and insurance, real estate, the service industries, and individuals. These four sectors together accounted for 83 percent of the growth in lending. While it is thought that over 60 percent of the borrowing by individuals can be attributed to housing loans, it is clear that there was significant growth in the remaining 40 percent. Almost certainly, a large proportion of funds supplied by the banks was borrowed for the purpose of investment in real estate or the stock market. Of course firms had other means of procuring funds including the Euro-market at lower rates of interest, and many made use of funds on hand to invest. Insurance companies and other financial institutions were active in these markets as well.

The price fluctuations of securities assets, which were the objects of all this investment and speculation, are illustrated in Fig. 7.12, which is based partly on data from Table 3.12, Chapter 3. The Nikkei stock price average had remained relatively stable at a level between ¥12,000 and ¥13,000 until the beginning of 1986, but it started to rise in the spring of that year and, recovering from two minor setbacks, went on rising steadily through the whole of 1988 and 1989. When it

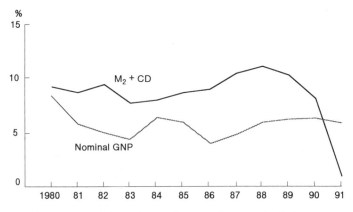

Figure 7.11. Money supply and annual rate of increase in GNP, 1980–91

Table 7.11. Outstanding Loans and Discounts by Industry

(¥ trillion)

	Total	Manu-facturing	Const-ruction	Wholesale and retail	Finance insurance	Real estate	Service industry	Individual	Other
1980	134.6	43.0	7.3	34.4	4.4	7.6	9.2	15.2	13.5
85	222.8	58.2	12.7	49.2	16.8	17.2	23.6	20.6	24.5
89	355.1	59.1	19.2	63.1	36.7	41.0	51.3	54.1	30.6
91	385.7	60.0	21.6	64.3	36.1	44.7	60.3	65.0	33.7
Increase from 1985–89	132.8	0.9	6.5	13.9	19.9	23.8	27.7	33.5	6.1
	(100)	(0.7)	(4.9)	(10.5)	(15.0)	(17.9)	(20.9)	(25.2)	(4.6)
~equipment funding									
1980	36.7	7.2	0.6	3.4	0.4	2.0	4.2	12.9	6.0
85	53.5	8.5	0.9	4.9	2.5	4.6	7.9	17.0	7.2
89	115.8	12.1	3.4	11.9	6.9	17.0	19.9	39.6	5.0
91	140.7	14.7	4.5	14.5	10.6	18.1	26.9	47.8	3.6
Increase from 1985–89	62.3	3.6	2.5	7.0	4.4	12.4	12.0	22.6	-2.2
	(100)	(5.8)	(4.0)	(11.2)	(7.1)	(19.9)	(19.3)	(36.3)	(-3.5)

Source: Bank of Japan survey.

peaked at ¥38,915 in December 1989, the average stood at three times its 1986 level. This meteoric ascent in share prices, which can only be called abnormal, encouraged more and more firms and individuals to trade on the stock market, and the average volume of trade at this time frequently exceeded 1 billion shares a day. In March 1989 the Bank of Japan started gradually to raise the official discount rate, and stock prices reached their highest level nine months later. The level of stock prices was indicative of the abundance of idle funds on the market. Prices started to fall again during 1990, and continued to plunge until the average was back down to the ¥14,000 mark in August 1992.

The rise in real estate, and particularly in land, prices was equally staggering. Table 3.12 showed that nationwide urban land prices, converted to 1970 values, had increased by an average 4.8 times in 1991, while land prices in the six major cities rocketed an average tenfold and by as much as twelve times in business districts. The rise in land prices picked up speed in 1986 and 1987, escalating first in urban business districts and then gradually spreading outwards. Rocketing land prices gave rise to many social problems as residents were victimized by land speculators and summarily evicted to make way for new office-building developments.

The total value of real estate held by the corporate sector, which amounted to ¥39 trillion in June 1985, rose to ¥81 trillion by June 1990 and ¥106 trillion by June 1992. The Ministry of Finance's annual *Corporate Statistics* show that stock holdings rose over the same period from ¥20 trillion to ¥41 trillion and ¥56 trillion. Since the later fall in prices for land or for stocks has likely been depreciated, these firms' latent losses remain hidden. Taking account of this situation, Fig. 7.13 plots the prices for land and stocks given in the national asset statistics, as multiples of GNP. Both ratios showed a continuous increase from 1986 to 1989, and rose abnormally in 1989 before beginning to fall. This is what was meant by the "bubble economy." It is worth mentioning that neither the rise and fall in the value of assets due to fluctuations in land and stock prices, nor the profits and losses resulting from the buying and selling of land and shares, figure in the national income accounts, except where businesses actually deal in land or stocks. Such fluctuations should therefore have no bearing on the rate of economic growth. However, the rise in the asset value of land and stocks undeniably raised their collateral value in the event of financial crisis, and caused a leap in land and share prices.

There was no immediate restraint of the money supply even after the March 1989 hike in the official discount rate, and asset prices

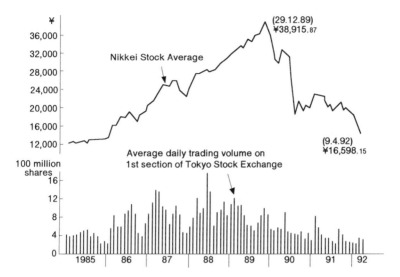

Figure 7.12. Nikkei Average stock price and volume of trading on Tokyo Stock Exchange, 1985–92
Source: Compiled from Nihon Keizai Shimbun.

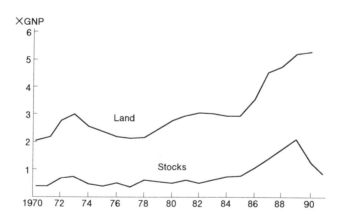

Figure 7.13. Ratio of asset values (land and stocks) to GNP, 1970–90
Source: Calculated from Economic Planning Agency, *Chōki Sokyū Shuyō Keiretsu Kokumin Keizai Keisan Hōkoku* [Long-term Retroactive National Economic Accounts for Major Business Groups].

continued to climb through the rest of 1989. There was a partial collapse of stock and real estate prices in 1990, but it was not until the summer of 1991 that it became clear the economy was in recession. This brought to an end the economic boom precipitated by the 1985 Plaza Agreement, but the boom had very considerable repercussions.

First, it raised Japan's international profile to new heights. Japan now led the world in terms of both the value of trade and the size of its net foreign claims. This meant the movements of the Japanese economy now had a much greater impact on the world. At the same time, however, there was great progress in the internationalization of the Japanese economy as measured, for example, by the level of imports of manufactured goods and the movement of capital. Japan's participation in the international system of division of labor had at last become a permanent feature of the economy.

The high-yen boom also enabled the economy to fully recover from the aftereffects of the two oil crises. From the late 1970s through the early 1980s the economy had been under constant pressure from such problems as the cumulative budget deficit and an excess of labor, but the boom of the late 1980s finally released it from this burden. The goals of "fiscal reconstruction without raising taxes" and overcoming the need to issue deficit-covering bonds had been thought practically impossible to achieve. Yet both were achieved in 1989, thanks to increased tax revenues, while the years 1987–88 had already seen the beginning of a serious labor shortage.

Note
1. Martin Feldstein, Chairman of the Council of Economic Advisors in the early days of the Reagan administration, explained the cause–effect relationship as follows. Curbing the money supply led to reduced demand, which led to a shortfall in tax revenues, which enlarged the budget deficit, and as a result of this chain reaction, bond issues increased, the government credit requirement increased, and high interest rates continued. Since this provoked an influx of capital from overseas, there was no depression of domestic equipment investment. But because high interest rates increased demand for the dollar, they pushed up the value of the currency, which slowed American exports and increased imports, inviting a trade deficit. This was the process that gave rise to the 'twin deficits.' (Toshida Seiichi?, "Reeganomikkusu" [Reaganomics], Chūkō Shinsho, 1986).

Epilogue

The 1990s

8

The Collapse of the Bubble Economy

The government pursued a low interest-rate policy and implemented a ¥6 trillion spending package (¥5 trillion in public works projects and ¥1 trillion in tax cuts) to combat the effects of the yen appreciation in 1986–87. But the high-yen recession, which had at first been expected to affect industry across the board, was only felt seriously by the export industries, and the economy started to rebound when the rest of industry eventually began to experience the benefits of the higher yen through lower import prices. Under a continued easy-money policy, the official discount rate was lowered to 2.5 percent in February 1987 and left at that level for two years and three months before being finally hiked to 3.25 percent in May 1989. During that period, as we have seen, the money supply increased rapidly, the money markets slackened, and there was massive speculation in stocks and real estate.

What was responsible for the abnormal rise in asset prices? The decisive factor is determined by comparing asset earnings (r) and the anticipated rise in asset prices (p) for the same period with the general interest rate (i). If we think of p increasing to a level p_e, then we can deduce the following relationships.[1]

$$i = \frac{r + (p_e - p)}{p}, \quad p = \frac{r + p_e}{1 + i}.$$

If no rise in asset prices is foreseen ($p = p_e$), then $p = \frac{r}{i}$ can be derived from $i = \frac{r}{p}$, showing the relation between base price and profits. The problem is how to determine p_e. It might be possible to predict the rise in asset prices from various objective factors, but the safest method is probably to accurately predict how the market itself expects prices to rise, and to follow its lead. Of course if everyone believes the market to be bullish, this will itself cause asset prices to rise. And monetary relaxation created the ideal conditions for this to happen.

The steep rise in stock and land prices during the second half of the 1980s should be thought of as having been created not just by the upturn in the business performance of firms due to the boom in the economy, or by the lack of commercial land in the big cities, but, over and above this, by people's expectations of higher prices based on the perceptions of a bullish market. The situation at this time closely resembles that at the time of the excess liquidity inflation of 1972–73. The high-yen recession gave rise to fiscal and monetary relaxation, and stock and real estate prices rose. The difference between the two periods is that whereas in 1972–73 there were sharp rises in general prices as well, during the bubble economy prices remained stable. The excess liquidity of the late 1980s was not seen as a serious problem because general prices had been tranquillized by the effect of lower import prices. Another factor which probably worked to keep the bubble inflated was the desire to maintain the differential between Japanese and U.S. interest rates. A further cause for hesitating to switch to a policy of monetary restraint was the New York stock market crash of October 19, 1987 ("Black Monday"), when stock prices tumbled 22.6 percent on Wall Street and prices on the Tokyo market collapsed by 14.9 percent on the following day. Hence, interest rates remained low and the money markets stayed sluggish until May 1989.

After the money supply was tightened, both stock and land prices continued to rise inexorably until the Nikkei stock price average (of 225 stocks) reached its record high level of ¥38,916 on December 29, 1989, after which stock prices nosedived. Land prices, however, continued their ascent until March 1990, when the Ministry of Finance introduced "real estate loan restrictions" which forced financial institutions to submit monthly reports of their real estate loans and limit the increase in such lending to a level below the rate of increase in their overall lending. The official discount rate was raised in stages until August 1990, when it stood at 6 percent. The rise in land prices was finally brought under control in the summer of 1990, but the loan restrictions remained in force until the end of that year. The official discount rate was again hiked to 5.5 percent in July 1991. Up to then the economy had remained on a steady course, and it was only in the summer of 1991 that the economic indicators started to turn down.

Subsequent recovery, however, was elusive, and the recession only bottomed out, with some difficulty, in the spring of 1993. The recession following monetary restraint owed its severity to a number of factors. First, many firms had problems coping with the latent losses they had sustained due to the decline in the value of their stock and land holdings. Second, industry was burdened with unplanned inventory increases, and the drawn-out process of adjustment inevitably led to a decline in production. Third, households reduced their consumption due to smaller bonuses and the decline in the value of their stocks and bonds. Those who profited most from speculation in land and stocks at the height of the "bubble economy" had the greatest difficulty in coping with its aftereffects. The distinctive feature of this recession was that it plunged into decline the very industries that had previously shown the most promising growth—automobiles and electronics. One reason the perception of a recession was so strong was that growth had slowed in the leading industries and no new growth industries had been built up to replace them.

By the spring of 1993 the end of the recession was in sight, but it was exports, once again, that had covered for the slump in domestic demand in 1991–92. The dollar-based value of exports rose from $275.2 billion in 1989 to $339.7 billion in 1992—an increase of $64.5 billion, or 23 percent, in three years. Meanwhile, reflecting the slowdown in domestic demand, imports hovered around the $230 billion mark, the trade surplus expanded, and friction between Japan and its trade partners flared up once again. At the same time, the value of the yen against the U.S. dollar, which had dropped temporarily to the ¥150 mark in 1990, rose to ¥120 in the second half of 1992 and had reached ¥110 by April 1993. This meant that yen income from exports did not increase even when more goods were being shipped, and the government had to implement a ¥13 trillion package of emergency pump-priming measures.

By 1992, Japan was the world's second largest exporter after Germany, ranked number one in terms of net foreign claims, and had also become the world's leading donor of foreign aid to the developing nations and of contributions to international organizations. The United States, which had been the world's strongest economic power, was overburdened with debt and started down the path to reconstruction, using funds from Germany and Japan.

Today, after the end of the Cold War and the dissolution of the Soviet Union, and with the U.S., despite its military power, unable any longer to boast of its economic prowess, the Japanese economy has become the focus of world attention. It is only natural that Japan is now expected to contribute to the world economy in a way that

Table 8.1. Indicators of Science and Technology Research and Development

	Japan		U.S.		Britain		Germany		France	
	1985	1990	85	90	85	90	85	90	85	90
Science and technology budget ($100m)	64.3	132.7	472.1	638.1	59.3	82.5*	43.4	94.8	66.9	147.9
Research expenditures ($100m)	340.3	790.8*	1137.5	1500.0	102.7	184.1†	172.6	344.8*	117.9	284.6
Ratio of research spending to GNP (%)	2.49	2.69*	2.83	2.74	2.21	2.19†	2.77	2.89*	2.27	2.33*
Proportion of research spending borne by govt. (%)	19.4	17.1*	45.8	46.1	42.2	36.7†	38.3	33.2	53.7	49.3*
Technology exports ($100m)	7.2	24.8	59.9	152.9	10.5	18.7†	5.5	11.5*	5.1	10.4*
Technology imports ($100m)	23.6	60.4	8.9	26.4	9.3	20.4†	9.9	21.5*	9.8	18.0*
Number of researchers (1000s)	381.3	484.3	849.2	949.2†	98.0	102.4†	147.6	165.6**	102.3	115.2

* denotes 1989, † 1988, and ** 1987.
Source: Science and Technology Agency, Kagaku Gijutsu Hakusho [White Paper on Science and Technology].

befits its status. Japan's international responsibility is all the greater in view of the fact that Germany now has to devote all its energy to the reconstruction of its formerly communist eastern sectors.

It will be an increasingly difficult task to steer the Japanese economy in the years ahead. The nation's leaders will have to address not only domestic policy objectives but the goal of fulfilling the nation's international obligations as well. The other nations of the world want to see Japan achieve a high growth rate and increase demand for imports. If, in response, Japan is to opt for a policy of stimulating domestic demand, at least over the next few years, it will not be possible to avoid increasing fiscal expenditure and issuing government bonds. This may well have the effect of upsetting the fiscal balance. On the other hand, if imports do not increase and the trade surplus continues, there is a strong possibility that the yen will continue to appreciate. The Japanese economy faces a dilemma which is quite outside its previous experience.

If the economy is to continue growing, Japan will probably have to develop new industries to complement the growth industries of the past. Previously, growth was expected of new industries like biotechnology and new materials, as well as electronics. But in the future Japan will have to look not only to these industries but to new forms of clean energy and new industries that are more friendly to the global environment.

As Table 8.1 shows, the level of Japan's current science and technology development investment ranks second in the world after that of the United States. Japan formerly assembled imported technology to develop its own production techniques. But now it has at last reached the stage where it has a comprehensive research and development capacity that includes basic technology.

Since the 1950s the Japanese economy has responded swiftly to the environment in which it found itself and has surmounted numerous difficulties to reach the position it is in today. If it is to respond to the demands of the world in taking on new and unfamiliar challenges, it must now demonstrate that same ability to the full. This is not necessarily the duty of government. It can probably best be achieved through the unremarkable but cumulative efforts of industry, without the need for any particular heroics.

Note

1. Noguchi Yukio, *Baburu no Keizaigaku* [The Economics of the Bubble Economy] (Tokyo: Nihon Keizai Shimbunsha, 1992).

Appendix

Cabinets and Major Events, 1935–1994

Cabinet	Term in office	Major events
Okada Keisuke	July 1934–March 1936	Repudiation of London Naval Disarmament Treaty (Dec. 1935)
Hirota Kōki	March 1936–Feb. 1937	February 26 Incident (Feb. 1936) Centralization of economic powers in the hands of the military begins
Hayashi Senjūrō	Feb.–June 1937	Anti-Comintern Pact (including secret mutual defense pact against the USSR) concluded with Germany (Nov. 1936) Army's Key Industries Five-year Plan (May 1937)
Konoe Fumimaro (1)	June 1937–Jan. 1939	War with China begins (July 1937) Nanking taken (Dec. 1937) Direct control of the economy begins (Sept. 1937) Planning Agency established, begins work on Materials Mobilization Plan (Oct. 1937) National General Mobilization Low (April 1938)
Hiranuma Kiichirō	Jan.–Aug. 1939	Abrogation of U.S.-Japan Trade and Navigation Treaty announced (July 1939)
Abe Nobuyuki	Aug. 1939–Jan. 1940	Beginning of war in Europe (Sept. 1939) Labor Conscription Order; Price Control Order (Sept. 1939)
Yonai Mitsumasa	Jan.–July 1940	Controls extended to all parts of the economy Military advances into French North Indochina (Sept. 1940)
Konoe Fumimaro (2) (3)	July 1940–Oct. 1941	Tripartite Alliance signed (Sept. 1940) Patriotic Industrial Associations formed (Nov. 1940) "New Economic Order" legislation (Dec. 1940) Military advances into French South Indochina (July 1941) U.S.-British-Dutch embargo on oil exports to Japan (July 1941) and freezing of Japanese funds "Control Associations" formed in key industries (Oct. 1941)

Prime Minister	Period	Events
Tōjō Hideki	Oct. 1941–July 1944	Pearl Harbor attack begins Pacific War (Dec. 1941)
		Control of Foodstuffs Law (Feb. 1942)
		Battle of Midway turns the tide of war toward the Allies after Japanese conquests in Singapore, Burma, the Philippines, and Dutch Indochina (June 1942)
		Guadalcanal falls to the Allies (Feb. 1943)
		Munitions Companies Act (Oct. 1943)
		Saipan taken by the Allies (July 1944)
Koiso Kuniaki	July 1944–April 1945	Intensive B-29 bombing of Tokyo Fall of Okinawa (April 1945)
Suzuku Kantarō	April–Aug. 1945	Potsdam Declaration (July 1945)
		Atomic bombing of Hiroshima and Nagasaki (Aug. 1945)
		USSR declares war on Japan and attacks Manchuria (Aug. 1945)
		Acceptance of Potsdam Declaration (Aug. 1945)
Higashikuninomiya (Prince) Naruhiko	Aug.–Oct. 1945	Beginning of Occupation by Allied Powers under Supreme Commander Douglas MacArthur (SCAP)
Shidehara Kijūrō	Oct. 1945–May 1946	"Democratization" of economic activity and free labor union activity and free labor union activity proposed by SCAP (Oct. 1945)
		Zaibatsu holdings frozen (Nov. 1945)
		Emergency Financial Measures establish and regulate currency (Feb. 1946)
		Trade Union Law (March 1946)
Yoshida Shigeru (1)	May 1946–May 1947	Economic Stabilization Office created (Aug. 1946)
		Labor Relations Adjustment Law (Sept. 1946)
		Land reform begins
		Constitution enacted (Nov. 1946)
		Labor Standards Law (April 1947)
		Anti-Monopoly Law (April 1947)
Katayama Tetsu	May 1947–March 1948	Elimination of Excessive Concentration of Economic Power Law stipulates breakup of large companies with control of their market (Dec. 1947)
		SCAP issues anti-strike order (March 1948); labor movement repressed

Cabinet	Term in office	Major events
Ashida Hitoshi	March–Oct. 1948	Draper Commission recommends reduced reparations payments (March 1948) Five-Year Economic Rehabilitation Plan (May 1948)
Yoshida Shigeru (2) (3) (4) (5)	Oct. 1948–Dec. 1954	Dodge Plan for Reconstruction (April 1949) Yen-dollar exchange rate set at ¥360/$1 (April 1949) 285,000 fired in so-called Red Purge (June 1949) War in Korea begins (June 1950); special procurement income begins to come in Japan Development Bank founded (April 1951) San Francisco Peace Treaty and U.S.-Japan Security Pact signed (Sept. 1951) First policies to promote capital accumulation (export subsidies, tax reductions for equipment investment, etc.) adopted Enterprise Rationalization Promotion Law (March 1952) Occupation ends (April 1952)
Hatoyama Ichirō (1) (2) (3)	Dec. 1954–Dec. 1956	Beginning of Spring Wage Offensive labor-management negotiation system (Jan. 1955) "Jimmu" boom (1956–57) spear-headed by the shipbuilding industry
Ishibashi Tanzan	Dec. 1956–Feb. 1957	Textile companies begin importing advanced technology and producing man-made fibers
Kishi Nobusuke (1) (2)	Feb. 1957–July 1960	Free trade and exchange policy adopted (March 1959) Short recession (1957–58) U.S.-Japan Security Treaty renewal (Jan. 1960) occasion for massive demonstrations, cancellation of Eisenhower visit (Apr.–June 1960) "Iwato" boom (1959–61)
Ikeda Hayato (1) (2) (3)	July 1960–Nov. 1964	Income-Doubling Plan (Dec. 1960) Basic Agricultural Law (June 1961) Short recession (1961–62)

Prime Minister (term)	Events
Satō Eisaku (1) (2) (3) Nov. 1964–July 1972	Temporary Measures for the Establishment of Specially Designated Industries proposed by MITI (March 1962) Japan becomes signatory to International Monetary Fund (April 1964) Membership in OECD (April 1964) Short recession (last half of 1964 through 1965) First postwar national bond issue (Nov. 1965) Beginning of explosive growth period which lasts until 1970 Merger of Yawata Steel and Fuji Steel companies to form Shin Nippon Steel (Oct. 1969) Growing public awareness of pollution problem (1970) U.S.-Japan textile negotiations (June 1970) Nixon announces U.S. withdrawal from Bretton Woods monetary system (Aug. 1971); collapse of postwar currency exchange system; free-floating yen-dollar exchange rates; reaction in Japan includes panic (autumn 1971) and extraordinary loose money policy (1971–72)
Tanaka Kakuei (1) (2) July 1972–Dec. 1974	OPEC announces steep increases in price of crude oil (October 1973); "energy crisis" leads to panic buying, slump First postwar minus growth rate (−1.3%) recorded in 1974
Miki Takeo Dec. 1974–Dec. 1976	Exports pick up again in 1975; balance of payments surplus of $990,000 recorded in 1976 Lockheed payoff scandal (Feb. 1976)
Fukuda Takeo Dec. 1976–Nov. 1978	Balance of payments surplus reaches $174,000,000 for 1977 Yen begins to appreciate dramatically in value, reaches postwar high of ¥180/$1 in late 1978
Ōhira Masayoshi (1) (2) Dec. 1978–June 1980	Tight-money policies instituted (April 1979) Tokyo Summit Conference (June 1979) Crude oil prices increased (June 1979)
Suzuki Zenkō July 1980–Nov. 1982	Exports of Japanese autos to the U.S. voluntarily curbed (May 1981) Market-opening measures package unveiled (May 1982)

Cabinet	Term in office	Major events
Nakasone Yasuhiro (1) (2) (3)	Nov. 1982–Nov. 1987	Former Prime Minister Tanaka found guilty in Lockheed payoff scandal (Oct. 1983) Farm trade agreement negotiated between Japan and the U.S. (April 1984) Plaza Agreement signed in New York (Sept. 1985) G-7 Summit held in Tokyo (June 1986) Wall Street crashes on "Black Monday" (Oct. 1987)
Takeshita Noboru	Nov. 1987–June 1989	Imports of American beef and citrus fruit liberalized (June 1988) Emperor Shōwa dies of duodenal cancer after three months' publicly acknowledged illness (Jan. 1989)
Uno Sōsuke	June 1989–Aug. 1989	Prime Minister Uno resigns after only weeks in office in wake of scandal
Kaifu Toshiki	Aug. 1989–Nov. 1991	Japanese firms make major financial and real estate acquisitions in the U.S. (Sept.–Oct. 1989) Iraq invades Kuwait, launching Persian Gulf War and opening foreign-policy debate in Japan (Aug. 1990) Gulf War ends; Japan's financial contributions total $13 billion (March 1991)
Miyazawa Kiichi	Nov. 1991–Aug. 1993	Trade war escalates with "America-bashing" remarks by government officials (Jan.–Feb. 1992) Self-Defense Forces sent to Cambodia on UN peace-keeping mission (June 1992) LDP falls from power after 38 years (July 1993)
Hosokawa Morihiro	Aug. 1993–April 1994	Coalition government formed under Prime Minister Hosokawa (Aug. 1993) Rice market opened to imports under GATT plan (Dec. 1993)
Hata Tsutomu	April 1994–June 1994	Prime Minister Hata resigns after two months; political realignment brings coalition between LDP and Socialist Party to power (June 1994)
Murayama Tomiichi	June 1994–	Yen rises beyond psychological barrier of ¥100/$1, to a postwar high of ¥99.50 (June 1994)

Index

Administrative guidance (*gyōsei shidō*), 18–19, 89, 91, 245
Agricultural cooperatives, 137, 139
Agricultural Land Act (1952), 182
Agriculture: commodity prices in, 184, 191; dispersion index, 180; imports in, 65, 89, 184; income from, 189; independent operators in, 188, 189; outmigration from 148, 149, 182, 186, 191; policy toward, 182–85; population employed in, 147, 148, 182, 183, 185; productivity in, 30, 187; technology in, 185. *See also* farmers; rice
Air Pollution Prevention Law, 120
Aircraft, wartime production of, 13
All Japan Congress of Industrial Unions (Sanbetsu), 30, 31, 42
Allied Powers, 24, 32, 33. *See also* Occupation; Supreme Commander for the Allied Powers
Aluminum industry, 27
Amagasaki Steel, 31
Anti-Monopoly Law (1947), 26, 51, 89, 168
Appliances, household electrical, 8, 100, 148
Army, economic power of, 3, 4, 7–8
Asahi Beer, 70
Asset-liability balance, 200, 249, 251
Asset stock, 115–16, 266, 271
Atomic bomb, 15
Automobile industry: competitiveness in, 27, 70; and pollution, 107; plant and equipment investment

in, 73, 260; recession in, 273; technological advances in, 77, 82
Automobiles: export of, 65; import restrictions on, 48

Baba Eiichi, 4, 7
Balance of payments: deficit, 4, 55, 57, 58, 60, 64, 141, 197; international disequilibrium in, 59; raising of ceiling on, 45, 46; surplus, 58, 61, 114, 141, 204, 205
Bank of Japan, 88, 127, 206, 207; and bonds, 35, 245; control by, 140–41, 142; debts to, 34; and discount rate, 204, 265; and inflation, 24, 214; loans by, 42; and Occupation, 35, 41, 136; during wartime, 4, 8, 18, 19, 135
Bank of Tokyo, 136, 138
Banks, 211–12; city, 135, 138; commercial, 136, 138; loans by, 264; ·mutual savings, 138, 139; regulation of, 245; trust, 137; zaibatsu, 135
Basic Agricultural Law, 184
Basic Environmental Pollution Prevention Law, 107, 120
Basic Small Business Law, 169
Beer industry, 27, 70
Black market, 10, 35, 36
Black Monday, 261, 272
Blumenthal, Michael, 221
Bonds, 42; deficit-covering, 244, 245, 268; national, 40, 125, 127, 129, 141, 142, 242, 275
Bonuses, 104, 156, 273